Educational Thoughts of Mahatma Gandhi

Educational Thoughts of Mahatma Gandhi

Dr. Sudharma Joshi

Crescent
CRESCENT
PUBLISHING CORPORATION

[The responsibility for the facts stated, conclusions reached and plagiarism, if any, in this book is entirely that of the Author. And the Publisher bears no responsibility for them, whatsoever.]

Educational Thoughts of Mahatma Gandhi

Edition : 2026

ISBN 978-81-8342-159-1

Published by:

CRESCENT PUBLISHING CORPORATION

4806/24, Mathur Lane,
Ansari Road, Darya Ganj,
New Delhi - 110002
Mob.: 9711991838, 9999021668
Ph.: 011-23244131
e-mail : crescentbook@gmail.com
Website : www.crescentpublishingcorp.weebly.com

Printed at :
Balaji Digital
Delhi

Preface

Although venerated by many as the architect of India's Independence, Mahatma Gandhi was an equal participant in the social reformation of the country. His stance on the caste system and support for the Harijans is quite well-known, and he was equally supportive of women's emancipation, religious harmony, and issues like development of the cottage industries. Within this framework of his social ideology was the equally relevant issue of education a matter to which he paid considerable attention and thought, resulting in a Gandhian philosophy which incorporated numerous elements of various educational philosophies and which has even tried and experimented with by Gandhi himself.

This book of the educational philosophies of renowned Indians explores the stance of the Father of the Nation on education. It explores various facets of the ideology of Gandhi, including his beliefs on the basic concept of education, the Hindustani medium of schools, vocational education, on, women's education, spirituality and morally in education, spirituality and morality in education, etc. In addition, it embarks on a brief discussion of his own educational experiences and how they moulded his ideology, as well as his tryst with Tolystoy Farm. Further it also analyses and critiques this philosophy and contrasts it with the ideologies of Gandhi's contemporaries.

It is hoped that the book's insight serves well for educators

Dr. Sudharma Joshi

Contents

	Prefac·	*v*
1.	Introduction	1
2.	Gandhiji on Meaning and Purpose of Education	18
3.	Educational Innovations	51
4.	Gandhi on Moral Education	117
5.	Gandhi's *Nayee Talim*	127
6.	Gandhi's Social Theory	154
7.	Gandhi on Educational Issues	170
8.	Gandhi on Language Education	215
9.	Gandhi on Women Education	243
10.	Gandhi on Religious Education	258
11.	Gandhian Values in Education	281
	Bibliography	292
	Index	294

1

Introduction

Mohandas Karamchand Gandhi (October 2, 1869 – January 30, 1948) was a major political and spiritual leader of India and the Indian independence movement. He was the pioneer of Satyagraha — the resistance of tyranny through mass civil disobedience, firmly founded upon ahimsa or total non-violence — which was one of the strongest driving philosophies of the Indian independence movement and inspired movements for civil rights and freedom across the world.

Gandhi is commonly known in India and across the world as Mahatma Gandhi and as Bapu. In India, he is officially accorded the honour of Father of the Nation and October 2nd, his birthday, is commemorated each year as Gandhi Jayanti, a national holiday. On 15 June 2007, the United Nations General Assembly unanimously adopted a resolution declaring October 2 to be the "International Day of Non-Violence."

As a British-educated lawyer, Gandhi first employed his ideas of peaceful civil disobedience in the Indian community's struggle for civil rights in South Africa. Upon his return to India, he organized poor farmers and labourers to protest against oppressive taxation and widespread discrimination. Assuming leadership of the Indian National Congress, Gandhi led nationwide campaigns for the alleviation of poverty, for the liberation of women, for brotherhood amongst differing religions and ethnicities, for an end to untouchability and caste discrimination, and for the economic self-sufficiency of the nation, but above all for Swaraj — the independence of India from foreign domination. Gandhi famously led Indians in the disobedience of the salt tax on the 400 kilometre (248 miles) Dandi Salt March in 1930, and in an open call for the British to Quit India in 1942. He was imprisoned for many years on numerous occasions in both South Africa and India.

Throughout his life, Gandhi remained committed to non-violence and truth even in the most extreme situations. A student of Hindu philosophy, he lived simply, organizing an ashram that was self-sufficient in its needs. Making his own clothes — the traditional Indian dhoti and shawl woven with a charkha, he lived on a simple vegetarian diet. He used rigorous fasts, for long periods, for both self-purification and protest.

Gandhi's Critique of Colonial Education

Rejection of the colonial education system, which the British administration had established in the early nineteenth century in India, was an important feature of the intellectual ferment generated by the struggle for freedom. Many eminent Indians, political leaders, social reformers and writers voiced this rejection. But no one rejected colonial education as sharply and as completely as Gandhi did, nor did anyone else put forward an alternative as radical as the one he proposed.

Gandhi's critique of colonial education was part of his overall critique of Western civilization. Colonization, including its educational agenda, was to Gandhi a negation of truth and non-violence, the two values he held uppermost. The fact that Westerners had spent 'all their energy, industry, and enterprise in plundering and destroying other races' was evidence enough for Gandhi that Western civilization was in a 'sorry mess'.Therefore, he thought, it could not possibly be a symbol of 'progress', or something worth imitating or transplanting in India.

It would be wrong to interpret Gandhi's response to colonial education as some kind of xenophobia. It would be equally wrong to see it as a symptom of a subtle revivalist dogma. If it were possible to read Gandhi's 'basic education' plan as an anonymous text in the history of world education, it would be conveniently classified in the tradition of Western radical humanists like Pestalozzi, Owen, Tolstoy and Dewey.

It does not lend itself to be read in the context of the East-West dichotomy that Gandhi did deal with in some of his other writings. Yet the fact remains that Gandhi wanted education-reconstructed along the lines he thought correct-to help India move away from the Western concept of progress, towards a different form of development more suited to its needs and more viable, for the world as a whole, than the Western model of development.

Basic Education Proposal

Gandhi was able to initiate an educational discourse outside the familiar East-West dichotomy yet forming part of the critique of the West by locating the problem of education in a different dialectic, that of man versus machine. In this dialectic, man represented the whole of mankind, not just India, and the machine represented the industrialized West.

Throughout his life Gandhi had perceived his personal life and the causes he fought for in a global context. This perception was no less operative in the final decade of his life, at the beginning of which he presented his 'basic education' proposal.The core of Gandhi's proposal was the introduction of productive handicrafts in the school curriculum. The idea was not simply to introduce handicrafts as a compulsory school subject, but to make the learning of a craft the axis of the entire teaching programme. It implied a radical restructuring of the sociology of school knowledge in India, where productive handicrafts had been associated with the lowest groups in the hierarchy of castes.

Knowledge of the production processes involved in crafts, such as spinning, weaving, leatherwork, pottery, metal-work, basket-making and book-binding, had been the monopoly of specific caste groups in the lowest stratum of the traditional social hierarchy. Many of them belonged to the category of 'untouchables'. India's indigenous tradition of education as well as the colonial education system had emphasized the skills (such as literacy) and knowledge of which the upper castes had a monopoly.

In terms of its epistemology, Gandhi's proposal intended to stand the education system on its head. The social philosophy and the curriculum of 'basic education' thus favoured the child belonging to the lowest stratum of society. This is how it implied a programme of social transformation. It sought to alter the symbolic meaning of 'education' and thereby to change the established structure of opportunities for education.

The rationale Gandhi proposed for the introduction of production processes in the school was not as startling as this interpretation. The rationale he proposed was that schools must be self-supporting, as far as possible, for two reasons. One was purely financial: namely, that a poor society could not provide education to all its children unless schools could generate the physical and financial resources to run them. The other was political:

that financial self-sufficiency alone could protect schools from dependence on the State and from interference by it.

As values, both self-sufficiency and autonomy were close to Gandhi's heart. They belonged to his vision of a society based on truth and non-violence. Financial selfsufficiency was linked to truth, and autonomy to non-violence. An individual or an institution that did not participate directly in the process of production for survival could afford to adhere to 'truth' for long. Such an individual or institution would have to depend on the State to an extent that would make violence, in one form or another, inevitable.

A State system of education was a contradiction of Gandhi's view of education. The possibility of the school developing the resources for its own maintenance showed a way out of this contradiction. The idea of productive schools clearly came from the two communities Gandhi had established in South Africa. Phoenix Farm, started in 1904, and Tolstoy Farm, which was established in 1910, provided him with a lasting interest and faith in the potential of life in a rural commune. The first of these experiments was apparently inspired by John Ruskin's Unto this last.

Gandhi drew three lessons from this book, or rather, as Louis Fischer has explained, Gandhi read three messages into the book.The first message was that the benefit of all is what a good economy is all about; the second was that earnings from manual work (such as that of a barber) have the same value as mental work (such as that of a lawyer); and the third one was that a life worth living was that of a labourer or craftsman. Gandhi recalls in his autobiography that he decided to put these messages into practice as soon as he had finished reading Ruskin's book on a train journey.

The kind of life that Gandhi's 'basic education' proposal projected as the 'good' life was first practised by him at Phoenix Farm and, somewhat more rigorously and ambitiously, at Tolstoy Farm a little later. As the name indicates, by the time of this latter experiment, Gandhi had read the works of, and had established contact with, the Russian writer and thinker Leo Tolstoy.

The inspiration Gandhi received from Tolstoy spanned a wide range of interests and concerns. Prominent among them was to fight the sources of violence in human society. Tolstoy's celebration of the individual's right to live in peace and freedom, and his negation of all forms of oppression, brought him close to Gandhi. Even though Gandhi did not read Tolstoy's articles on education in the journal Yasnaya polyana, Tolstoy's view that 'education as a premeditate formation of men according to certain patterns is sterile, unlawful, and impossible'could well have been expressed by Gandhi.

The right to autonomy that Gandhi's educational plan assigns to the teacher in the context of the school's daily curriculum is consistent with the libertarian principles he shared with Tolstoy. Gandhi wanted to free the Indian teacher from the slavery of the bureaucracy. The schoolteacher's job had come to be defined under colonial rule as one transmitting and elucidating the forms and content of knowledge selected by bureaucratic authorities for inclusion in the prescribed textbook.

Exposing the link between the mandatory use of textbooks and the feeble position of the teacher, Gandhi wrote: 'If textbooks are treated as a vehicle for education, the living word of the teacher has very little value. A teacher who teaches from textbooks does not impart originality to his pupils.

'Gandhi's basic education plan implied the end of the teacher's subservience to the prescribed textbook and the curriculum. For one thing, it presented a concept of learning that could not be fully implemented with the help of textbooks. More important, however, was the freedom and authority that the basic education plan gave to the teacher in matters concerning the curriculum. It was a libertarian plan inasmuch as it denied the State the power to decide precisely what the teacher must do in the classroom. In accordance with his wider philosophy of social life and politics, this aspect of Gandhi's educational plan implied a dramatic reduction of the State's sphere of authority.

Concept of Self Sufficiency

Having assembled a conceptual outline of Gandhi's plan, we can now return to its core concern and probe it more deeply. Basic education was an embodiment of Gandhi's perception of an ideal society as one consisting of small, self-reliant communities. To him, Indian villages were capable of becoming such communities; indeed, he believed that Indian villages were historically self-reliant, and the great task now was to restore their autonomy and to create the conditions necessary for economic self-sufficiency and political dignity in villages. Colonial rule, he thought, had damaged the village economy, subjecting it to exploitation by citydwellers.

Freedom from colonial rule would mean empowerment of the village and its development as a viable community. The basic education plan was meant to develop the village along these lines, by training children for productive work and by imparting to them attitudes and values conducive to living in a co-operative community. This programme of development was rooted in Gandhi's view of industrialization as a threat to human sanity. Much debate has taken place about Gandhi's 'real' view of technology. It is not clear whether he was against the spirit of modern science and technology, or whether his opposition to Western-type modernity was confined to the manner in which science and technology had been used to exploit non-European societies. In the vast body of responses contained in his collected works, one finds ample evidence on both sides.

Perhaps it is wrong to look for an either/or kind of position in Gandhi on this matter (and several others), for he was not so much a theorist of action as a person always ready to react and engage in action. Preparing for action by developing a symbolic model first was not his style. In the context of science and industrialization, he appears to have worked towards slowing down the march of capitalism and industrial development in India. He wanted India to develop socially and politically first, so as to be in a position of power to exercise options in the face of technological and market pressures coming from the industrialized West and from the capitalist lobby within Indian society.

His programme can be understood as a chronological ordering of priorities in which the consolidation of a viable political system would come first, and the development of productive processes through the use of machines would come second. According to Gandhi, a viable political system for India had to be centred on village republics, organized like 'oceanic circles'.

The metaphor was meant to convey the principle of local power in combination with commitment to the larger society. He wanted such a political system to develop before the modernization of the means of production so that the masses, who lived in villages, would not lack the power to protect their interests under the imperatives of modernization.His educational plan fits nicely in this ordering of priorities. If the march of industrialization could be slowed down and shaped in accordance with a plan for social and political progress, basic education could serve a definite purpose in such progress.

More specifically, if purposeful industrialization meant protecting the right of villages to produce what they could without competition with large-scale mechanized establishments, basic education could enhance the productive capacities of village children under such a plan. The ideal citizen in Gandhi's Utopia was an industrious, self-respecting and generous individual living in a small community. This is the image underlying his educational plan.

This image of man and the production system sustaining it brings to mind the American philosopher John Dewey (1859-1952), and it is useful to probe the similarities between the educational visions of these two contemporaries. Dewey grew up in a country whose frontiers were still developing. The small community of skilled, hard-working men and women, whose individual personalities mattered to the community, seemed the ideal democratic unit in Dewey's youth.

The growing capitalist economy had not yet revealed the nature of politics and culture that it would demand. In his famous book, Democracy and education, published in 1916, Dewey had rooted his work-based model of teaching in the idealized small community of responsible individuals. Linking productive work with education was at the heart of Gandhi's model too, and it was rooted in the idealized village republic of his Utopia not much different from Dewey's. But whereas Dewey sketched his democratic community rather late in terms of his country's development along the path of capitalism,

Gandhi sketched his ideal village community at a point when he thought there was still time to make choices. Furthermore, Dewey's plans were not as dependent on traditional craft-based production processes as Gandhi's were. Both, however, were products of the ethos of early capitalist development. In retrospect, Dewey's educational proposal reads like a plea for protecting a special space for children in the midst of rampant, dehumanizing, capitalist advancement.

Gandhi' proposal, on the other hand, reads like a plea for delaying the growth of capitalism, for buying time to strengthen the capacities of men and women to live with machines. If we take this comparison between Gandhi and Dewey a step further, we shall discover another similarity between the two educators: both propagated a purely secular pedagogy.

This is indeed somewhat startling in the case of Gandhi because, in every sphere of action except education, Gandhi acted as a man with deep religious feelings. In the context of education too he seemed reluctant to commit himself to a purely secular position, but the fact remains that his basic education plan provides no room for religious teaching. In June 1938 he had to explain the matter in some detail because a delegation of educators demanded to know precisely what his view was on this matter. His answer was:

'We have left out the teaching of religion from the Wardha scheme of education because we are afraid that religions as they are taught and practised today lead to conflict rather than unity. But on the other hand, I hold that the truths that are common to all religions can and should be taught to all children. These truths cannot be taught through words or through books-the children can learn these truths only through the daily life of the teacher. If the teacher himself lives up to the tenets of truth and justice, then alone can the children learn that Truth and Justice are the basis of all religions.7 Apparently, Gandhi resolved the conflict in his mind between the religious role of education in which he believed and the secular programme of basic education by upholding the moral image of the teacher. By arguing that the teacher can convey the basic truths of all religions-which are similar, he says-by practising them, Gandhi was surely making an extraordinary demand.

Whether the practical impossibility of the demand bothered him or not is a secondary matter. Most probably it did not, for he was used to overlooking the limitations-physical, intellectual or moral -within which ordinary people worked. And it is true that as a great educator active in politics he made many ordinary people do extraordinary things. The important thing for us to note is that by demanding the daily example of moral correctness in the teacher's conduct Gandhi was opting for a religious, as opposed to a purely professional, role for the teacher.

Also, he was using a familiar Indian motif, that of guru living in his ashram in the company of his disciples. In the ideal ashram community, the teacher was expected to set an example of the life worth living, and from this high pedestal of daily existence he was permitted to demand any conceivable form of sacrifice from the students. This quasi-mythologized image seems to have served an important rhetorical function in Gandhi's plea for reform in education along the lines of his basic education proposal. It promised to place what was a modern concept of education and pedagogy within the halo of Indian tradition.

Opposition to Gandhi's Educational Proposals

This modest strategy, however, could not protect basic

education from the attacks, indifference and undermining to which it was subjected from the beginning. The hostility that Gandhi's proposal faced cannot be separated from the political battles of the final decade of India's struggle for independence. Basic education was described as a 'Hindu ploy' by the leaders of the Muslim League in northern India. These critics chose to miss the secular character of Gandhi's plan. On the other hand, they paid exaggerated attention to a scheme that happened to synchronize with Gandhi's proposal and had some features similar to it. This other scheme was initiated by Ravi Shankar Shukla in the Central Provinces under the name of Vidya mandir, which literally meant 'temple of knowledge'.

The rural schools Shukla wanted to start under this scheme and, more than that, the known absence of liberal, secular elements in his personality, made them vulnerable to attack. It was purely by metonymic logic that the attack covered Gandhi's original proposal. The attack found an audience wide enough to include members of the committee appointed by the Central Advisory Board of Education to discuss basic education in the perspective of State policy.Another perspective from which Gandhi's plan received suspicion and criticism was that of planning for industrial development in India.

The basic education proposal coincided with the setting up of the National Planning Committee (NPC) by the Congress Party. The specific aim of the NPC was to formulate a plan for India's industrialization with the aim of 'economic regeneration' after independence. Its chairman, Jawaharlal Nehru, had believed for a long time that large-scale industrialization alone could solve India's problems of poverty and unemployment. But apart from Nehru's own beliefs, the NPC's reports on different spheres of development reflected the vision of a powerful and growing class of industrialists, their supporters in politics and intellectuals with high qualifications in different areas, including science and technology.

The projection of a centrally controlled economy and rapid expansion of large-scale industries in the NPC's reports could hardly have pleased Gandhi. He had been unhappy with the news of the NPC's meetings and work, and had said so. The conflict between Gandhi's view and the NPC's was not confined to the role and proportion of large-scale industries in the national economy; it extended to the rationale underlying industrial development. Apart from the material prosperity of India, the NPC's reports used India's security as a major rationale for the growth of heavy industries. Militarization and development were to go hand in hand, as in the West. This association was not something we might regard as cheerful rhetoric to please Gandhi.

The NPC's sub-committee on general and technical education did not acknowledge this conflict, perhaps because it was not necessary to talk about larger conceptual issues in the context of education. But the sub-committee's report showed great reluctance in recommending a shift from the existing system to the one suggested by Gandhi. It argued that there had been a sudden increase since 1938 in the efficiency of primary schools under the Congress ministries (the data provided to support this claim were confined to Bombay). 'It would, therefore, be wrong', the report said, 'to displace the movement by one in favour of basic education. The introduction of basic education should be a process of grafting it on to the elementary education possible.'

Obviously, the sub-committee saw serious problems in the Wardha scheme of basic education. The major problem had to do with the importance given to the teaching of productive skills. The sub-committee's argument against this was that 'too much stress on vocation at such [an] age is spiritually harmful and teaching of general subjects through such [a] single narrow-down medium makes the knowledge of subject superficial and defective'.The other major objection was related to this first one. The idea that the output of children's work at school should financially sustain the school was unacceptable to the sub-committee. 'To a certain extent such a system will mean [the] existence of child labour in schools', the report said.These were familiar arguments, and they were consistent with the general approach perspective adopted by the NPC.

A broad, liberal curriculum for elementary education, and expansion of facilities for technical education, were the major thrusts of the recommended plan. Financial responsibility for compulsory primary education was assigned to be that of the State. This was indeed the staple of modernist thought, compared to which Gandhian ideas looked obsolete and conservative.

In contrast to Gandhi's Utopia of village republics enjoying considerable autonomy but offering a modest standard of life dependent on rudimentary production processes, the modernist Utopia featured a strong centralized State responsible for building an industrial infrastructure in order to ensure a high standard of living for all. A liberal curriculum under State-supported arrangements for elementary schooling was part of the modernist vision. The pedagogical strengths of such a system were indicated by Nehru in one of his few reflections on education which figured at the end of a sub-chapter entitled 'The Congress and Industry', in The Discovery of India:

It is well recognized now that a child's education should be intimately associated with some craft or manual activity. The mind is stimulated thereby and there is a co-ordination between the activities of the mind and the hands. So also the mind of a growing boy or girl is stimulated by the machine. It grows under the machine's impact (under proper conditions, of course, and not as an exploited and unhappy worker in a factory) and opens out new horizons. Simple scientific experiments, peeps into the microscope and an explanation of the ordinary phenomenon of nature bring excitement in their train, an understanding of some of life's processes, and a desire to experiment and find out instead of relying on set phrases and old formulae. Self-confidence and the co-operative spirit grow, and frustration, arising out of the miasma of the past, lessens. A civilization based on ever-changing and advancing mechanical techniques leads to this. Such a civilization is a marked change, a jump almost from the older type, and is intimately connected with modern industrialization.

There can be little doubt that, while writing these words, Nehru was engaging in a dialogue with Gandhi's basic education plan. He starts by agreeing with the main pedagogical assumption underlying basic education, namely that a craft or manual activity stimulates the child's mind. Then, by the force of analogy between craft and machine, he goes off along another argument that challenges the main economic assumption underlying basic education, without identifying it.

The starting point of a dialogue with Gandhi's proposal turns, after two sentences, into a statement regarding the pedagogical value of scientific experiments and the relation such experiments have with an industrial civilization. Nehru was, of course, correct in pointing out this relationship, and also in stressing the enormous role that an experiment-based pedagogy of science could play in revitalizing education in India. He shared the hope of such revitalization with many Indian intellectuals who were committed to rapid modernization and who found Gandhi's educational plan unacceptable. One of them was the well-known novelist Mulk Raj Anand, who wrote in his book On education published at the time of independence:

The dream of perfecting good little minds on the basis of Khadi and non-violence, so that these morons vegetate within the limits of their self-sufficient communities, is not only impossible in an India where every village is already inundated with cheap machine-made goods produced by foreign and indigenous capitalists, but is likely to bring about the very opposite of all those qualities which the Mahatma seeks to create in the average Indian. Clearly, from the modernists' point of view, Gandhi's plan was an invitation to take India backward. Furthermore, they believed that modernization of children's education could be accomplished within the foreseeable future with the help of available resources.

IMPLEMENTATION

Not all responses to Gandhi's scheme of education were hostile. Many eminent educators welcomed basic education, and they prepared extensive plans to implement it. As might be expected, the ways in which Gandhi's idea was interpreted differed widely. At one extreme were educators and leaders who understood the scheme in the context of progressive educational thought associated with thinkers like Pestalozzi and Dewey. At the other extreme were those who lived by the letter of Gandhi's thoughts and who saw basic education as a fixed charter, a matter of orthodoxy.

The fact remains that despite this range in the interpretations that Gandhi's proposal received, and despite imaginable administrative and financial problems, the scheme of basic schools was implemented on a considerable scale in several parts of India after independence. It is customary to look back at this implementation as a big failure, a conclusion that may not appear to be particularly sound if examined in the light of historical circumstances. But that is another story.

The only fact that ought to be recorded here is that the implementation of Gandhi's plan could not survive the 'development decade' of the 1960s when the Indian economy and its politics entered into a new phase featuring the penetration of Indian agriculture by the advanced economies of the West and the centralization of power.

2

Gandhiji on Meaning and Purpose of Education

Gandhiji understood the Indian people, the Indian nation and the Indian national heritage ver well. The entire world accepts the clarity of his perception and his assessment of the shape of future trends so much so that with the passage of time the relevance of his thoughts and ideas is gaining greater significance globally. Born during the first phase of industrial and scientific revolution and living through its second and third stages, Gandhiji saw both the positive and humane aspects of science and technology as well as their destructive possibilities and potentialities for misutilization which could lead to a growing wedge between the 'haves' and 'have nots' and hence to destruction. Realizing something definitely wrong with the consumeristic way of life that many people were chasing in a society oriented to violence, exhibitionism, consumerism, a life far removed from Nature and moving in a direction that was not conducive to a balanced life or would promote equality of opportunity amongst people of different nations, races, castes, colours and creeds, Gandhiji began his quest for the alternatives which got even further reinforced and broadened with his experiences in South Africa.

Gandhiji's innovative approach to political activism, passive resistance, belief in non-violence, firm faith in 'satyagraha' against oppressive regime came as the biggest surprise to one and all across the globe. People became curious and attentive when he not only preached but also practised his doctrine in action as part of his personal life as a staunch believer in personal example than in mere precept, that efforts have to be made to eliminate the misdeeds of the oppressor rather than the oppressor himself. Truth, non-violence and satyagraha were successfully used and their credibility as an effective instrument of the social and political transformation was established. Though the world saw the success of his faith, strategy and effort in achieving his goals yet the Mahatma himself was not fully satisfied.

Gandhiji was convinced that injustice, violence and oppression manifest from human heart and that education can play an effective role in developing a wholesome human personality capable of resisting war, violence, injustice and oppression and building a social order wherein man can live in peace and harmony with others. Since education is a potential instrument of man-making and social engineering, he concentrated on an education that could draw out the best in the child—body, mind and spirit—for developing a peace loving human personality.

Gandhian philosophy is, indeed, rich in its educational and social values. It can transform the destiny of man and is capable of establishing an alternative social order if it is practised sincerely and honestly in its true perspective. Gandhiji's educational philosophy, which evolved during his lifetime in the form of Gandhian School of Educational Thought, has not received adequate attention in policy formulations during last five decades. Globally, it is being realized that his views were dynamic and futuristic in nature. Fully understanding inadequacies of our over-dependence on the alien model of education and the needs of the weakest, the poorest and the neglected, he evolved an indigenous strategy to provide equality of opportunity and success to each and every individual of this category.

Gandhiji's ideas on meaning and aims of education are described in this chapter in his own words. It will provide an insight into the vastness of his vision and the expanse of his thought-process.

Gandhiji on Meaning of Education

True Value of Education

The real difficulty is that people have no idea of what education truly is. We assess the value of education in the same manner as we assess the value of land or of shares in the stock-exchange market. We want to provide only such education as would enable the student to earn more. We hardly give any thought to the improvement of the character of the educated. The girls, we say, do not have to earn; so why should they be educated? As long as such ideas persist there is no hope of our ever knowing the true value of education.

Not Mere Literacy

In Western countries education is so highly valued that senior teachers are treated with much respect. There are at present in England, schools that have been running for hundreds of years and have turned out many renowned men. One of these famous schools is Eton. A few months ago the Old Boys of Eton presented an address to the Head Master, Dr. Weir, who is well known throughout the British Empire. Writing about the occasion, *The Pall Mall Gazette*, a well-known journal in England, has explained the nature of real education. Its comments deserve the attention of us all. The writer in *The Pall Mall Gazette* says:

> We hold that real education does not consist merely in acquainting oneself with ancient or modern books. It consists in the habits which one knowingly or unknowingly imbibes from the atmosphere, one's surroundings and the company one keeps and above all in work. It is all very well to acquire a stock of knowledge from good books or from other sources. But the more important thing is to learn humanity. The primary function of teachers is, therefore, not to teach the alphabet, but to inculcate humanity. Aristotle said that virtue is not learnt by reading big volumes. It is by doing good deeds that we learn virtue. Another great writer also says that it is well for one to know what is good, but one will be considered a happy person only if one acts upon that knowledge.

Judged by these standards, English schools will not be found wanting. If we think of English schools as places for turning out human beings, we shall see that they give us statesmen and administrators. Those educated in German schools may have greater knowledge, but if they become also men of action like the pupils of Eton, it is not by virtue of their training in the schools. Despite the defects that may exist in English schools, it is these that produce true men. They are men who are ever ready to meet an enemy threatening at the gates of England.

We can readily realize how a country that invests education with such a noble purpose becomes prosperous. India's star will shine bright when Indian children receive such education. Parents, teachers and pupils ought to ponder over the passage quoted above. It would not do merely to know it, it is necessary to act upon it. That is to say, parents should provide for excellent education, teachers should discharge their responsibility and pupils should recognize that mere literacy is not education.

Education as Service

True education lies in serving others, oblige them without

the least feeling of one-uppishness. The more mature you grow, the more you will realise this. A great deal of religious obligations on us are fulfilled when we nurse the sick. I am not worried about your bookish learning so long as you perform your duties and observe solemn ethical conduct. For me carrying out the fundamentals of ethics is *duty*. I shall support you if you want to study further out of your love for it or for excellence. But I won' t scold you if you do not do it. Try your best to carry out the decisions you have made. Write to me what you do at the press, at what time do you get up and about your work at the farm.

Service Before Self

I was extremely glad to read your letter of the 21st (ultimo) about Mr. West. I read the letter twice. I felt proud of you and thanked God that I had such a son. I wish you to remain such for ever. To do good to others and serve them without any sense of egoism—this is real education. You will realize this more and more as you grow up. What better way of life can there be than serving the sick? Most of religion is covered by it.

Moral Path

The true occupation of man is to build his character. It is not quite necessary to learn something special for earning [one's livelihood]. He who does not leave the path of morality never starves, and is not afraid if such a contingency arises.

Living a Good Life

The service you are rendering to Mr. West and others is the best study for you. He who does his duty is all the while studying. You say that you had to leave your studies; but it is not so. You are certainly studying when you are serving. It would be correct to say that you had to give up reading books. There is no harm in thus leaving studies. One can get academic education later on. One cannot say that one will get an opportunity of serving others later on...' Let this be inscribed in your heart that, since your mind is pure, you will not fall ill while serving others. And even if you fall ill, I will not worry. You and I, all of us, will achieve perfection only by being moulded in this manner. Learning to live a good life is in itself education. All else is useless.

Laying Strong Foundation

What is the meaning of education? It simply means a knowledge of letters. It is merely an instrument, and an instrument may be well used or abused. The same instrument that may be used to cure a patient may be used to take his life, and so may a knowledge of letters. We daily observe that many men abuse it and very few make good use of it; and if this is a correct statement, we have proved that more harm has been done by it than good.

The ordinary meaning of education is a knowledge of letters. To teach boys reading, writing and arithmetic is called primary education. A peasant earns his bread honestly. He has ordinary knowledge of the world. He knows fairly well how he should behave towards his parents, his wife, his children and his fellow villagers. He understands and observes the rules of morality. But he cannot write his own name. What do you propose to do by giving him a knowledge of letters? Will you add an inch to his happiness? Do you wish to make him discontented with his cottage or his lot? And even if you want to do that, he will not need such an education. Carried away by the flood of Western thought we came to the conclusion, without weighing pros and cons, that we should give this kind of education to the people.

Now let us take higher education. I have learned Geography, Astronomy, Algebra, Geometry etc. What of that? In what way have I benefited myself or those around me? Why have I learned these things? Professor Huxley has thus defined education:

> That man, I think, has had a liberal education who has been so trained in youth that his body is the ready servant of his will and does with ease and pleasure all the work that as a mechanism it is capable of; whose intellect is a clear, cold, logic engine with all its parts of equal strength and in smooth working order; . . . whose mind is stored with a knowledge of the fundamental truths of nature;. . . whose passions are trained to come to heel by a vigorous will, the servant of a tender conscience; . . . who has learnt to hate all vileness and to respect others as himself . Such a one and no other, I conceive, has had a liberal education, for he is in harmony with nature. He will make the best of her and she of him.

If this is true education, I must emphatically say that the sciences I have enumerated above I have never been able to use for controlling my senses. Therefore, whether you take elementary education or higher education, it is not required for the main thing. It does not make men of us. It does not enable us to do our duty.

Reader: If that is so, I shall have to ask you another question: What enables you to tell all these things to me? If you had not received higher education, how would you have been able to explain to me the things that you have?

Editor: You have spoken well. But my answer is simple: I do not, for one moment, believe that my life would have been wasted, had I not received higher or lower education. Nor do I consider that I necessarily serve because I speak. But I do desire to serve and in endeavouring to fulfil that desire, I make use of the education I have received. And, if I am making good use of it, even then it is not for the millions, but I can use it only for such as you, and this supports my contention. Both you and I have come under the bane of what is mainly false education. I claim to have become free from its ill effect, and I am trying to give you the benefit of my experience and in doing so, I am demonstrating the rottenness of this education.

Moreover, I have not run down a knowledge of letters in all circumstances. All I have now shown is that we must not make of it a fetish. It is not our *Kamadhuk*. In its place it can be of use and it has its place when we have brought our senses under subjection and put our ethics on a firm foundation. And then, if we feel inclined to receive that education, we may make good use of it. As an ornament it is likely to sit well on us. It now follows that it is not necessary to make this education compulsory. Our ancient school system is enough. Character-building has the first place in it and that is primary education. A building erected on that foundation will last.

The Three R's

But although much good and useful work can be done without a knowledge of the three R's, it is my firm belief that we cannot always do without such knowledge. It develops and sharpens one's intellect, and it increases our capacity of doing good. I have never placed an unnecessarily high value on the knowledge of the three R's. I am only attempting to assign its proper place to it. Again, the true knowledge of self is unattainable by the millions who lack such education. Many a book is full of innocent pleasure, and this will be denied to us without education. It is no exaggeration to say that a human being without education is not far removed from an animal. Education, therefore, is necessary for women as it is for men.

Education as Liberation

"That is true education which leads to freedom." That

alone is true education which enables us to preserve our dharma. This is the motto accepted by our university. The idea has appealed to me very much: "That is true education which leads to freedom." That which liberates is education. Liberation is of two kinds. One form of liberation consists in securing the freedom of the country from foreign rule. Such freedom may prove short-lived. The other kind of liberation is for all time. In order to attain *moksha*, which we describe as our *paramadharma*, we should have freedom in the worldly sense as well. He who is ridden with many fears cannot attain the ultimate *moksha*. If one would attain this, would achieve the highest end of human effort, one has no choice but to attain that *moksha* which is nearest to one. That education which delays our freedom is to be shunned, it is Satanic, it is sinful. Whatever the quality of the education given in Government schools and colleges, it is to be shunned because the Government which imparts it is Satanic and deserves to be shunned.

Education as Assimilation

But I must advise you, students, to read these prize-books carefully, to reflect over their real import and, keeping in mind all the profound truths set out in them, follow the path enjoined by religion. Whether you are a girl or a boy, you will grow up one day and have to carry a heavy burden of worldly duties; give some thought, therefore, to the future.

Truth is revealed not only in our scriptures but in the scriptures of other religions as well.It is the duty of students to assimilate whatever they have learnt. They should have religious and moral instruction, as much of it as they can usefully apply. They need education in such measure that it would not become too much of a useless burden on them. I should like to address a few words exclusively to students.

Men and women students, you will benefit from what you have learnt only to the extent that you have assimilated it. That should be the object of this institution too. You should ponder over the element of truth in whatever books of religion you read. If you cling to truth, success is yours. I would advise you from my experience, to profit well from your education. That will be to your advantage and to your country's as well.

Overcoming Fear

Speaking about the timidity induced by their education, Gandhiji said: We may feel in our heart any measure of devotion for Tilak Maharaj, but where is the student who will express it freely?

For us, fear has become synonymous with life. What is the use of that education which does not help us to overcome fear, but which, on the contrary, strengthens it? What kind of an education is it which does not teach us to follow truth and to cultivate devotion for the country?

Culture of the Heart

There is one thing which, as I am speaking to you occurs to me, which comes to me from my early studies of the Bible. It seized me immediately. I read the passage:

But seek ye first the Kingdom of God, and his righteousness; and all these things shall be added unto you.

I tell you that if you will understand, appreciate and act up to the spirit of this passage, you won't even need to know what place Jesus or any other teacher occupies in your heart. If you will do the proper scavenger's work, clean and purify your hearts and get them ready, you will find that all these mighty teachers will take their places without invitation from us. That, to my mind, is the basis of all sound education . Culture of the mind must be subservient to the culture of the heart. May God help you to become pure!

Learning and Courage

Let them (students) realize that learning without courage is like a waxen statue beautiful to look at but bound to melt at the least touch of a hot substance.

Character vs Knowledge

In brief, formation of character should have priority over knowledge of the alphabet. If this order is reversed, the attempt would be like putting the cart before the horse and making it push the cart with its nose, and would meet with the same success as the latter course.

Education as Contemplation

Education, character and religion should be regarded as convertible terms. There is no true education which does not tend to produce character, and there is no true religion which does not determine character. Education should contemplate the whole life. Mere memorizing and book-learning is not education. I have no faith in the so-called systems of education which produce men of learning without the backbone of character.

Education of the Whole Child

Education does not mean a knowledge of the alphabet. This type of knowledge is only a means to education. Education implies a child's learning how to put his mind and all his senses to good use. That is to say, he really learns how to use his hands, feet and other organs of action and his nose, ear and other organs of sense.

A child who has acquired the knowledge that he should not use his hands for stealing or for killing flies nor for beating up his companions or younger brothers and sisters has already begun his education. He has started it, we can say, when he understands the necessity of keeping his body, his teeth, tongue, ears, head, nails, etc., clean and keeps them clean. That child has made good progress in education who does not indulge in mischief while eating and drinking, eats and drinks alone or in society in a proper manner, sits properly and chooses pure foodstuffs knowing the difference between pure and impure foodstuffs, does not eat like a glutton, does not clamour for whatever he sees and remains calm even if he does not get what he wants. Even that child has advanced on the road to education whose pronunciation is correct, who can recount to us the history and geography of the country surrounding him without knowing those terms and who understands what his country means. That child has made very good progress in his education who can understand the difference between truth and untruth, worth and worthlessness and chooses the good and the true, while rejecting the bad and the untrue.

Education as Self-discipline

All your scholarship, all your study of Shakespeare and Wordsworth would be vain if at the same time you do not build your character, and attain mastery over your thoughts and actions. When you have attained self-mastery and learnt to control your passions you will not utter notes of despair. You cannot give your hearts and profess poverty of action. To give one's heart is to give all. You must, to start with, have hearts to give. And this you can do if you will cultivate them.

Right Learning

I have been all this time looking at the motto in front of me: "Learning owes its worth to dharma." What the motto says is true. I have discovered in the course of my travels in India that, without dharma, learning is barren. This raises the question: "What is right learning?" I have given my reply often enough. We shall settle afterwards the issue of what manner of learning to provide. For the present, we may follow one definite method and include religious instruction in it. Religion is not a matter for reflection but of conduct. It is not a subject for talking about, be it noted. Teachers can create the thing only by their conduct. Gurjarat itself should produce such teachers; it is shameful to go looking for them outside.

Becoming Strong

In the circumstances in which you pursue your studies, you can only learn to fear man. I would say, on the other hand, that he alone is a real M.A. who has given up the fear of man and has learnt to fear God. Any education you receive will have justified itself only when you have become so strong that you will not beg of anyone for your living. It will have justified itself when the feeling has grown in you that, so long as you are strong of limb, you need not humble yourselves before anyone for a livelihood.

Literary Training

Literary training by itself adds not an inch to one's moral height and that character-building is independent of literary training.

Development of Body, Mind and Spirit

The English word 'education' etymologically means 'drawing out'. That means an endeavour to develop our latent talents. The same is the meaning of *kilavani*, the Gujarati word for education. When we say that we develop a certain thing, it does not mean that we change its kind or quality, but that we bring out the qualities latent in it. Hence 'education' can also mean 'unfoldment'.

In this sense, we cannot look upon knowledge of the alphabet as education. This is true even if that knowledge gains us the M.A. degree or enables us to adorn the place of a Shastri1 in some *pathshala* with the requisite knowledge of Sanskrit. It may well be that the highest literary knowledge is a fine instrument for education or unfoldment, but it certainly does not itself constitute education.

True education is something different. Man is made of three constituents, the body, mind and spirit. Of them, spirit is the one permanent element in man. The body and the mind function on account of it. Hence we can call that education which reveals the qualities of spirit. That is why the seal of the Vidyapith carries the dictum 'Education is that which leads to *moksha*'.

Education can also be understood in another sense; that is, whatever leads to a full or maximum development of all the three, the body, mind and spirit, may also be called education. The knowledge that is being imparted today may possibly develop the mind a little, but certainly it does not develop the body and spirit. I have a doubt about the development of the mind too, because it does not mean that the mind has developed if we have filled it with a lot of information. We cannot therefore say that we have educated our mind.

A well-educated mind serves man in the desired manner. Our literate mind of today pulls us hither and thither. That is what a wild horse does. Only when a wild horse is broken in can we call it a trained horse. How many 'educated' young men of today are so trained?

Now let us examine our body. Are we supposed to cultivate the body by playing tennis, football or cricket for an hour every day? It does, certainly, build up the body. Like a wild horse, however, the body will be strong but not trained. A trained body is healthy, vigorous and sinewy. The hands and feet can do any desired work. A pickaxe, a shovel, a hammer, etc. are like ornaments to a trained hand and it can wield them. That hand can ply the spinning-wheel well as also the ring and the comb while the feet work a loom. A well trained body does not get tired in trudging 30 miles. It can scale mountains without getting breathless. Does the student acquire such physical culture? We can assert that modern curricula do not impart physical education in this sense.

The less said about the spirit the better. Only a seer or a seeker can enlighten the soul. Who will awaken that dormant spiritual energy in us all? Teachers can be had through an advertisement. Is there a column for spiritual quest in the testimonials which they have to produce? Even if there is one, what is its value? How can we get through advertisements teachers who are seekers after self-realization? And education without such enlightenment is like a wall without a foundation or, to employ an English saying, like a whited sepulchre. Inside it there is only a corpse eaten up or being eaten by insects.

Science and Responsibility

At the time when emphasis in education is put more upon literary knowledge than upon character building, the following from the article of Principal Jacks in the *Sunday School Chronicle* will be read with profit:

> Our life presents itself as an endless movement, in which the march of science never quite overtakes the final problem of its own application. The point where responsibility rests upon us all is always just ahead of the last point reached by advancing science. The more the pursuer quickened his pace the more the fugitive quickens his. This inability of science to overtake responsibility is

> what I mean by its limitations. Applied science will tell you how to make a gun, but it will not tell you when to shoot nor whom to shoot at. You say that moral science will look after that. I answer that moral science in revealing the right use of my gun, inevitably reveals the wrong use also, and since the wrong will often serve my selfish purpose better than the right, my neighbours run a new risk of being shot at and plundered. A bad man armed with moral science is another name for the devil. If Mephistopheles had been examined in moral science in the University of London, he would have carried off all the prizes. At that point moral science and natural science are both in the same boat. How shall we name this fugitive thing which science never catches? I have called it life, others call it spirit or soul or sense, or perhaps the will. I do not think it matters greatly what we call it, so long as we recognize that it exists and that it carries in its arms the fortunes of mankind. Let education look to that. This is the point where all the enterprise of education and all the activities of religion come to their focus—the point of responsibility. If we do it at all other points and leave the point of responsibility uncared for, we shall inevitably come to grief.

Against Atheism

My association with the students of our country dates back to 10 years, since my return to India. I know the hardships and the difficulties of the students. I have been seeing them every day. I also know their weak points. It has been my privilege to have a corner in their hearts. They have not hesitated to open their hearts to me, to tell me even what they had concealed from their parents. I do not know how I could bring them peace, or what message I could give them. I share in their sorrows, and I have been striving to alleviate their hardships. But in this world, we have to look only to God for help. None other could render any effectual help. There is no sin equal to that of disbelieving in Him, in denying Him. Amongst the students of today the spirit of atheism is gaining ground. I am deeply grieved that things should be so.

Whenever I see Hindu students, I ask them to think of God, to pray, to repeat Ramanama. They ask me where is God, where is Rama and such other questions. When I see Mussalman youths and ask them to read the Koran, and to live the life enjoined therein, they also ask me similar questions. The education which leads to the negation of God cannot make for the service of the country nor of humanity. In your address, you have referred to my service to my country. Whatever I have been doing is done with a sense of my duty to God. And this I consider to be the right thing. God is not seated in the skies, in the heavens, or elsewhere. He is enshrined in the heart of everyone—be he a Hindu, Mohammedan, Christian or Jew, man or woman.

Education and Culture

"Culture" means refinement of feelings and "education" means knowledge of literature. Education is a means and culture is the end. The latter is possible even without education. For instance, if a child is brought up in a truly cultured family, it will unconsciously imbibe culture from its environment. In our country at any rate, present-day education and culture have no connection with each other. If the educated still retain some culture, that is in spite of their education. This fact shows that the roots of our culture are deep.

Strengthening of Character

In my wanderings among the students I made the discovery at an early stage of the movement that in order to conduct a movement of this kind character must be the foundation. We also found that real education consists not in packing the brain with so many facts and figures, not in passing examinations by reading numerous books but in developing character. I do not know to what extent you students of France lay stress upon character rather than upon intellectual studies, but I can say this that if you explore the possibilities of non-violence you will find that without character it will prove a profitless study.

Knowledge of the Self

True education is that which helps us to know the *atman*, our true self, God and Truth. To acquire this knowledge, some persons may feel the need for a study of literature, some for a study of physical sciences and some others for art. But every branch of knowledge should have as its goal knowledge of the self. That is so in the Ashram. We carry on numerous activities with that aim in view. All of them are, in my sense of the term, true education. Those activities can also be carried on without any reference to the goal of knowledge of the self. When they are so carried on, they may serve as a means of livelihood or of something else, but they are not education. In an activity carried on as education, a proper understanding of its meaning, devotion to duty and the spirit of service are necessary.

Ideal Education

When it is remembered that the primary aim of all education is, or should be, the moulding of the character of pupils, a teacher who has a character to keep need not lose heart.

Real Education

Real education has to draw out the best from the boys and girls to be educated. This can never be done by packing ill-assorted and unwanted information into the heads of the pupils. It becomes a dead weight crushing all originality in them and turning them into mere automata.

Book of Humanity

Real education consists in drawing the best out of yourself. What better book can there be than the book of humanity?

Education of the Hand

Literary education should follow the education of the hand—the one gift that visibly distinguishes man from beast. It is a superstition to think that the fullest development of man is impossible without a knowledge of the art of reading and writing. That knowledge undoubtedly adds grace to life, but it is in no way indispensable for man's moral, physical, or material growth.

Fighting Social Evils

All this means education of a character that will revolutionize the mentality of the youth of the nation. Unfortunately the system of education has no connection with our surroundings which therefore remain practically untouched by the education received by a microscopic minority of the boys and girls of the nation.

Whilst, therefore, whatever can be done to abate the evil must be done, it is clear to me that this evil and many others which can be named can only be tackled if there is education which responds to the rapidly changing conditions of the country. How is it that so many boys and girls who have even passed through colleges are found unable or unwilling to resist the manifestly evil custom which affects their future so intimately as marriage does? Why should educated girls be found to commit suicide because they are not suited? Of what value is their education if it does not enable them to dare to defy a custom which is wholly indefensible and repugnant to one's moral sense? The answer is clear.

There is something radically wrong in the system of education that fails to arm girls and boys to fight against social or other evils. That education alone is of value which draws out the faculties of a student so as to enable him or her to solve correctly the problems of life in every department.

Making the Whole Man

Man is neither mere intellect, nor the gross animal body, nor the heart or soul alone. A proper and harmonious combination of all the three is required for the making of the whole man and constitutes the true economics of education...

I hold that true education of the intellect can only come through a proper exercise and training of the bodily organs, e.g., hands, feet, eyes, ears, nose, etc. In other words an intelligent use of the bodily organs in a child provide the best and quickest way of developing his intellect. But unless the development of the mind and body goes hand in hand with a corresponding awakening of the soul, the former alone would prove to be poor lop-sided affair. By spiritual training I mean education of the heart. A proper and all-round development of the mind, therefore, can take place only when it proceeds *pari passu* with the education of the physical and spiritual faculties of the child. They constitute an indivisible whole. According to this theory, therefore, it would be a gross fallacy to suppose that they can be developed piecemeal or independently of one another.

Self-supporting Schools

By education I mean an all-round drawing out of the best in child and man—body, mind and spirit. Literacy is not the end of education nor even the beginning. It is only one of the means whereby man and woman can be educated. Literacy in itself is no education. I would therefore begin the child's education by teaching it a useful handicraft and enabling it to produce from the moment it begins its training. Thus every school can be made self-supporting, the condition being that the State takes over the manufactures of these schools.

Training in Crafts

Do not think that I say this because I wish to run down book-learning. I fully understand its value. You will not easily come across many men who put such knowledge to better use than I do. My purpose in saying this is to put training in crafts on the same footing as education in letters. Those who thoroughly understand this point will never be eager for a literal education at the cost of training in crafts. Their book-learning will shine better and also prove of greater benefit to the people.

Nayee Taleem

It is necessary to understand the newness of *Nayee Taleem*. The new scheme of basic education will retain whatever was good in the old system. However, it will have newness in abundance. If there is something genuinely new in it, it should result in hope taking up place of despondency, food of poverty, work of unemployment, unity of dissensions and in our boys and girls learning along with reading and writing some craft, for only through the latter will they gain the knowledge of the alphabet.

Making the Right Choice

Our education has got to be revolutionized. The brain must be educated through the hand. If I were a poet, I could write poetry on the possibilities of the five fingers. Why should you think that the mind is everything and the hands and feet nothing? Those who do not train their hands, who go through the ordinary rut of education, lack 'music' in their life. All their faculties are not trained. Mere book knowledge does not interest the child so as to hold his attention fully. The brain gets weary of mere words, and the child's mind begins to wander.

The hand does the things it ought not to do, the eye sees the things it ought not to see, the ear hears the things it ought not to hear, and they do not do, see, or hear, respectively, what they ought to. They are not taught to make the right choice and so their education often proves their ruin. An education which does not teach us to discriminate between good and bad, to assimilate the one and eschew the other is a misnomer.

Freedom from Servitude

The ancient aphorism, "Education is that which liberates", is as true today as it was before. Education here does not mean mere spiritual knowledge, nor does liberation signify only spiritual liberation after death. Knowledge includes all training that is useful for the service of mankind and liberation means freedom from all manner of servitude even in the present life. Servitude is of two kinds: slavery to domination from outside and to one's own artificial needs. The knowledge acquired in the pursuit of this ideal alone constitutes true study.

Culture as the Foundation

I attach far more importance to the cultural aspect of education than to the literary. Culture is the foundation, the primary thing which the girls ought to get from here. It should show in the smallest detail of your conduct and personal behaviour, how you sit, how you walk, how you dress, etc., so that anybody might be able to see at a glance that you are the products of this institution. Inner culture must be reflected in your speech, the way in which you treat visitors and guests, and behave towards one another and your teachers and elders.

GANDHIJI ON PURPOSE OF EDUCATION

Nationalism

Education is just a means. If it is not accompanied by truthfulness, firmness, patience and other virtues, it remains sterile, and sometimes does harm instead of good. The object of education is not to be able to earn money, but to improve oneself and to serve the country. If this object is not realized, it must be taken that the money spent on education has been wasted.

Public Good

The Indian community has a moral to learn from this case. Without the right kind of education, the community will not only remain backward, but become increasingly so. Education in England, the study of English, world history and of the sciences—all these are essential in the world of today. Without them one is crippled. It is also necessary to learn how to put the knowledge thus acquired to proper use.

In itself knowledge is only a means. It can be employed for good, for making money, and in the service of public causes. Knowledge is justified only when it is put to good use and employed in the public cause. Otherwise, as we pointed out once earlier and as everyone will readily admit, it is like poison.

Cardinal Virtues

If you practise the three virtues1 if they become part of your life so far as I am concerned, you will have completed your education—your training. Armed with them, believe me, you will earn your bread in any part of the world and you will have paved the way to acquire a true knowledge of the soul, yourself and God. This does not mean that you should not receive instruction in letters. That you should and you are doing. But it is a thing over which you need not fret yourself. You have plenty of time for it and after all you are to receive such instruction in order that your training may be of use to the others.

Not Mere Employment

You—the students of Madras as well as students all over India—are you receiving an education which will make you worthy to realise that idea and which will draw the best out of you, or is it an education which has become a factory for making Government employees or clerks in commercial offices? Is the goal of the education that you are receiving that of mere employment whether in the Government departments or other departments? If that be the goal of your education, if that is the goal that you have set before yourselves, I feel and I fear that the vision which the poet3 pictured for himself is far from being realised.

National Service

Pupils are to receive education which will incline them to do nothing but national service when their studies are over. If, on growing up, they leave the Ashram, the education will have failed to that extent. Should any occasion of the kind arise, the student will be free [to follow his inclination]. It is not the aim, however, that the students should return to their parents and get lost in the sea of practical affairs.

Thinking and Becoming

But I am afraid that most of the students do not pay any

regard to the real aim of education. They go to school merely because it is the custom to do so. Some go to be able to obtain employment later on. In my opinion, to think of education as a means of earning a living betrays an unworthy disposition of mind.

The body is the means of earning a living while the school is the place for building character. To regard the latter as the means of fulfilling one's bodily needs is like killing a buffalo for a small piece of hide. The body should be maintained through doing physical work. How can the *atma*, the spirit, be employed for this purpose? You earn your bread by the sweat of your brow—this is one of the most significant sayings of Christ. The Gita also seems to say the same.

Students who attend school without taking thought as to the true aim of education, should first make sure what it should be. Such a student may resolve this very day that, henceforth, he will regard school as a place for building character. I am sure that he will effect a change for the better in his character in the course of a month and that his companions will also bear witness to his having done so. The shastras assert that we become what we think.

Knowing the Self

As I have earlier pointed out, most of the students look listless and devoid of energy. Many have asked me what they should do to overcome lethargy and serve the country? What should they do to earn their living? I have the impression that they are anxious about this matter. Before answering these questions it is necessary to find out the aim of education. Huxley has said that the aim of education is the building up of character. Our seers aver that, if in spite of his knowledge of the Vedas and shastras, a man fails to know himself and acquire the power to liberate himself from all bonds, his knowledge is useless. They have also said: "He who has known the Self knows all." Knowledge of the Self is possible without any literary education.

Prophet Mohammed was an illiterate man. Christ too did not attend school. But it would be impudent to deny that these great men had acquired knowledge of the Self. Though they did not pass any examination, yet we hold them in high esteem and worship them. They were in possession of all the fruits of learning. They were *mahatmas*—men of great spiritual attainment.

Building Character

All education must aim at building character. I cannot see how this can be done except through religion. We are yet to realize that gradually we are being reduced to a state in which we shall have lost our own without having acquired the new. I cannot go more into this, but I have met hundreds of teachers and they sighed in pain as they told me of their experiences... If pupils in schools lose their character, everything will have been lost.

Manliness and Self-Respect

If education is to be bought at the price of manliness and self-respect, the price is too heavy. "Man does not live by bread alone." Self-respect and character are above means of livelihood or a career. I am sorry that so many students have taken their expulsion so much to heart. The parents as well as students must revise their ideas about education. Education is treated merely as a means of earning a livelihood and acquiring a status in society. These are not unworthy ambitions. But they are not everything in life.

There are many other honourable means of acquiring wealth and status. There are many independent activities in life which one may undertake without having to contemplate loss of self-respect. And there is no better or cleaner passport to status in society than honesty and selfless service of fellow-beings. If, therefore, after due effort, the college door remains banged in the students' faces, they should not lose heart but seek other means of livelihood. And if the other students will empty the recalcitrant colleges as a matter of respectful protest, they and India will not be losers, but both will be considerable gainers.

Kindness to All

He said the essence of all education was kindness—kindness to all, friends, foes, men and beasts. The chief object of education was the building of character which could be done by strict observance of *brahmacharya*. Mr. Gandhi then explained to the students the necessity of learning Hindi and spinning and said that if the whole younger generation was educated in the manner in which they were trained in national schools then there would not have been any difficulty in getting swaraj.

Knowledge to Character

That is certainly what we mean. Even imparting knowledge should aim at character-building. Knowledge is the means and character-building is the end.

Reaching the Ideal

In my humble opinion, knowledge should never be used for acquiring wealth. Business should be the only means of doing so. The means of livelihood should be labour, i.e., weaving, carpentry, tailoring and such other occupations essential for maintaining human life. I believe that one of the chief reasons for our moral fall is that doctors, lawyers, teachers and others acquire their knowledge mainly for getting money and, in fact, use it for that purpose. What I have set out is, of course, an ideal, which we cannot attain. I have no doubt, however, that the nearer we get to it, the better for us.

Making a True Student

The education that you are receiving is intended for swaraj. I have taken up the responsibilities of a chancellor in Gujarat. That too I have done in my capacity as a fighter for freedom and with the intention of training students to be fighters for freedom. I landed in England on 4th of August, 1914. What did I see there? As the War spread, the Inns of Courts went on closing. Many faculties in Oxford and Cambridge were also closed. During the War, they allotted a minor role to education. And why should they not? The outcome of education is that the student becomes an ideal citizen, an ideal patriot and an ornament to his family, his community and his nation.

Service of Humanity

In asking them to study the lives of lawyers like Ghose, Mahatma Gandhi asked them not merely to be satisfied with the heritage those great lawyers had left for them, but wished the present generation to do better. They should become the poor man's friend in every sense and then alone would they be able to justify the legal profession. Their end was not to get more than a decent livelihood or how to shine in life, but to serve humanity in order to serve the motherland. They ought not to become lawyers in order to increase cases.

The education they received ought not to be prostituted to the base use of earning a livelihood, it ought to be used to promote moral growth to enable them to realize themselves, to understand that there was the Maker who saw everything and registered all thoughts, pure and impure, and the learning they derived should be dedicated to a vigorous self-analysis and not prostituted.

Fearlessness

The little boys of the school had all been waiting in the sun with the handsome purse they had collected and they had the lesson of fearlessness from Gandhiji's lips:

Fearlessness is the foundation of all education, the beginning and not the end. If you do not build on that foundation, the edifice of all your education will topple over.

And to send the lesson home to them he told them the story of Prahlada and exhorted them to declare the truth courteously and bravely without regard for the consequences as the twelve-year-old Prahlada did.

Purity of Personal Life

Purity of personal life is the one indispensable condition for building a sound education. And my meetings with thousands of students and the correspondence which I continuously have with the students in which they pour out their innermost feelings and take me into their confidence show me quite clearly that there is much left to be desired. I am sure that all of you understand thoroughly what I mean.

In our languages, there is a beautiful word, equivalent for the word student, that is, *brahmachari*. *Vidyarthi* is a coined word and a poor equivalent for *brahmachari*. And I hope you know what the word *brahmachari* means. It means searcher after God, one who conducts himself so as to bring himself nearest to God in the least possible time. And all the great religions of the world, however much they may differ, are absolutely one on this fundamental thing that no man or woman with an impure heart can possibly appear before the Great White Throne. All our learning or recitation of the Vedas, correct knowledge of Sanskrit, Latin, Greek and what not will avail us nothing if they do not enable us to cultivate absolute purity of heart. The end of all knowledge must be building of character.

Freedom from Bondage

You have asked for my blessings. Them you certainly have. But you have them on the condition that you impart lustre to this Vidyalaya and its name. The Patidars also should benefit by it and should disgrace neither the Vallabh Vidyalaya nor my name. I do not care for the sort of Vidyalaya which may prove a millstone round my neck and be a burden to me. Education liberates us, frees us from bondage, helps us to shine, adds to the country's wealth, enriches character: our boys and girls become smart and intelligent thereby. This Vidyalaya has been established with this end in view. May this end be realized.

Quest for Truth

True education is that which helps us to know the *atman*, our true self, God and Truth. To acquire this knowledge, some persons may feel the need for a study of literature, some for a study of physical sciences and some others for art. But every branch of knowledge should have as its goal, knowledge of the self. That is so in the Ashram. We carry on numerous activities with that aim in view. All of them are, in my sense of the term, true education. Those activities can also be carried on without any reference to the goal of knowledge of the self. When they are so carried on, they may serve as a means of livelihood or of something else, but they are not education. In an activity carried on as education, a proper understanding of its meaning, devotion to duty and the spirit of service are necessary. The first necessarily brings about development of the intellect. In doing any piece of work, however small, we should be inspired by a holy aim and, while doing it, we should try to understand the purpose which it will serve and the scientific method of doing it. There is a science of every type of work—whether it be cooking, sanitation, carpentry or spinning. Everybody who does his work with the attitude of a student knows its science or discovers it.

Sparing the Rod

Our aim is not just to impart education to children or teach them discipline, but to build character in them. Education, discipline, etc., are means to that end. If the result of building character in them is that education and discipline are neglected, let that be so. I understand your arguments, though. I also see that there is no ill will behind your use of the rod. But there are certainly anger and impatience behind them. May I make a suggestion? Call a meeting of the children. If any of them, say, "You may punish us, and in this manner, if we play mischief or disobey you", you may punish them in the manner which they suggest.

Selfless Service

Studies should be undertaken only with the aim of equipping oneself for service. Since, however, service of others gives one the highest joy, one may say that studies are for joy. I have not heard of anyone, however, who found unbroken joy in life through literary pursuits alone without devoting himself to service.

National Character

What is your goal in education when India obtains self-rule?

Character-building. I would try to develop courage, strength, virtue, the ability to forget oneself in working towards great aims. This is more important than literacy, academic learning is only a means to this greater end. That is why India's great lack of literacy, deplorable as it is, does not appeal to me nor make me feel that India is unfit for self-rule.

Would you try to bring about any specific kind of social organization through education. I would feel that if we succeed in building the character of the individual, society will take care of itself. I would be quite willing to trust the organization of society to individuals so developed.In developing the new national spirit in India would you like to make patriotic feelings so strong that duty to one's country would be a higher good than obeying one's personal conscience? I hope that will never be. One's own inner convictions come first always. But in a nation where character is developed in all individuals, there can be no conflict between the dictates of one's own conscience and those of the State.

Self Control

The true aim of education is spiritual development. One should, therefore, go in for such kind of education as will bring it about. It need not be of one fixed type. Hence it is not necessary to say anything on that subject. One should lead a life of self-control.

Humility

With this introduction I would like to tell the students, boys and girls, that humility is the primary thing to be acquired. One who is not humble cannot put one's learning to proper use. What does it matter if he has obtained double first class or has stood first? One does not achieve everything by just passing an examination. It is possible that it may help in securing a good job or a good marriage alliance. But, if learning is to be put to proper use, if it is to be used only for the sake of service, one should acquire more and more humility every day. No service is possible without it.

Developing Independent Thinking

At present, the minds of the students become dull there. They can only imitate. Instead of this, they must acquire the power of independent thinking. We are born into this world not for indulging in sensuous activities but for sacrifice, for restraint. The purpose of education is that we know God and progress towards the ideal, and get closer to Him. It is the strict law of God that anyone who desires to be close to Him should renounce the world and yet be in it. This is what the first *mantra* of the *Ishopanishad* exhorts us to do. This thing is difficult and yet easy at the same time. It is easy if we believe that we have to live for service. We acquire learning not for sensuous pleasures and for earning but for *mukti*. Education is considered necessary to save ourselves from darkness, sensuous pleasures and capricious behaviour.

Wholesome Educational Environment

That boy will grow into a courageous, healthy and service-minded boy, provided he gets a wholesome, environment.[1] His body as well as his mind will develop in right proportion. He will be free of any fraud or immorality. Staying in the village he will serve the villagers and will be content to live on the subsistence provided by the villagers. Through his service and the knowledge acquired by him he will provide proper guidance to the people around him and thus train more young men. I expect that a student trained under the Nayee Talim would develop on these lines.

3

Educational Innovations

Throughout the world today, people find themselves trapped in overwhelming socio-cultural, moral, and spiritual crises. We see the distress signals: rapid increases in crimes, unemployment, environmental degradation, endangered species, loss of languages, poverty, malnutrition, disease, militarism, and violent death, especially in the last fifty years. Yet also in this time, the amount of money, capital, technology, and trade worldwide has increased manifold, as have the number of health facilities and schools. Clearly, the Utopia that these institutions promised is very far from being realized. In fact, for many they have brought little better than dehumanized hell.

Visionaries of India's past – Gandhi, Tagore, Aurobindo, and Krishnamurti, among others –left us with several alternatives. In their writings and their experiments, each tried to envision a better reality for India, one unmarred by the greed and destruction of Western- style development and by the colonization and debilitation of Western-style schooling. They believed that India could only grow and regenerate itself by seeking out those beliefs, values, languages, cultures, knowledges and wisdoms upon which she had developed and lived. At the same time, they did not romanticize the past. Rather, they engaged in a critical traditionalism, believing that the injustices and problems within traditions and customs required self-correcting mechanisms. Thus, in their own unique ways, these innovators tried to create alternative visions of living and paths for India. Today, as we feel ourselves increasingly being swept away by these glo-cal (global-local) crises, and especially the crises of 'schooling,' perhaps it is time to revisit their ideas and experiments in education.

Why are we focusing on these four individuals? After all, a multitude of thinkers and experimenters have emerged throughout India's rich and diverse history. However, what distinguishes Gandhi, Tagore, Aurobindo, and Krishnamurti from the rest is their effort to situate education in a complete spiritual, political, socio-cultural, and economic vision of transformation. For them, education germinated from a context and it was just as important to transform this context, as it was to transform the system of education. To varying degrees, all four were engaged in India's freedom struggle, and their experiences around this struggle inspired them to imagine a different conception of freedom and, with it, a different India. They beautifully and forcefully expressed themselves in writings, poetry, speeches and meditations, and illustrated their ideas in extremely different parts of India: Gujarat/Madhya Pradesh/Maharashtra; Bengal; Pondicherry; and Andhra Pradesh/Karnataka.

Finally, and perhaps most importantly, while many people still refer to them, few really know what they envisioned, and even fewer know how to evolve their ideas/experiments or re-contextualize them to today's rapidly changing world. The current crises of the 'schooled' and of schooling require radical new thinking, new dialogue, and new action. While this radical discourse is being driven by thinkers in other parts of the world (mainly from industrialized countries), learning from the radicalism of these four visionaries could do much to resuscitate the intellectually-stagnated discourse on education in India. By deeply probing into their critiques, frameworks and experiments, we hope to invigorate the education discourse and offer fresh insight into the development of learning societies for 21st century India.

Education was arguably the most important arena for the introduction of modernity in India. Designed as it was by the colonial masters, besides remaining generally divorced from India tradition, it was also oblivious to the needs and problems of the teeming millions in the countryside. Gandhi's basic education scheme was primarily a system of rural education and handicraft constituted the medium of instruction. Spinning and weaving was again Gandhi's preference among the crafts and so his entire pedagogy and educational philosophy was intermeshed with his khadi based approach to life.

From his earliest days in Indian public life Gandhi was critical of the Western system of education for much of what it stood for in his opinion. A sample of his critique can be read below:

> "The system of education at present in vogue is wholly unsuited to India's needs, is a bad copy of the Western model and it has by reason of the medium of instruction being a foreign language sapped the energy of the youths who had passed through our schools and colleges and has produced an army of clerks and office-seekers. It has dried up all originality, impoverished the vernaculars and has deprived the masses of the benefit of higher knowledge which would otherwise have percolated through the intercourse of the education classes with them. The system has resulted in creating a gulf between educated India and the masses. It has stimulated the brain but starved the spirit for want o f a religious basis for education and emaciated the body for want of training in handicrafts. It has criminally neglected the greatest need of agricultural training worth the name..."

Judith Brown has rightly observed, it is difficult to appreciate quite how radical and abrasive Gandhi would have sounded to educated Indians as he castigated their educational training and their values and told them they were traitors to their mother land by being willing 'victims' of the current system'. Despite their opposition to British rule, most their nationalists did not reject the British rule, most other nationalists did not reject the British system of education outright, since they viewed it as a means by which India could became a materially advance nation. But form the beginning of his career Gandhi thought differently.

Alongside Champaran Satyagraha, his earliest foray into local politics, he launched his experiment in education. In November 1917 the first school was opened in Barharwa just a week after. The experiment grew mature and eventually in 1937 after Wardha Conference fully developed was announced, although system was announced although it was indeed a modified version of Gandhi's won scheme of education. Even in June 1921, writing in Young India he had outlined his views with a great deal of clarity:

> "I can see nothing wrong in the children, from the very threshold of their education, paying for it in work. The simplest handicraft, suitable for all, required for the whole of India undoubtedly spinning along with the previous processes. If we introduced this in our educational institutions, we should fulfill three purposes. If we introduced this in our educational institutions, we should fulfill three purpose: make education self – supporting, train the bodies of the children as well as their minds and pave the way for a complete boycott of foreign yarn and cloth. Moreover, the children thus equipped will become self-reliant and independent.

Gandhiji's experiments in education are described in this chapter in his own words. It will provide an insight into the vastness of his vision on education.

Experiments in South Africa

Education of Children

When I landed at Durban in January 1897, I had three children with me, my sister's son ten years old, and my own sons nine and five years of age. Where was I to educate them?

I could have sent them to the schools for European children, but only as a matter of favour and exception. No other Indian children were allowed to attend them. For these there were schools established by Christian missions, but I was not prepared to send my children there, as I did not like the education imparted in those schools. For one thing, the medium of instruction would be only English, or perhaps incorrect Tamil or Hindi; this too could only have been arranged with difficulty. I could not possibly put up with this and other disadvantages. In the meantime I was making my own attempt to teach them. But that was at best irregular, and I could not get hold of a suitable Gujarati teacher.

I was at my wit's end. I advertised for an English teacher who should teach the children under my direction. Some regular instruction was to be given them by this teacher, and for the rest they should be satisfied with what little I could give them irregularly. So I engaged an English governess on £7 a month. This went on for some time, but not to my satisfaction.

The boys acquired some knowledge of Gujarati through my conversation and intercourse with them, which was strictly in the mother tongue. I was loath to send them back to India, for I believed even then that young children should not be separated from their parents. The education that children naturally imbibe in a well-ordered household is impossible to obtain in hostels. I therefore kept my children with me. I did send my nephew and elder son to be educated at residential schools in India for a few months, but I soon had to recall them.

Later, the eldest son, long after he had come of age, broke away from me, and went to India to join a High School in Ahmedabad. I have an impression that the nephew was satisfied with what I could give him. Unfortunately he died in the prime of youth after a brief illness. The other three of my sons have never been at a public school, though they did get some regular schooling in an improvised school which I started for the children of Satyagrahi parents in South Africa.

These experiments were all inadequate. I could not devote to the children all the time I had wanted to give them. My inability to give them enough attention and other unavoidable causes prevented me from providing them with the literary education I had desired, and all my sons have had complaints to make against me in this matter. Whenever they come across an M.A. or a B.A., or even a matriculate, they seem to feel the handicap of a want of school education.

Nevertheless I am of opinion that, if I had insisted on their being educated somehow at public schools, they would have been deprived of the training that can be had only at the school of experience, or from constant contact with the parents. I should never have been free, as I am today, from anxiety on their score, and the artificial education that they could have had in England or South Africa, torn from me, would never have taught them the simplicity and the spirit of service that they show in their lives today, while their artificial ways of living might have been a serious handicap in my public work.

Therefore, though I have not been able to give them a literary education either to their or to my satisfaction, I am not quite sure, as I look back on my past years, that I have not done my duty by them to the best of my capacity. Nor do I regret not having sent them to public schools. I have always felt that the undesirable traits I see today in my eldest son are an echo of my own undisciplined and unformulated early life. I regard that time as a period of half-baked knowledge and indulgence.

It coincided with the most impressionable years of my eldest son, and naturally he has refused to regard it as my time of indulgence and inexperience. He has on the contrary believed that that was the brightest period of my life, and the changes, effected later, have been due to delusion, miscalled enlightenment. And well he might. Why should he not think that my earlier years represented a period of awakening, and the later years of radical change, years of delusion and egotism? Often have I been confronted with various posers from friends: What harm had there been, if I had given my boys an academical education? What right had I thus to clip their wings? Why should I have come in the way of their taking degrees and choosing their own careers?

I do not think that there is much point in these questions. I have come in contact with numerous students. I have tried myself or through others to impose my educational 'fads' on other children too and have seen the results thereof. There are within my knowledge a number of young men today contemporaneous with my sons. I do not think that man to man they are any better than my sons, or that my sons have much to learn from them.

But the ultimate result of my experiments is in the womb of the future. My object in discussing this subject here is that a student of the history of civilization may have some measure of the difference between disciplined home education and school education, and also of the effect produced on children through changes introduced by parents in their lives. The purpose of this chapter is also to show the lengths to which a votary of truth is driven by his experiments with truth, as also to show the votary of liberty how many are the sacrifices demanded by that stern goddess. Had I been without a sense of self-respect and satisfied myself with having for my children the education that other children could not get, I should have deprived them of the object-lesson in liberty and self-respect that I gave them at the cost of the literary training. And where a choice has to be made between liberty and learning, who will not say that the former has to be preferred a thousand times to latter.

A Peep into the Household

I introduced as much simplicity as was possible in a barrister's house. It was impossible to do without a certain amount of furniture. The change was more internal than external. The liking for doing personally all the physical labour increased. I therefore began to bring my children also under that discipline.

Instead of buying baker's bread, we began to prepare unleavened wholemeal bread at home according to Kuhne's recipe. Common mill flour was no good for this, and the use of handground flour, it was thought, would ensure more simplicity, health and economy. So I purchased a hand-mill for £7. The iron wheel was too heavy to be tackled by one man, but easy for two. Polak and I and the children usually worked it. My wife also occasionally lent a hand, though the grinding hour was her usual time for commencing kitchen work. Mrs. Polak now joined us on her arrival.

The grinding proved a very beneficial exercise for the children. Neither this nor any other work was ever imposed on them, but it was a pastime to them to come and lend a hand, and they were at liberty to break off whenever tired. But the children, including those whom I shall have occasion to introduce later, as a rule never failed me. Not that I had no laggards at all, but most did their work cheerfully enough. I can recall few youngsters in those days fighting shy of work or pleading fatigue.

We had engaged a servant to look after the house. He lived with us as a member of the family, and the children used to help him in his work. The municipal sweeper removed the night-soil, but we personally attended to the cleaning of the closet instead of asking or expecting the servant to do it. This proved a good training for the children.

The result was that none of my sons developed any aversion for scavenger's work, and they naturally got a good grounding in general sanitation. There was hardly any illness in the home at Johannesburg, but whenever there was any, the nursing was willingly done by the children. I will not say that I was indifferent to their literary education, but I certainly did not hesitate to sacrifice it. My sons have therefore some reason for a grievance against me. Indeed they have occasionally given expression to it, and I must plead guilty to a certain extent. The desire to give them a literary education was there. I even endeavoured to give it to them myself, but every now and then there was some hitch or other. As I had made no other arrangement for their private tuition, I used to get them to walk with me daily to the office and back home—a distance of about 5 miles in all. This gave them and me a fair amount of exercise. I tried to instruct them by conversation during these walks, if there was no one else claiming my attention.

All my children, excepting the eldest, Harilal, who had stayed away in India, were brought up in Johannesburg in this manner. Had I been able to devote at least an hour to their literary education with strict regularity, I should have given them, in my opinion, an ideal education. But it has been their, as also my, regret that I failed to ensure them enough literary training.

The eldest son has often given vent to his distress privately before me and publicly in the press; the other sons have generously forgiven the failure as unavoidable. I am not heart-broken over it, and the regret, if any, is that I did not prove an ideal father. But I hold that I sacrificed their literary training to what I genuinely, though may be wrongly, believed to be service to the community. I am quite clear that I have not been negligent in doing whatever was needful for building up their character. I believe it is the bounden duty of every parent to provide for this properly. Whenever, in spite of my endeavour, my sons have been found wanting, it is my certain conviction that they have reflected, not want of care on my part, but the defects of both their parents.

Children inherit the qualities of the parents, no less than their physical features. Environment does play an important part, but the original capital on which a child starts in life is inherited from its ancestors. I have also seen children successfully surmounting the effects of an evil inheritance. That is due to purity being an inherent attribute of the soul.

Curriculum

The main object of this school is to strengthen the pupils' character. It is said that real education consists in teaching the pupil the art of learning. In other words, a desire for knowledge should grow in him. Knowledge, however, is of many kinds. There is some knowledge which is harmful. If, therefore, the boys' character is not formed well, they will acquire the wrong kind of knowledge. Because of lack of proper planning in education, we observe that some persons grow to be atheists and some, though highly educated, fall a prey to vices. It is therefore the main object of this school to assist in building the moral character of boys. We can see this aim realized in Mr. Hassan Mia and Mr. Ravikrishna. We can form some idea of what Mr. Hassan Mia has been doing in England. Mr. Ravikrishna is in gaol today for the sake of the country. Both these have gone out from the school at Phoenix.

Boys will be taught their own language, that is, Gujarati or Hindi and, if possible, Tamil, as also English, arithmetic, history, geography, botany and zoology. Advanced pupils will also be taught algebra and geometry. It is expected that they can be brought up to the matriculation level.

For purposes of religious instruction, parents will be allowed to send any religious teacher of their choice. Hindu boys will be taught the fundamentals of the Hindu religion in any manner that may be desired by their parents. Indian Christians will be taught the elements of Christian religion by Mr. West and Mr. Cordes on the basis of the teachings of Theosophy. For boys of the Muslim faith, we want to arrange for a Moulvi, if possible. They will be permitted to go to Durban on Fridays. We believe that the education of any people is fruitless without religious instruction. Therefore, it is the duty of parents with a religious bent of mind to provide their children with both religious and secular education. We shall find on reflection that what we call secular education is also for strengthening the religious instinct. We think education imparted without any such aim is often harmful.

Boys will be taught the history of ancient and modern India so as to inculcate in them love of India and help them grow patriotic. Apart from this, there is no other information to be given. We hope that those who want to send their boys will do so indeed. As for the difficulty about the building, it is the duty of the parents to remove it. It is hardly necessary to mention that a report on the school and a statement of accounts will be published regularly.

Tolstoy Farm

As the Farm grew, it was found necessary to make some provision for the education of its boys and girls. There were, among these, Hindu, Musalman, Parsi and Christian boys and some Hindu girls. It was not possible, and I did not think it necessary, to engage special teachers for them. It was not possible, for qualified Indian teachers were scarce, and even when available, none would be ready to go to a place 21 miles distant from Johannesburg on a small salary. Also we were certainly not overflowing with money. And I did not think it necessary to import teachers from outside the Farm. I did not believe in the existing system of education, and I had a mind to find out by experience and experiment the true system. Only this much I knew,—that, under ideal conditions, true education could be imparted only by the parents, and that then there should be the minimum of outside help, that Tolstoy Farm was a family, in which I occupied the place of the father, and that I should so far as possible shoulder the responsibility for the training of the young.

The conception no doubt was not without its flaws. All the young people had not been with me since their childhood, they had been brought up in different conditions and environments, and they did not belong to the same religion. How could I do full justice to the young people, thus circumstanced, even if I assumed the place of paterfamilias?

But I had always given the first place to the culture of the heart or the building of character, and as I felt confident that moral training could be given to all alike, no matter how different their ages and their upbringing, I decided to live amongst them all the twenty-four hours of the day as their father. I regarded character building as the proper foundation for their education and, if the foundation was firmly laid, I was sure that the children could learn all the other things themselves or with the assistance of friends.

But as I fully appreciated the necessity of a literary training in addition, I started some classes with the help of Mr. Kallenbach and Sjt. Pragji Desai. Nor did I underrate the building up of the body. This they got in the course of their daily routine. For there were no servants on the Farm, and all the work, from cooking down to scavenging, was done by the inmates. There were many fruit trees to be looked after, and enough gardening to be done as well. Mr. Kallenbach was fond of gardening and had gained some experience of this work in one of the Governmental model gardens. It was obligatory on all, young and old, who were not engaged in the kitchen, to give some time to gardening .

The children had the lion's share of this work, which included digging pits, felling timber and lifting loads. This gave them ample exercise. They took delight in the work, and so they did not generally need any other exercise or games. Of course some of them, and sometimes all of them, malingered and shirked . Sometimes I connived at their pranks, but often I was strict with them. I dare say they did not like the strictness, but I do not recollect their having resisted it.

Whenever I was strict, I would, by argument, convince them that it was not right to play with one's work. The conviction would, however, be short-lived, the next moment they would again leave their work and go to play. All the same we got along, and at any rate they built up fine physiques. There was scarcely any illness on the Farm, though it must be said that good air and water and regular hours of food were not a little responsible for this.

A word about vocational training. It was my intention to teach every one of the youngsters some useful manual vocation. For this purpose Mr. Kallenbach went to a Trappist monastery and returned having learnt shoe-making. I learnt it from him and taught the art to such as were ready to take it up. Mr. Kallenbach had some experience of carpentry, and there was another inmate who knew it; so we had a small class in carpentry. Cooking almost all the youngsters knew.

All this was new to them. They had never even dreamt that they would have to learn these things some day. For generally the only training that Indian children received in South Africa was in the three R's.

On Tolstoy Farm we made it a rule that the youngsters should not be asked to do what the teachers did not do, and therefore, when they were asked to do any work, there was always a teacher co-operating and actually working with them. Hence whatever the youngsters learnt, they learnt cheerfully.

Literary Training

Literary training, however, was a more difficult matter. I had neither the resources nor the literary equipment necessary; and I had not the time I would have wished to devote to the subject. The physical work that I was doing used to leave me thoroughly exhausted at the end of the day, and I used to have the classes just when I was most in need of some rest. Instead, therefore, of my being fresh for the class, I could with the greatest difficulty keep myself awake. The mornings had to be devoted to work on the farm and domestic duties, so the school hours had to be kept after the midday meal. There was no other time suitable for the school.

We gave three periods at the most to literary training. Hindi, Tamil, Gujarati and Urdu were all taught, and tuition was given through the vernaculars of the boys. English was taught as well. It was also necessary to acquaint the Gujarati Hindu children with a little Sanskrit, and to teach all the children elementary history, geography and arithmetic.

I had undertaken to teach Tamil and Urdu. The little Tamil I knew was acquired during voyages and in jail. I had not got beyond Pope's excellent Tamil handbook. My knowledge of the Urdu script was all that I had acquired on a single voyage, and my knowledge of the language was confined to the familiar Persian and Arabic words that I had learnt from contact with Musalman friends. Of Samskrit I knew no more than I had learnt at the high school, even my Gujarati was no better than that which one acquires at the school.

Such was the capital with which I had to carry on. In poverty of literary equipment my colleagues went one better than I. But my love for the languages of my country, my confidence in my capacity as a teacher, as also the ignorance of my pupils, and more than that, their generosity, stood me in good stead.

The Tamil boys were all born in South Africa, and therefore knew very little Tamil, and did not know the script at all. So I had to teach them the script and the rudiments of grammar. That was easy enough. My pupils knew that they could any day beat me in Tamil conversation, and when Tamilians, not knowing English, came to see me, they became my interpreters. I got along merrily, because I never attempted to disguise my ignorance from my pupils. In all respects I showed myself to them exactly as I really was. Therefore in spite of my colossal ignorance of the language I never lost their love and respect. It was comparatively easier to teach the Musalman boys Urdu. They knew the script. I had simply to stimulate in them an interest in reading and to improve their handwriting.

These youngsters were for the most part unlettered and unschooled. But I found in the course of my work that I had very little to teach them, beyond weaning them from their laziness, and supervising their studies. As I was content with this, I could pull on with boys of different ages and learning different subjects in one and the same class room.

Of text-books, about which we hear so much, I never felt the want. I do not even remember having made much use of the books that were available. I did not find it at all necessary to load the boys with quantities of books. I have always felt that the true text-book for the pupil is his teacher. I remember very little that my teachers taught me from books, but I have even now a clear recollection of the things they taught me independently of books.

Children take in much more and with less labour through their ears than through their eyes. I do not remember having read any book from cover to cover with my boys. But I gave them, in my own language, all that I had digested from my reading of various books, and I dare say they are still carrying a recollection of it in their minds. It was laborious for them to remember what they learnt from books, but what I imparted to them by word of mouth they could repeat with the greatest ease. Reading was a task for them, but listening to me was a pleasure, when I did not bore them by failure to make my subject interesting. And from the questions that my talks prompted them to put I had a measure of their power of understanding.

Training of the Spirit

The spiritual training of the boys was a much more difficult matter than their physical and mental training. I relied little on religious books for the training of the spirit. Of course I believed that every student should be acquainted with the elements of his own religion and have a general knowledge of his own scriptures, and therefore I provided for such knowledge as best I could. But that, to my mind, was part of the intellectual training. Long before I undertook the education of the youngsters of the Tolstoy Farm I had realized that the training of the spirit was a thing by itself. To develop the spirit is to build character and to enable one to work towards a knowledge of God and self-realization. And I held that this was an essential part of the training of the young, and that all training without culture of the spirit was of no use, and might be even harmful.

I am familiar with the superstition that self-realization is possible only in the fourth stage of life, i.e., *sannyasa* (renunciation). But it is a matter of common knowledge that those who defer preparation for this invaluable experience until the last stage of life attain not self-realization but old age amounting to a second and pitiable childhood, living as a burden on this earth. I have a full recollection that I held these views even whilst I was teaching, i.e, in 1911–12, though I might not then have expressed them in identical language.

How then was this spiritual training to be given? I made the children memorize and recite hymns, and read to them from books on moral training. But that was far from satisfying me. As I came into closer contact with them I saw that it was not through books that one could impart training of the spirit. Just as physical training was to be imparted through physical exercise, and intellectual through intellectual exercise, even so the training of the spirit was possible only through the exercise of the spirit. And the exercise of the spirit entirely depended on the life and character of the teacher. The teacher had always to be mindful of his p's and q's, whether he was in the midst of his boys or not.

It is possible for a teacher situated miles away to affect the spirit of the pupils by his way of living. It would be idle for me, if I were a liar, to teach boys to tell the truth. A cowardly teacher would never succeed in making his boys valiant, and a stranger to self-restraint could never teach his pupils the value of self-restraint. I saw, therefore, that I must be an eternal object-lesson to the boys and girls living with me. They thus became my teachers, and I learnt I must be good and live straight, if only for their sakes. I may say that the increasing discipline and restraint I imposed on myself at Tolstoy Farm was mostly due to those wards of mine.

One of them was wild, unruly, given to lying, and quarrelsome. On one occasion he broke out most violently. I was exasperated. I never punished my boys, but this time I was very angry. I tried to reason with him. But he was adamant and even tried to over-reach me. At last I picked up a ruler lying at hand and delivered a blow on his arm. I trembled as I struck him. I dare say he noticed it. This was an entirely novel experience for them all. The boy cried out and begged to be forgiven. He cried not because the beating was painful to him; he could, if he had been so minded, have paid me back in the same coin, being a stoutly built youth of seventeen; but he realized my pain in being driven to this violent resource. Never again after this incident did he disobey me. But I still repent that violence. I am afraid I exhibited before him that day not the spirit, but the brute, in me.

I have always been opposed to corporal punishment. I remember only one occasion on which I physically punished one of my sons. I have therefore never until this day been able to decide whether I was right or wrong in using the ruler. Probably it was improper, for it was prompted by anger and a desire to punish. Had it been an expression only of my distress, I should have considered it justified. But the motive in this case was mixed.

This incident set me thinking and taught me a better method of correcting students. I do not know whether that method would have availed on the occasion in question. The youngster soon forgot the incident, and I do not think he ever showed great improvement. But the incident made me understand better the duty of a teacher towards his pupils.

Cases of misconduct on the part of the boys often occurred after this, but I never resorted to corporal punishment. Thus in my endeavour to impart spiritual training to the boys and girls under me, I came to understand better and better the power of the spirit.

Tares Among the Wheat

It was at Tolstoy Farm that Mr. Kallenbach drew my attention to problem that had never before struck me. As I have already said, some of the boys at the Farm were bad and unruly. There were loafers, too, amongst them. With these my three boys came in daily contact, as also did other children of the same type as my own sons. This troubled Mr. Kallenbach, but his attention was centred on impropriety of keeping *my* boys with these un-truly youngsters.

One day he spoke out: 'Your way of mixing your own boys with the bad ones does not appeal to me. It can have only one result. They will become demoralized through this bad company.'

I do not remember whether the question puzzled me at the moment, but I recollect what I said to him:

'How can I distinguish between my boys and the loafers? I am equally responsible for both. The youngsters have come because I invited them. If I were to dismiss them with some money, they would immediately run off to Johannesburg and fall back into their old ways. To tell you the truth, it is quite likely that they and their guardians believe that, by having come here, they have laid me under an obligation. That they have to put up with a good deal of inconvenience here, you and I know very well. But my duty is clear. I must have them here, and therefore my boys also must need live with them.

And surely you do not want me to teach my boys to feel from today that they are superior to other boys. To put that sense of superiority into their heads would be to lead them astray. This association with other boys will be a good discipline for them. They will, of their own accord, learn to discriminate between good and evil. Why should we not believe that, if there is really anything good in them, it is bound to react on their companions? However that may be, I cannot help keeping them here, and if that means some risk, we must run it.'

Mr. Kallenbach shook his head.

The result, I think, cannot be said to have been bad. I do not consider my sons were any the worse for the experiment. On the contrary I can see that they gained something. If there was the slightest trace of superiority in them, it was destroyed and they learnt to mix with all kinds of children. They were tested and disciplined.

This and similar experiments have shown me that, if good children are taught together with bad ones and thrown into their company, they will lose nothing, provided the experiment is conducted under the watchful care of their parents and guardians.

Children wrapped up in cottonwool are not always proof against all temptation or contamination. It is true, however, that when boys and girls of all kinds of upbringing are kept and taught together, the parents and the teachers are put to the severest test. They have constantly to be on the alert.

Fasting as Penance

Day by day it became increasingly clear to me how very difficult it was to bring up and educate boys and girls in the right way. If I was to be their real teacher and guardian, I must touch their hearts, I must share their joys and sorrows, I must help them to solve the problems that faced them, and I must take along the right channel the surging aspirations of their youth.

I hold, however, that some occasions do call for this drastic remedy. But it presupposes clearness of vision and spiritual fitness. Where there is no true love between the teacher and the pupil, where the pupil's delinquency has not touched the very being of the teacher and where the pupil has no respect for the teacher, fasting is out of place and may even be harmful. Though there is thus room for doubting the propriety of fasts in such cases, there is no question about the teacher's responsibility for the errors of his pupil.

Experiments in India

Shantiniketan

From Rajkot I proceeded to Shantiniketan. The teachers and students overwhelmed me with affection. The reception was a beautiful combination of simplicity, art and love.

The Phoenix family had been assigned separate quarters at Shantiniketan. Maganlal Gandhi was at their head, and he had made it his business to see that all the rules of the Phoenix Ashram should be scrupulously observed. I saw that, by dint of his love, knowledge and perseverance, he had made his fragrance felt in the whole of Shantiniketan.Andrews was there, and also Pearson. Amongst the Bengali teachers with whom we came in fairly close contact were Jagadanandbabu, Nepalbabu, Santoshbabu, Kshitimohanbabu, Nagenbabu, Sharadbabu and Kalibabu.

As is my wont, I quickly mixed with the teachers and students, and engaged them in a discussion on self-help. I put it to the teachers that, if they and the boys dispensed with the services of paid cooks and cooked their food themselves, it would enable the teachers to control the kitchen from the point of view the boys' physical and moral health, and it would afford to the students an object-lesson in self-help. One or two of them were inclined to shake their heads. Some of them strongly approved of the proposal. The boys welcomed it, if only because of their instinctive taste for novelty. So we launched the experiment. When I invited the Poet to express his opinion, he said that he did not mind it provided the teachers were favourable. To the boys he said, ' The experiment contains the key to Swaraj.'

Pearson began to wear away his body in making the experiment a success. He threw himself into it with zest. A batch was formed to cut vegetables, another to clean the grain, and so on. Nagenbabu and others undertook to see the sanitary cleaning of the kitchen and its surroundings. It was a delight to me to see them working spade in hand.

But it was too much to expect the hundred and twenty-five boys with their teachers to take to this work of physical labour like ducks to water. There used to be daily discussion. Some began early to show fatigue. But Pearson was not the man to be tired. One would always find him with his smiling face doing something or other in or about the kitchen. He had taken upon himself the cleaning of the bigger utensils. A party of students played on their sitar before this cleaning party in order to beguile the tedium of the operation. All alike took the thing up with zest and Shantiniketan became a busy hive.

Changes like these when once begun always develop. Not only was the Phoenix party's kitchen self-conducted, but the food cooked in it was of the simplest. Condiments were eschewed. Rice, dal, vegetables and even wheat flour were all cooked at one and the same time in a steam cooker. And Shantiniketan boys started a similar kitchen with a view to introducing reform in the Bengali kitchen. One or two teachers and some students ran this kitchen.

The experiment was, however, dropped after some time. I am of opinion that the famous institution lost nothing by having conducted the experiment for a brief interval, and some of the experiences gained could not but be of help to the teachers.

Satyagraha Ashram Experiment

The Ashram experiment in education was a trial for us as nothing else was.

We saw at once that the women and children in the Ashram should be taught to read and write, and a little later on that there should be similar facilities for even the illiterate men that came to the Ashram. Those who had already joined the Ashram could not undertake to teach. If capable teachers were to be attracted to the Ashram, the rule of brahmacharya had to be relaxed in their case. The Ashram was therefore divided into two sections, the 'teachers' quarters and the Ashram proper.

Human beings cannot overcome their weakness all at once. As soon as the two sections came into being, a feeling of superiority and inferiority poisoned the Ashram atmosphere in spite of all our efforts to scotch it. The Ashramites developed spiritual pride, which the teachers could not tolerate. This pride was an obstacle in the attainment of the Ashram ideal and therefore an aspect of untruth as well.

If brahmacharya was to be observed in its perfection, the division was inevitable. But the brahmacharis had no reason to think too highly of themselves. It may be that the brahmacharis who sinned mentally in spite of themselves were retrogressing while those who did not claim to be brahmacharis but liked brahmacharya were making progress. This was clear to the intellect but it was not easy for all of us to put it into practice.

Then again there were differences of opinion as regards the method of education which gave rise to difficulties in administration. There were bitter discussions, but at last all calmed down and learned the lesson of forbearance. This was in my view a triumph of truth, the goal of all Ashram endeavour. Those who held divergent views harboured no evil intentions in their minds, and were indeed grieved at the divergence. They wished to practise truth as they saw it. Their partiality for their own stand-point came in the way of their giving due weight to the arguments of their opponents. Hence the quarrels which put our charity to a severe test.

I have my own perhaps peculiar views on education which have not been accepted by my colleagues in full, and here they are:

1. Young boys and girls should have co-education till they are eight years of age.
2. Their education should mainly consist in manual training under the supervision of an educationist.
3. The special aptitudes of each child should be recognized in determining the kind of work he or she should do.
4. The reasons for every process should be explained when the process is being carried.

5. General knowledge should be imparted to each child as he begins to understand things. Learning to read or write should come later.
6. The child should first be taught to draw simple geometrical figures, and when he has learnt to draw these with ease, he should be taught to write the alphabet. If this is done he will write a good hand from the very first.
7. Reading should come before writing. The letters should be treated as pictures to be recognized and later on to be copied.
8. A child taught on these lines will have acquired considerable knowledge according to his capacity by the time he is eight.
9. Nothing should be taught to a child by force.
10. He should be interested in everything taught to him.
11. Education should appear to the child like play. Play is an essential part of education.
12. All education should be imparted through the mother tongue.
13. The child should be taught Hindi-Urdu as the national language, before he learns letters.
14. Religious education is indispensable and the child should get it by watching the teacher's conduct and by hearing him talk about it.
15. Nine to sixteen constitutes the second stage in the child's education.
16. It is desirable that boys and girls should have co-education during the second stage also as far as possible.
17. Hindu children should now be taught Sanskrit, and Muslim children Arabic.

18. Manual training should be continued during the second stage. Literary education should be allotted more time according to necessity.
19. The boys during this stage should be taught their parents' vocation in such a way that they will by their own choice obtain their livelihood by practising the hereditary craft. This does not apply to the girls.
20. During this stage the child should acquire a general knowledge of world history and geography, botany, astronomy, arithmetic, geometry and algebra.
21. Each child should now be taught to sew and to cook.
22. Sixteen to twenty-five is the third stage, during which every young person should have an education according to his or her wishes and circumstances.
23. During the second stage (9–16) education should be self-supporting; that is, the child, all the time that he is learning, is working upon some industry, the proceeds of which will meet the expenditure of the school.
24. Production starts from the very beginning, but during the first stage it does not still catch up with the expenditure.
25. Teachers should be paid not very high salaries but only a living wage. They should be inspired by a spirit of service. It is a despicable thing to take any Tom, Dick or Harry as a teacher in the primary stage. All teachers should be men of character.
26. Big and expensive buildings are not necessary for educational institutions.
27. English should be taught only as one of several languages. As Hindi is the national language, English is to be used in dealing with other nations and international commerce.

As for women's education I am not sure whether it should be different from men's and when it should begin. But I am strongly of opinion that women should have the same facilities as men and even special facilities where necessary.

There should be night schools for illiterate adults. But I do not think that they must be taught the three R's; they must be helped to acquire general knowledge through lectures, etc., and if they wish, we should arrange to teach them the three R's also.

Experiments in the Ashram have convinced us of one thing, viz., that industry in general and spinning in particular should have pride of place in education, which must be largely self-supporting as well as related to and tending to the betterment of rural life.

In these experiments we have achieved the largest measure of success with the women, who have imbibed the spirit of freedom and self-confidence as no other class of women have done to my knowledge. This success is due to the Ashram atmosphere.

Women in the Ashram are not subject to any restraint which is not imposed on the men as well. They are placed on a footing of absolute equality with the men in all activities. Not a single Ashram task is assigned to the women to the exclusion of the men. Cooking is attended to by both. Women are of course exempted from work which is beyond their strength; otherwise men and women work together everywhere. There is no such thing as purdah or laj in the Ashram. No matter from where she has come, a woman, as soon as she enters the Ashram, breathes the air of freedom and casts out all fear from her mind. And I believe that the Ashram observance of brahmacharya has made a big contribution to this state of things. Adult girls live in the Ashram as virgins. We are aware that this experiment is fraught with risk but we feel that no awakening among women is possible without incurring it.

Women cannot make any progress so long as there are child marriages. All girls are supposed to be in duty bound to marry and that too before menstruation commences, and widow re-marriage is not permitted. Women, therefore, when they join the Ashram, are told that these social customs are wrong and irreligious. But they are not shocked as they find the Ashram practising what it preaches.

Not much of what is usually called education will be observed in the Ashram. Still we find that the old as well as the young, women as well as men are eager to acquire knowledge and complain that they have no time for it. This is a good sign.

Real education begins after a child has left school. One who has appreciated the value of studies is a student all his life. His knowledge must increase from day to day while he is discharging his duty in a conscientious manner. And this is well understood in the Ashram.

The superstition that no education is possible without a teacher is an obstacle in the path of educational progress. A man's real teacher is himself. And nowadays there numerous aids available for self -education. A diligent person can easily acquire knowledge about many things by himself and obtain the assistance of a teacher when it is needed. Experience is the biggest of all schools. Quite a number of crafts cannot be learnt at school but only in the workshop. Knowledge of these acquired at school is often only parrot-like. Other subjects can be learnt with the help of books. Therefore what adults need is not so much a school as a thirst for knowledge, diligence and self-confidence.

The education of children is primarily a duty to be discharged by the parents. Therefore the creation of a vital educational atmosphere is more important than the foundation of numerous schools. When once this atmosphere has been established on a firm footing the schools will come in due course.

National Gujarati School

For many years past, several friends and I have felt that our present education is not national and that in consequence people do not get from it the benefit they ought to. Our children languish as a result of this education. They become incapable of any great achievement and the knowledge they acquire does not spread among the masses—not even in their families. Nor do the young people have any aim in mind in taking this modern education except to get a job and make money. It is one of the fundamental principles of education that it should be planned with a view to the needs of the people. This idea finds no place at all in our schools.

Wherever I have travelled in India, I have discussed this question with the leaders and, without exception, almost every one has admitted that our educational system must change.

To look to the Government for this will be sheer waste of time. The Government will wait on public opinion and, being foreign, move very timidly; it cannot understand our needs, its advisers may be ill-informed or they may have interests of their own to serve. For a variety of such reasons, it will probably be quite long before there is any serious change in the present system; the time that passes meanwhile is so much loss to the people.

It is, however, not intended to suggest here that we should not try to get the Government to move. Let petitions be made to it and let public opinion be ascertained. But the best petition to the Government will be an actual demonstration by us and this will also be the easiest way of cultivating public opinion. It has accordingly been decided, in consultation with some educated gentlemen, to start a national school.

Basic principle: The education will be physical, intellectual and religious.

For physical education, there will be training in agriculture and hand-weaving and in the use of carpenter's and blacksmith's tools incidental to these. That will provide sufficient exercise for the pupils. In addition, they will be given drill, which is both an entertainment [and a practical utility] and, as part of this, they will be taught how to march in squads and how each one may work with quiet efficiency in case of accidents such as fire.

They will have instruction on how to preserve health and on home remedies for ordinary ailments, with as much of physiology and botany as may be necessary for the purpose.

For intellectual training, they will study Gujarati, Marathi, Hindi and Sanskrit as compulsory subjects. Urdu, Tamil and Bengali will also be taught.

There will be no teaching of English during the first three years.

In addition, the pupils will be taught Mathematics (Arithmetic, Algebra and Geometry). Instruction in multiplication tables, Indian book-keeping and the measures, weights, etc., currently in use will begin at once and the rest of the curriculum will be covered progressively.

There will be instruction in History, Geography, Elements of Astronomy and Elements of Chemistry.

By way of instruction in religion, pupils will be taught general ethical principles and we are hopeful that the teachers will demonstrate by their conduct that the essence of religion is good character.

All teaching will be through Gujarati, right up to the highest stage, and most of it will be oral during the first few years. The intention is to put across to the children, before they learn to read and write, quite a few things orally by way of stories, as was the practice in old days, and so help their minds to grow, and to give them some general knowledge as they play about, rather than repress them by doing nothing more than remarking, "Oh dear, dear! How dirty", and so on.

The aim at present is that after a few years of such education, the student's equipment will approximate to that of a well-informed graduate. That is, he will have a reduced load by way of learning English and, during the time so saved, he will be given all the useful knowledge a graduate acquires. He will be freed from the fear of examinations. All the students will be tested from time to time, but that will be by the teachers of the school itself. The use to which the student puts his abilities after leaving school will be the true measure of the worth of his education.

Every opportunity will be taken to rid his mind of the fallacious notion that the aim of education is to get employment. And, finally, every pupil joining this school is likely to develop such self-confidence in a few years that he will not be troubled with doubts or fears about how he will make a living. A pupil who has been in the school for five years will be fixed up, if he so desires, in some work in the school itself and be paid for it. The school will make arrangements with some factories, etc., so that they provide training in vocations and give a start to those who wish to set themselves up independently. If, after ten years of study, anyone wants to pursue a subject further, necessary arrangements for the purpose are left to the future.

Free Education

No fees will be charged in this school, the expenses being met from donations received.

Teachers

Paid teachers will be engaged and will be, all of them, grown-up men who have reached the college level or possess equivalent attainments. The idea is that children should have the best teachers in the early stages.

Objects of School

1. To adopt a new method of education.
2. To pay special attention to character-building, the aim being that ten per cent of the pupils at any rate get trained for national service.
3. To raise the status of the Gujarati language.
4. To work for the spread of the national language, Hindi.
5. To open schools of the new pattern in every place, and make this school a model for them, and for Government as well, to copy. The aim is to have teachers trained in this school who will then go to villages and run schools there.
6. To get the new pattern adopted by the Government.

Requirements for Teachers

1. Knowledge of Hindi and Marathi
2. Proficiency in weaving
3. Well-preserved health
4. Travel in India
5. Readiness for other work besides that in the school, that is, for work in the Ashram or as secretary to Bapu

Work to be Attended to by Teachers, Apart from Teaching

1. Text-books
2. Vocabulary of technical terms

Co-Education

I am myself in favour of co-education, but I don't insist on it if the teachers hold a different opinion.

I am not in favour of common residence. Girls should not be kept in a hostel. I am of the view that they must live under the constant supervision of their mothers and nowhere else.

There should be holidays in summer and the school should be shifted to a cooler place. This, I believe, will enable the teachers and the pupils to work very much better at other times. The teachers and the pupils should spend the holidays together.

English should be an optional subject. One should know good, at any rate correct, English. It would be excellent if we could get an English teacher for the purpose, but I can think of no one at present except Miss Schlesin. If only she would come, we could want nothing better. She is a very capable person. A pupil of the school should be able to talk in English with any Englishman without being nervous.

Drawing will be taught not as a fine art but because the pupil should be able to draw for practical purposes, draw maps, for instance, and straight lines, have a good hand-writing and should know memory drawing.

Rules should be framed for discipline in the school, but no compulsion should be used to enforce obedience to them; they [the pupil] should feel inclined to obey them on their own. One should keep a watch on them whether they do. If any of them does not, we should express our disapproval and advise him.

To start with, 100 pupils should be admitted to the school, all of whom can pay for their own expenses. Nothing may be spent from the School Fund for any of the pupils. If there is a good but poor student, we may secure help for him from one of our friends and beg of another for his fees; but the School Fund cannot be used for the purpose.

History, Geography, Science and Hygiene can be part of Gujarati.

We have necessarily to come into contact with people from the South, and this is to our benefit too; everyone should, therefore, know Marathi.

True National Education

Our teachers must be men of high moral character. Conditions must be created to enable the poorest Indian to receive the best possible education. There must be a happy union of literary knowledge and Dharma. Education must be related to the conditions of life in our country. And the heavy burden on the minds of our young men resulting from the use of an alien language as the medium of instruction must be removed. Unless we reshape our education so as to fulfil the foregoing the level of the life of our people cannot be raised.

True national education should be imparted through the language of each province. The teachers must be men of high ability. The school should be located at a place where students would get clean drinking water, pure air and a peaceful atmosphere. The surroundings must be perfectly healthy. The scheme of education must provide for securing to the students a knowledge of the main occupations and religions of India.

[Except] . . . the first five years of a child's life, the rest of his education is given through a foreign language. Besides, in the first five years, which are in some respects the most useful and of the greatest importance, education is usually imparted by the most ordinary type of teachers. Then begins English. At this stage the boys pass as if into a different world altogether. The education which is given to them has no relation to the life at home. The boys who till then were quite happy to do their lessons sitting on the ground now have benches.

At home, even today, the prevailing custom in most homes is to sit on the floor. Until then, the boy, if he was a Hindu, was content to wear a dhoti, a kurta and the angarakha and, if a Muslim, to wear the payjamas instead of the dhoti; but now he uses a coat and trousers. Until then, he could do with the homely kalam, but now he has a pen with a steel nib. Thus, many significant changes take place in his outer living and a wide gulf divides the home and the school. Gradually, but definitely, this change begins to enter his inner life too. How are these changes in the outer life and the inner mental make-up of the boy going to affect his home and the way his people live at home? His parents have no idea at all as to what sort of education the boy is getting and their faith in that education is negligible.

Parents only know that it will help the boy to earn money. And this satisfies them. If this situation lasts long, we might all become foreigners! What is worse even the Swaraj for which we are struggling may become foreign in character when we finally get it, with the result that the very burden under which we are crushed today may continue even after Swaraj. There is only one way to escape this danger. It is to change and overhaul our system of education. In the national education to be evolved:

1. Education must be imparted through the mother-tongue.

2. There must be accord between the education a child receives at school and the environment of the home.
3. It must be so planned as to meet the needs of the majority of the people.
4. The teachers in primary classes must be competent men of good character right from the first class.
5. Education must be free.
6. Overall control must be in the hands of the people.

Education must be imparted through the mother-tongue. It is a pity that we are required to prove this self-evident truth. If we had not been dazzled by the lure of English, there should have been no need to prove this most obvious truth. The advocates of English say:

1. It is through English that an awakening has been created in the country.
2. English literature is so rich and vast that to give it up would be a great misfortune. It is not possible to translate it all into our language.
3. We can achieve unity only through English. To try to encourage and promote the different languages of India would amount to disrupting this unity and retarding the growing feeling that we are one nation.
4. English is the language of the rulers.

These are the main arguments of the advocates of English. They have many other things to say, but they have no more substance or importance than is included in the above.

To say that all the awakening we see in the country has been brought about through English is only a half-truth. The fact is that all the education in the country is being imparted through English. And because the Hindus are not absolute blockheads they have imbibed and utilized the good they have found in it. And yet the overall result which this education has yielded has been disappointing. Everybody admits that the present system of education suffers from some grave defects. We have not received from it the results which we are entitled to expect of an education which has now lasted for more than fifty years. Why is it so? If it had been imparted from the beginning through the mother-tongue it would have produced much good by this time. What only a few English-knowing people know at present would have spread and reached crores of our people—who would have shown the spirit and the strength which is now shown only by the English-knowing handful.

At present, our young men, when they pass out of the college, appear to be devoid of all energy and just wander about in search of jobs. Instead, if they had been educated through the mother-tongue, then having been spared the strain of cramming, they would have been stronger both in body and mind and would have therefore rejected Government service as something inferior.

No one suggests that English literature should be given up. We should have translated what is precious in it into our different languages. Japan and South Africa have done it. In Japan, they taught German and French to some who then translated good books from German and French into Japanese. It is not that German has nothing to borrow from English. Even so, not all Germans learn English. No German receives his education through English. Only a few Germans learn English and then translate into German whatever they think will be of value to their nation, and thus serve their mother-tongue. We should do the same.

As to the assumption that we have received a sense of unity by using English, the fact is that we become sharply aware of the illusion of our separateness from one another only after this alien language was introduced into our country, though it may be admitted that once we had seen through that illusion we strove to throw it off and regain our national solidarity. We observe that in many countries the oneness of the people is not always due to the oneness of the language. There are two languages in South Africa. But the people are striving to achieve unity because their interests are the same. Similar is the case with Canada.

In England, Scotland and Wales they still speak three different languages. Mr. Lloyd George is making great efforts to revive Welsh, the language of Wales. And, yet, in all the three parts of Great Britain there is a strong feeling that they are one nation. Development of the regional languages of our country will produce social, political and economic awakening amongst our people. They will have a better appreciation of their condition and position in the picture of the wider whole of the country. They will know that though belonging to different provinces they are sailing in the same boat. Thus they will forget differences of language, appreciate the unity of their interests and be ready to fight for it, and protect it from dangers. Besides, the better educated amongst us will have to learn Hindi—as the common medium of speech. The effort required to learn Hindi is as nothing compared to that needed to learn English.

That English is the language of the rulers proves nothing beyond the fact that some of us have to master this alien tongue. I do not dislike English; I am only pleading that it be put in its proper place. Then, we can truly appreciate its merits, and derive such benefit as we can. It cannot, however, continue to be the medium of our education; nor can it be the language of inter-provincial communication. In our schools and colleges we must provide for imparting even the highest education through the mother-tongue.

There must be accord between the education given in the school and the home. The reason for this is obvious. Today, there is no such accord between the two. In national education, we must see that such accord is achieved and maintained.

We will now pass on to the third attribute of national education, namely, that it should be so designed as to meet the needs of the majority of the people. The great bulk of our people are peasants. So, if our boys had been given, from the very beginning, a knowledge of agriculture and weaving and if they had cultivated an appreciation of the needs of these two classes, and if these classes had received the scientific training in these vocations, our peasants today would have been happy and prosperous.

Our cattle would not have been weak and diseased as they are today. Our peasants would not have been crushed with the weight of debt—incurred by poverty. Our produce would not have first gone to foreign countries as raw material and then brought back to us in the shape of finished goods to drain us of wealth. Today, we feel ashamed of such a state of affairs. We could not have paid England 85 crores rupees a year for cotton cloth. The prevailing system of education has made slaves of us instead of masters.

In the lower stages of primary education teachers must be men of high character. There is a proverb in English: 'The child is the father of the man.' We have a similar proverb: 'A child, even while in the cradle, shows signs of what he is going to be in the future.' If we entrust our children, in their most impressionable years, to incompetent teachers, we have no right to expect that they will grow to be men of good and strong character. That would be as absurd as to sow the seeds of kauvach and expect from them the flowers of mogra. We must procure the best teachers for our children whatever it may cost. In ancient times, our children received their education from learned and wise Rishis and Munis.

The fifth requirement of national education is that it should be free. Education should not be made to depend on money . Just as the sun gives light to all equally and rain pours down for all, even so learning must be made available to all.

Lastly, the people themselves must have control over the planning and carrying out of education. In the exercise of this control lies education too. People will then have faith in the education meted out to their children, and feel their responsibility towards it. When this stage is reached and education occupies an important place in the life of our people, it will be possible for us to obtain Swaraj with no trouble at all. Therefore, it is our duty to initiate such education. It is also our right to ask the Government for it. But we can approach the Government about this matter only after we start the ball rolling ourselves. However, it is beyond the scope of this article to discuss the steps we should take for organizing such a type of national education. Let people first accept the view expressed herein.

National Higher Education

I have done a good many things in my life; some of them I feel proud of, though some others I regret. A few of them were very responsible undertakings. But I should like to state here—I am sure I am guilty of no exaggeration—that nothing I have done so far can stand comparison with what we are about to do today. I am aware of a great risk in this undertaking, but not because I fear that it may prove harmful to the nation; what pains me, or rather the incongruity I feel, is this that I am not fit for the task I have undertaken. I do not say this as a matter of formality, I speak from the heart. If I knew that the present undertaking related to education in the real sense of the term, this preface would not have been necessary. This Mahavidyalaya is not being established with the sole object of imparting education; it [also] aims at helping the student to acquire a means of livelihood and when, in this respect, I compare it with Gujarat College and other similar institutions, I simply shudder.

In this, too, I am not exaggerating. What comparison is possible between Gujarat College and other similar colleges, on the one hand, and this small Mahavidyalaya of ours? To my mind, of course, it is great, but I am afraid that in your eyes, as you compare this Vidyalaya with the colleges you have in India, this Maha-vidyalaya1 probably appears an Anuvidyalaya2. You are very likely thinking in terms of brick and mortar. Of this, to be sure, I see more in Gujarat College.

Today, not an inch of the ground is ours. Everything belongs to the Government. This land, these trees, everything belongs to Government, even this body, and I have now begun to doubt whether our soul also is ours. Placed in this pitiable condition, why go looking for good buildings to house our Mahavidyalaya? How can we afford to wait till we had found men of great learning? Even if the most ignorant of ignorant men, a mere simpleton, were to come forward and could succeed in convincing us that our atman had been starved, that this country had lost its light—its knowledge of things of the spirit—I would appoint him as the principal. I am not sure that you would be ready to appoint a shepherd as principal and so we have had to find Shri Gidwani1. I have not been attracted by the position he occupied. Perhaps you do not know him apart from that position. I should, however, like you to adopt a different criterion, some another touchstone, for judging the worth of this Vidyalaya if you test it on the common touchstone, it will seem to be brass but it will be found to be gold if you test it on the touchstone of character.

The coming together of [talented] men for educational work here is like the holy confluence of rivers. We have men of character assembled here. Fine men from Sind, Maharashtra and Gujarat have banded together here. How could we have, ordinarily, secured this?

I shall first address my prayer to the sisters and brothers who have come here for the function. You are witnesses to the establishment of this Mahavidyalaya. If there are any among you who feel that what is taking place is a farce, I would ask them not to be so conscientious and sit through the function. They should remain only if they wish to give their blessings. With the blessings of you all, the Mahavidyalalya will earn a name as a great institution. But they should not be blessings merely uttered with the lips; bless it from your heart. This you can do only by offering your sons and daughters to the institution. People in India have plenty of capacity to contribute money.

In no field is progress held up for lack of funds. It is held up for want of men—of teachers or leaders, or if a leader is forthcoming, for want of pupils, i.e., soldiers. It is my belief that, if the leader is worthy, there will be no lack of soldiers. A carpenter will not quarrel with his tools, however bad they may be. He will handle the bluntest of them with the utmost ease. Likewise, if the leader is a real artisan, whatever the quality of the material, he will produce gold from it, will produce gold from the country's clay. This is my prayer to the principal.

You, principal and teachers, have been inspired by one ideal only in joining this institution. You have undertaken to secure freedom through the miracle not of learning but of character, secure it not by meeting the Government, sword against its shining sword, but with peaceful, spiritual effort—howsoever imperfect it be—

against its aggressive, Satanic way. We want just now to sow the seed of freedom and afterwards we will water the plant and rear it into a tree. This tree can be raised only through character, with pure, spiritual strength. So long as the principal and the teachers go on working with their eyes on this one aim, we shall never be put to shame.

May God justify in your experience the faith which is mine. Were it not for this unshakable faith of mine, I would not at all have accepted the sacred position of chancellor. I am ready to live and die for this cause, thinking that to die in this cause is to live; it is because I know that this is also true of you that I live among you and have accepted this exalted position.

We are establishing this Vidyalaya, not with an educational, but with a national aim in view. Advising that students be taught to cultivate strength and character, I have been saying everywhere that in the measure we succeed with them we shall make ourselves fit for Swaraj in the country. Swaraj cannot be secured in any other way. No amount of money we can spend or strength of character we can employ to ensure the success of such colleges will be enough.

This is a time not for words but for action. I have placed my thoughts before you as they came. I asked of you what you could give. Now I shall ask something of the students as well. There is no doubt at all that they have in them the courage which takes risks. I shall not look upon them-upon those who have already joined—as mere students and, therefore, I will not treat them as being free from responsibility. Those who have registered their names here are half teachers. It is they who have provided the foundation for the Mahavidyalaya. It is on them that the structure of the institution has been raised.

Had they not joined, this Mahavidya-laya could not have been started. They also, therefore, share equal responsibility. You are equal partners in this and, if you do not play your part well, no efforts on the part of the teachers will succeed or, at any rate, succeed completely. Students who have left their colleges should understand why they have joined here and what they should expect to gain. May God grant them the strength to go on with their work, no matter how long this grim war continues. If they do, I am sure that, even if they are a mere handful, this Mahavidyalaya will shine forth and be a model institution for the whole country.

The reason will not be that Gujarat has wealth or that it has learning; it will be rather, that non-co-operation had its origin here. The seed was sown and watered here, the required tapas-charaya was performed here. Do not think from this that I am a conceited man to speak in this manner, or that all the tapascharaya has been mine and the seed was sown by me. I merely gave the mantra, I fulfilled the function of a rishi, if a Vanik's son can do so.

I have done nothing more than this. The planting was done by my co-workers. It is because their faith was greater than mine that we have succeeded. I claim the knowledge which comes from direct perception. Even if the gods came down and tried to persuade me to the contrary, my faith would not be shaken. As surely as I see, with my eyes, the trees in front of me, so surely I know that there is no salvation for India except through non-violent non-co-operation. As for my co-workers, however, they have believed this through logic or reasoning or accepted it on faith.

My co-workers have laid the foundation. Many of them are Gujaratis; there are Maharashtrians, too, but having been in Gujarat, they have become half or three-quarters Gujaratis or, perhaps, more Gujaratis than the

Gujaratis themselves. They have made this a weapon of shining strength. We have not yet seen all its miraculous power. Within six months, you will see more of the miraculous power of this programme for which young girls handed over their bangles to me. But the source of it all—the visible image—is this Mahavidyalaya. Hindus are worshippers of images and we are proud of being so. This image has its various limbs: one of them is the chancellor and that is myself.

The teachers, the principal and the students are other limbs. I am, myself, an old man, a withering leaf, and busy with other work. The falling away of such a leaf as I am can do no harm to a tree. The principal and the teachers, too, are no more than leaves, though green leaves as yet. In a short while, they also will grow old and, perhaps, fall off. The students, however, are the branches of this beautiful tree and it is on them that principals and teachers will grow as leaves.

I request them to put the same faith in their teachers as they do in me. Should they, however, see that the principal or any of the teachers is weak, let them burn him to ashes with the fire which was Prahlad's and go ahead with their work. This is my prayer to God and my blessings to the students.

I shall end with a prayer to God and I want you all to say "amen" to it. Join me in my prayer, all of you, with a pure heart, "God! Make this Mahavidyalaya of such worth that through it we may win the freedom for which we offer prayers day and night and grant it that, through that freedom, not only India but the entire world, in which India is but a dot, may be happy."

National Institutions

Since some of the staunchest supporters of non-co-operation have lost faith in it and since the numbers attending national institutions are dwindling, what is the use of holding on to these tottering schools and colleges and wasting good money after bad institutions?

My believing eye detects a flaw in this argument. My faith in non-co-operation remaining as staunch as ever, I can find it possible to reconcile myself to the existing national institutions even though the attendance may be reduced to half a dozen. For the half a dozen will be the makers of Swaraj whenever it comes. When virgins are required to perform certain sacred ceremonies, others are not accepted as substitute if no virgin is found. And even one virgin if found is enough to save the situation. So will it be with the planting of the Swaraj flag-post. The flags will be unfurled with the unsullied hands of those, be they ever so few, who have remained true to their original creed.

I do not therefore regard it as waste of money to continue the national institutions. They are so many oases in the desert. They give the water of life to the souls thirsting for freedom. In writing this I cast no reflection upon those who attend or otherwise support Government schools. They are entitled to hold the view if they choose that theirs is the only way or also a way to freedom. National institutions are meant for those whose thirst for freedom is not satisfied by the ones managed or patronized by the Government. Few as they are, insignificant though they may appear, they supply a felt want and contain in them the seeds, as it appears to non-co-operators, of true and lasting freedom.

The final success of these institutions depends upon the worth of the teachers. "But they are deserting the national schools and colleges," says the critic. So some of them are. It tries the faith of the survivors. Have they the courage to stand alone? Are there enough monied men to support the surviving national institutions? On the correct answer to these questions depends the future of the national institutions and with them the freedom of the country, and so far as I can judge, there are teachers enough to stand the severest test and there are monied men enough to support them. I know no organization that has died for want of funds. Organi-zations die always for want of men, i.e., honesty, efficiency and self-sacrifice. And it is my certain knowledge that where there are teachers, pupils are not wanting.

But the pupils have perhaps the largest share of responsibility on their shoulders. The future depends upon their ability, integrity, application, and patriotism. The teachers cannot give what the pupils have not. The teachers can help to 'draw out' in the pupils what they have. If it were otherwise, if the teachers were capable of putting something into their pupils, all the latter receiving instruction under them will be alike, whereas we know as a matter of fact that no two pupils have been yet known to be alike.

The pupils must therefore have initiative. They must cease to be mere imitators. They must learn to think and act for themselves and yet be thoroughly obedient and disciplined. The highest form of freedom carries with it the greatest measure of discipline and humility. Freedom that comes from discipline and humility cannot be denied; unbridled licence is a sign of vulgarity injurious alike to self and one's neighbours.

Non-Co-operation Movement's First University

Kakasaheb is writing about what Gujarat Vidyapith has done and what it is trying to achieve. There is one bit of criticism, however, to which he cannot reply. Some say that the Vidyapith has met with disaster since he took charge of it. If it has been ruined, I am responsible for it, not Kakasaheb. This is because so long as the people are enamoured of me or are fond of me and largely accept my advice, I am responsible for the changes that have been made in the Vidyapith. I was primarily responsible for the boycott of Government schools and for formulating a policy for national education. This I must humbly say or admit. It was I who brought over Acharya Gidwani and it is I who asked him to step down. Kakasaheb was connected with the Vidyapith ever since its inception. Again, it was I who took him away from the Vidyapith.

During Acharya Gidwani's term of office, the Vidyapith attracted students, land was bought for it and buildings were erected. Perhaps the Vidyapith would not be there if there were no Acharya Gidwani. He had promised me twice that he would readily come over whenever I summoned him. I received Vallabhabhai's telegram in Bhiwani in which he had suggested that Acharya Gidwani should take charge of the Vidyapith. He immediately agreed to do so. And in a few days, the first non-co-operation university in India was launched.

The treaty that was made between Gujarat and Sind by bringing him over to the former place is still there. I withdrew Acharya Gidwani because of a difference of opinion that arose in the Vidyapith. That did not imply any slur on anyone. It is my conviction that even today, Acharya Gidwani belongs to Gujarat. He went over to Prem Mahavidyalaya because Gujarat sent him there. And today he is in Karachi, only as a delegate from Gujarat. At all the three places, it is hoped, the national view-point will be fostered. At all the three places, there will certainly be propaganda for Khadi.

Acharya Kripalani was borrowed from the Kashi Ashram, which is his own creation. I relieved him as I had promised to do so. Under his leadership, too, the Vidyapith has not taken a retrograde step. At the time of the students' strike, we saw that he had stolen the hearts of the students. Acharya Kripalani was a second gift that Sind gave to Gujarat.

Even today, he belongs to Gujarat. In my opinion, under his leadership also the Vidyapith has progressed. Although all may have a common ideal, there is naturally a difference in the work and character of every man. And, it is in accordance with this that an institution which is in charge of a particular person develops and takes on a distinct colour. However, in regard to the Vidyapith, I have felt that this variety has been as beautiful as the variety in the colours of a rainbow. Whereas one principal has strengthened one aspect of it, another has done the same for another aspect of it. The result has only been good.

At present the rudder is in the hands of Kakasaheb. He has been moulding the Vidyapith. The Vidyapith has not crumbled; it is going ahead. So long as Kakasaheb is at the helm, all that needs to be said with regard to it is that anyone who has any doubts about it should go there and inspect it. Just as all the three principals have been complementary to one another, the periods to which they belonged also stand in the same relationship to one another. As all the three are fruits of the same tree, there is a continuity hidden behind their work. Not even one of them has wiped out what had been achieved before, but has added to the sum total of its achievements.

The present state of the Vidyapith, itself bears testimony to this. At the very inception of the Vidyapith, I had suggested a test for judging it; that holds good even today. The Vidyapith is going to be judged neither by its buildings nor by the number of its students, nor again by the knowledge of English that its students possess. It is going to be judged by the patriotism of its students, by their capacity to give to others the knowledge of the subjects which they have learnt, by their knowledge of Hindi by their knowledge of the science of the spinning-wheel, by the strength of character of its students and teachers, and by their turning towards the villages.

Judged by these standards, it is my confirmed belief that the Vidyapith has taken forward strides and anyone who wishes to ascertain this can do so by going over to examine it. Just as a tree is judged by its fruit, the Vidyapith can be examined in a similar manner. It is not a distant institution about which an investigator would need a testimonial from me or from anyone else.

Moreover, it is fair to scrutinize a thing personally, wherever this is possible and where such a scrutiny is necessary. After conducting this inquiry if it is felt that the Vidyapith has made continuous progress and has augmented its capacity to serve, it is only fitting that contributions should flow in to its doors.

Salt Satyagraha

It has been often said that the money spent on national education in general and the Gujarat Vidyapith in particular has been so much waste. In my opinion the Gujarat Vidyapith by its supreme sacrifice has more than justified its existence, the hopes entertained by its authors and the grants made to it by donors. For the Vidyapith has suspended its literary activities save for boys under 16 who are already under training there. The teachers and students of over 15 years of age have offered their services as volunteers and nearly forty students with the teachers are already in the field.

A class for giving fifteen days' emergency training in connection with Satyagraha has been opened for the sake of those who may need such training. I congratulate the students and the teachers on the promptitude with which they have acted. I may state that twenty of these are with me on the march. They are divided into two parties, both preceding the 80 pilgrims to make preparations in advance and assisting the villagers. They are under orders not to offer civil resistance till the 80 are arrested and immediately to replace them as soon as they are arrested.

I am sure that every national educational institution will copy the noble example of the Gujarat Vidyapith which was the first to come into being in response to the call of non-co-operation in 1920. And I hope that the Government and aided institutions will also copy the example. Every revolution of modern times has found students in the forefront. This, because it is peaceful, ought not to offer less attraction to the students.

Freedom Struggle

I learnt what happened in India after my arrest in Karadi only through the newspapers. Later on, after my release, I also heard about it from the people. I have heard so much about the part that the Vidyapiths—our national schools and colleges—have played in the movement that I am really overwhelmed with joy. I have come to know more about the Gujarat Vidyapith as also of the Bihar and Kashi Vidyapiths. It is no small matter that the teachers and students from all these three institutions cast aside their books and came to join the fight for freedom. When the history of this fight comes to be written the world will be glad to know of the great part played in it by the students and the national Vidyapiths.

While in jail, whenever I read anything in the newspapers about the students and the teachers, I would at once make a comparison between them and those in Government schools. As a result of which it became clear to me how correct we were in launching the programme of the boycott of Government schools in 1920. It is true that the Government schools are yet as crowded with students as they used to be. And it is even more tragic that the students are so eager to enter them that they ask for pardon, pay fines and somehow secure admission into them. This so far emboldens the heads of the colleges, or the authorities of the education department, that they send circulars that before admitting the students who have taken a direct or indirect part in the fight or who have gone to jail the matter should first be referred to the head of the education department. It is he who is to permit their admission after studying their cases. What are we to think of students who thus seek entrance into Government schools and colleges at the cost of their self-respect, and what of the authorities of the education department who insist on such conditions?

So much about the achievement of our college section. Let me now draw your attention to Appendix III of the Report of the Vidyapith. It mentions the names of the teachers and students who had gone to jail. Kakasaheb has said that what the students have learnt in the past one year, they had never learnt before, though the Vidyapith was the same; it was no less national then, and yet we did not then achieve as much as in the past year. And in future too whenever there is a call for the fight and we fill the jails, we will again have the satisfaction of having done our duty which is the greatest gift of knowledge. We believe that when we do so we shall be true teachers and students.

The point is that the Snataka and Gramseva-Dikshitas should not think that they are the product of any ordinary school. What can we do; we too have to earn a living; fate has brought us to the Vidyapith, so willy-nilly we must act as we are asked to! You should never entertain such thoughts in your mind even for a moment. Even though superficially you may appear to be only a handful, really you are like a sea, while the others, though they may appear to be as big as a sea, are really a phantom which has no existence. It is difficult, if not impossible, to instil in them the courage and the power to win Swaraj. As to the cultivation of that power in national schools, we can see it in these students. Those who have seen their work will bear witness to the fact that we have not lost anything in setting up these Vidyapiths. On the contrary, we have fully recovered with interest the money gifted for it.

The Spinning Wheel Message

The real work of the Vidyapith lies in the villages. I have been stressing this point ever since the inception of the Vidyapith, but until a couple of years ago, when it was declared an illegal organization and most of our professors and boys were imprisoned, we laboured under the impression that the work could be carried on only through a central institute situated in the capital town of Gujarat. But under the altered conditions and now that we have some breathing time to put our heads together and to collect our thoughts, we shall do well to hark back to the original conception and think of our future work in its terms. Each member of a live institution must be a living embodiment of the ideals of the institution, wherever he may be, and when such a state of things is brought about, it is the same thing whether the institution has a habitation and a corporate existence or not.

I would, therefore, expect every one of you who has cherished the ideals of the Vidyapith and who is pledged to serve it to go straight to the villages and start living those ideals there. Each one of you will thus be a peripatetic Vidyapith, teaching the ideals by means of his own personal example. It is quite conceivable that a host of workers, after having lived the life in the villages according to the ideals of the Vidyapith, re-establish the central institute in a village. But we are not in that position today. We have yet to gain all that experience on which alone you can build the new Vidyapith.

The centre of this village worker's life will be the spinning-wheel. I am sorry I have not been able yet to bring home to anyone the message of the spinning-wheel in all its implication. The reason is that my life itself is not a true echo of the message. But it came home to me again and again during my nine months' peregrinations in India. We have not yet sufficiently realized that hand-spinning is a supplementary industry of universal application and scope in India.

The village weaver cannot live but for the spinning-wheel. He gets his yarn no doubt from the mills, but he is doomed to destruction, if he is to remain for ever dependent on the mills. Today, the spinning-wheel has established itself in our economic life only to the extent that it is needed to minister to the clothing needs of the new class of khadi weavers that has sprung up during the past decade. But a large body like the Spinners' Association cannot justify its existence to fulfil that limited object. The idea at the back of khadi is that it is an industry supplementary to agriculture and co-extensive with it, that it is the life-breath of millions of Harijan weavers who derive their sustenance from it.

The spinning-wheel cannot be said to have been established in its own proper place in our life, until we can banish idleness from our villages and make every village home a busy hive. Unemployment and idleness of millions must lead to bloody strife. Khadi is the only alternative to this and not the so called socialism, which presupposes industrialism. The socialism that India can assimilate is the socialism of the spinning-wheel. Let the village worker, therefore, make the wheel the central point of his activities.

The worker will not be spinning regularly but will be working for his bread with the adze or the spade or the last, as the case may be. All his hours minus the eight hours of sleep and rest will be fully occupied with some work. He will have no time to waste. He will allow himself no laziness and allow others none. His life will be a constant lesson to his neighbours in ceaseless and joy-giving industry. Bodily sustenance should come from body labour, and intellectual labour is necessary for the culture of the mind.

Division of labour there will necessarily be, but it will be a division into various species of body labour and not a division into intellectual labour to be confined to one class and body labour to be confined to another class. Our compulsory or voluntary idleness has to go. If it does not go, no panacea will be of any avail, and semi-starvation will remain the eternal problem that it is. He who eats two grains must produce four. Unless the law is accepted as universal, no amount of reduction in population would serve to solve the problem. If the law is accepted and observed, we have room enough to accommodate millions more to come.

The village worker will thus be a living embodiment of industry. He will master all the process of khadi, from cotton-sowing and picking to weaving, and will devote all his thought to perfecting them. If he treats it as a science, it won't jar on him, but he will derive fresh joy from it everyday, as he realizes more and more its great possibilities. If he will go to the village as a teacher, he will go there no less as a learner. He will soon find that he has much to learn from the simple villagers. He will enter into every detail of village life, he will discover the village handicrafts and investigate the possibilities of their growth and their improvement. He may find the villagers completely apathetic to the message of khadi, but he will, by his life of service compel interest and attention. Of course, he will not forget his limitations and will not engage in, for him, the futile task of solving the problem of agricultural indebtedness.

Sanitation and hygiene will engage a good part of his attention. His home and his surroundings will not only be a model of cleanliness, but he will help to promote sanitation in the whole village by taking the broom and the basket round.

He will not attempt to set-up a village dispensary or to become the village doctor. These are traps which must be avoided. I happened during my Harijan tour to come across a village where one of our workers who should have known better had built a pretentious building in which he had housed a dispensary and was distributing free medicine to the villages around. In fact, the medicines were being taken from home to home by volunteers and the dispensary was described as boasting a register of 1,200 patients a month! I had naturally to criticize this severely. That was not the way to do village work, I told him. His duty was to inculcate lessons of hygiene and sanitation in the village folk and thus to show them the way of preventing illness, rather than attempt to cure them. I asked him to leave the palace-like building and to hire it out to the Local Board and to settle in thatched huts. All that one need stock in the way of drugs is quinine, castor oil and iodine and the like. The worker should concentrate more on helping people realize the value of personal and village cleanliness and maintaining it at all cost.

Then he will interest himself in the welfare of the village Harijans. His home will be open to them. In fact, they will turn to him naturally for help in their troubles and difficulties. If the village folk will not suffer him to have the Harijan friends in his house situated in their midst, he must take up his residence in the Harijan quarters.

A word about the knowledge of the alphabet. It has its place, but I should warn you against a misplaced emphasis on it. Do not proceed on the assumption that you cannot proceed with rural instruction without first teaching the children or adults how to read and write. Lots of useful information on current affairs, history, geography and elementary arithmetic, can be given by word of mouth before the alphabet is touched.

The eyes, the ears and the tongue come before the hand. Reading comes before writing and drawing before tracing the letters of the alphabet. If this natural method is followed, the understanding of the children will have a much better opportunity of development than when it is under check by beginning the children's training with the alphabet.

The worker's life will be in tune with the village life. He will not pose as a litterateur buried in his book, loath to listen to details of humdrum life. On the contrary, the people, whenever they see him, will find him busy with his tools—spinning-wheel, loom, adze, spade, etc.—and always responsive to their meanest inquiries. He will always insist on working for his bread. God has given to everyone the capacity of producing more than his daily needs and, if he will only use his resourcefulness, he will not be in want of an occupation suited to his capacities, however poor they may be. It is more likely than not that the people will gladly maintain him, but it is not improbable that in some places he may be given a cold shoulder. He will still plod on. It is likely that in some villages he may be boycotted for his pro-Harijan proclivities.

Let him in that case approach the Harijans and look to them to provide him with food. The labourer is always worthy of his hire and, if he conscientiously serves them, let him not hesitate to accept his food from the Harijans always, provided that he gives more than he takes. In the very early stages of course, he will draw his meagre allowance from a central fund where such is possible.

I have deliberately left out the question of the cow. The village worker will find it difficult to tackle the question and will not attempt it, except to the extent of educating the people in the theory of it. We have not yet hit upon the best way of curing dead cattle's hide and dyeing it, as also the best means of protecting the cow. In Gujarat the buffalo problem complicates the situation. We have got to make people realize that to encourage the buffalo is to allow the cow to die. But more of this some other time.

Remember that our weapons are spiritual. It is a force that works irresistibly, if imperceptibly. Its progress is geometrical rather than arithmetical. It never ceases so long as there is a propeller behind. The background of all your activities has therefore, to be spiritual. Hence the necessity for the strictest purity of conduct and character.

You will not tell me that this is an impossible programme, that you have not the qualifications for it. That you have not fulfilled it so far should be no impediment in your way. If it appeals to your reason and your heart, you must not hesitate. Do not fight shy of the experiment. The experiment will itself provide the momentum for more and more effort.

Village Schools

"The cruelest irony of the new Reforms lies in the fact that we are left with nothing but the liquor revenue to fall back upon in order to give our children education," said Gandhiji in one of the numerous talks he has been giving on the subject, ever since the Congress Ministers took up office. "That is the educational puzzle but it should not baffle us. We have to solve it and the solution must not involve the compromise of our ideal of prohibition cost whatever else it may. It must be shameful and humiliating to think that unless we got the drink revenue, our children would be starved of their education. But if it comes to it, we should prefer it as a lesser evil. If only we will refuse to be obsessed by the figures and by the supposed necessity of giving our children the exact kind of education that they get today, the problem should not baffle us." That explains Gandhiji's emphasis on our educationists putting their heads together in order to evolve a system of education which is at once inexpensive and also in consonance with the needs of our vast rural population.

"Then you would really abolish what is called secondary education and give the whole education up to matriculation in the village schools?" asked a questioner in great surprise.

"Certainly. What is your secondary education but compelling the poor boys to learn in a foreign language in seven years what they should learn in the course of a couple of years in their own mother-tongue? If you can but make up your minds to free the children from the incubus of learning their subjects in a foreign tongue, and if you teach them to use their hands and feet profitably, the educational puzzle is solved. You can sacrifice without compunction the whole of the drink revenue. But you must resolve to sacrifice this revenue first, and think of the ways and means about education later. Make the beginning by taking the big step."

Self-supporting Education

In spite of the weak state of his health and the quantities of rest that he needs, Gandhiji has shown his readiness to discuss his theory of self-supporting education with anyone who has thought about the subject and wants to contribute his share to making the new experiment a success.

The discussions have been, in view of his health, necessarily few and brief, but every now and then something new has emerged, and whenever he has talked, he has had some fresh suggestion to make and fresh light to throw. Thus on one occasion he sounded a warning against the assumption that the idea of self-supporting education sprang from the necessity of achieving total prohibition as soon as possible. "Both are independent necessities," he said. "You have to start with the conviction that total prohibition has to be achieved revenue or no revenue, education or no education.

Similarly, you have to start with the conviction that looking to the needs of the villages of India our rural education ought to be made self-supporting if it is to be compulsory."

"I have the first conviction deep down in me," said an educationist who carried on the discussion. "Prohibition to me is an end in itself, and I regard it as a great education in itself. I should, therefore, sacrifice education altogether to make prohibition a success. But the other conviction is lacking. I cannot yet believe that education can be made self-supporting."

"There, too, I want you to start with the conviction. The ways and means will come as you begin to work it out. I regret that I woke up to the necessity of this at this very late age. Otherwise I should have made the experiment my self. Even now, God willing, I shall do what I can to show that it can be self-supporting. But my time has been taken up by other things all these years, equally important perhaps; but it is this stay in Segaon that brought the conviction home to me. We have up to now concentrated on stuffing children's minds with all kinds of information, without ever thinking of stimulating and developing them. Let us now cry a halt and concentrate on educating the child properly through manual work, not as a side activity, but as the prime means of intellectual training."

"I see that too. But why should it also support the school?"

"That will be the test of its value. The child at the age of 14, that is, after finishing a seven years' course, should be discharged as an earning unit. Even now the poor people's children automatically lend a helping hand to their parents—the feeling at the back of their minds being, what shall my parents eat and what shall they give me to eat if I do not also work with them? That is an education in itself. Even so the State takes charge of the child at seven and returns it to the family as an earning unit. You impart education and simultaneously cut at the root of unemployment. You have to train the boys in one occupation or another. Round this special occupation you will train up his mind, his body, his writing, his artistic sense, and so on. He will be master of the craft he learns."

"But supposing a boy takes up the art and science of making Khadi. Do you think it must occupy him all the seven years to master the craft?"

"Yes. It must, if he will not learn it mechanically. Why do we give years to the study of history or to the study of languages? Is a craft any the less important than these subjects which have been up to now given an artificial importance?"

"But as you have been mainly thinking of spinning and weaving, evidently you are thinking of making of these schools so many weaving schools. A child may have no aptitude for weaving and may have it for something else."

"Quite so. Then we will teach him some other craft. But you must know that one school will not teach many crafts. The idea is that we should have one teacher for twenty-five boys, and you may have as many classes or schools of twenty-five boys as you have teachers available, and have each of these schools specializing in a separate craft—carpentry, smithy, tanning or shoe-making.

Only you must bear in mind the fact that you develop the child's mind through each of these crafts. And I would emphasize one more thing. You must forget the cities and concentrate on the villages. They are an ocean. The cities are a mere drop in the ocean. That is why you cannot think of subjects like brick-making. If they must be civil and mechanical engineers, they will after the seven years' course go to the special colleges meant for these higher and specialized courses.

"And let me emphasize one more fact. We are apt to think lightly of the village crafts because we have divorced educational from manual training. Manual work has been regarded as something inferior, and owing to the wretched distortion of the varna we came to regard spinners and weavers and carpenters and shoe-makers as belonging to the inferior castes, the proletariat. We have had no Cromptons and Hargreaves because of this vicious system of considering the crafts as something inferior, divorced from the skilled. If they had been regarded as callings having an independent status that learning enjoyed, we should have had great inventors from among our craftsmen. Of course the 'Spinning Jenny' led on to the discovery of water-power and other things which made the mill displace the labour of thousands of people. That was, in my view, a monstrosity. We will by concentrating on the villages see that the inventive skill that an intensive learning of the craft will stimulate will subserve the needs of the villages as a whole."

Education Through Craft

Speaking about education through a craft Gandhiji said:

"If such education is given, the direct result will be that it will be self-supporting. But the test of success is not its self-supporting character, but that the whole man has been drawn out through the teaching of the handicraft in a scientific manner. In fact I would reject a teacher who would promise to make it self-supporting under any circumstances. The self-supporting part will be the logical corollary of the fact that the pupil has learnt the use of every one of his faculties. If a boy who works at a handicraft for three hours a day will surely earn his keep, how much more a boy who adds to the work a development of his mind and soul!"

Basic Education

This Basic Education has grown out of the atmosphere surrounding us in the country and is in response to it. It is, therefore, designed to cope with that atmosphere. This atmosphere pervades India's seven hundred thousand villages and its millions of inhabitants. Forget them and you forget India. India is not to be found in her cities. It is in her innumerable villages.

The following are the fundamentals of Basic Education:

1. All education to be true must be self-supporting, that is to say, in the end it will pay its expenses excepting the capital which will remain intact.
2. In it the cunning of the hand will be utilized even up to the final stage, that is to say, hands of the pupils will be skilfully working at some industry for some period during the day.
3. All education must be imparted through the medium of the provincial language.

4. In this there is no room for giving sectional religious training. Fundamental universal ethics will have full scope.
5. This education, whether it is confined to children or adults, male or female, will find its way to the homes of the pupils.
6. Since millions of students receiving this education will consider themselves as of the whole of India, they must learn an inter-provincial language. This common inter-provincial speech can only be Hindustani written in Nagari or Urdu script. Therefore, pupils have to master both the scripts.

Intellectual Development

During my recent wanderings in Travancore and Madras I found that most of the students and 'intellectuals' who came into touch with me were an instance of intellectual dissipation rather than intellectual development. The fault lies in the modern system of education which encourages this vicious tendency, misdirects the mind, and thereby hinders its development instead of helping it. My experiments in Segaon have only confirmed this impression. But they are as yet too incomplete to be cited as evidence. The views on education that I am now going to set forth have been held by me right from the time of the founding of the Phoenix Settlement in South Africa in the year 1904.

I hold that true education of the intellect can only come through a proper exercise and training of the bodily organs, e.g. hands, feet, eyes, ears, nose, etc. In other words, an intelligent use of the bodily organs in a child provides the best and quickest way of developing his intellect. But unless the development of the mind and body goes hand in hand with a corresponding awakening of the soul, the former alone would prove to be a poor lop-sided affair. By spiritual training I mean education of the heart. A proper and all-round development of the mind, therefore, can take place only when it proceeds pari passu with the education of the physical and spiritual faculties of the child. They constitute an indivisible whole. According to this theory, therefore, it would be a gross fallacy to suppose that they can be developed piecemeal or independently of one another.

The baneful effects of absence of proper co-ordination and harmony among the various faculties of body, mind and soul respectively are obvious. They are all around us; only we have lost perception of them owing to our present perverse associations. Take the case of our village folk. From their childhood upward they toil and labour in their fields, from morning till night, like their cattle in the midst of whom they live. Their existence is a weary endless round of mechanical drudgery unrelieved by a spark of intelligence or higher graces of life. Deprived of all scope for developing their mind and soul, they have sunk to the level of the beast.

Life to them is a sorry bungle which they muddle through anyhow. On the other hand, what goes by the name of education in our schools and colleges in the cities today is in reality only intellectual dissipation. Intellectual training is there looked upon as something altogether unrelated to manual or physical work. But since the body must have some sort of physical exercise to keep it in health, they vainly try to attain that end by means of an artificial and otherwise barren system of physical culture which would be ridiculous beyond words if the result was not so tragic. The young man who emerges from this system can in no way compete in physical endurance with an ordinary labourer. The slightest physical exertion gives him a headache; a mild exposure to the sun is enough to cause him giddiness. And what is more, all this is looked upon as quite 'natural'. As for the faculties of the heart, they are simply allowed to run to seed or to grow anyhow in a wild undisciplined manner. The result is moral and spiritual anarchy. And it is regarded as something laudable!

As against this, take the case of a child in whom the education of the heart is attended to from the very beginning. Supposing he is set to some useful occupation like spinning, carpentry, agriculture, etc., for his education and in that connection is given a thorough comprehensive knowledge relating to the theory of the various operations that he is to perform and the use and construction of the tools that he would be wielding. He would not only develop a fine healthy body but also a sound, vigorous intellect that is not merely academic but is firmly rooted in and is tested from day to day by experience. His intellectual education would include a knowledge of mathematics and various other sciences that are useful for an intelligent and efficient exercise of his avocation. If to this is added literature by way of recreation, it would give him a perfect well-balanced, all-round education in which the intellect, the body and the spirit have all full play and develop together into a natural, harmonious whole.

Man is neither mere intellect, nor the gross animal body, nor the heart of soul alone. A proper and harmonious combination of all the three is required for the making of the whole man and constitutes the true economics of education. To say that this kind of education can only be given after we have attained our independence would, I am afraid, be like putting the cart before the horse. The advent of independence would be incredibly hastened if we could educate millions of our people through an intelligent exercise of their respective vocations like this and teach them that they live for the common good of all.

4

Gandhi on Moral Education

Mahatma Gandhi was one of those people who believed strongly in the goodness of family life and therefore he never endorsed the view of separating young children from their parents for studies or any other reason. His opinion on the subject is well summed up in his own words: "The education that a child imbibes in a well-ordered household is impossible to obtain in hostels". This statement made by him almost half a century ago, in fact still holds true in todays' fast paced world, a world in which we see children who are not even a year old being left in crèches. This is of course the case only because both the parents of the child are busy with their careers and therefore do not have time to spare for the child.

Most parents perhaps overlook the fact that the children undergo their most formative part of their life in the first six years of their life. In fact it is in this phase that 80% of their mental make-up takes place. And it is this fact coupled with the state of parenting that exists today, that makes one wonder about what sort of legacy we are passing on to the next generation. In fact, it makes one wonder whether there is any legacy to talk about at all.

Gandhi's views on parenting and the importance of parenting can be summed up in another belief that was held by him and as stated by him: "for proper upbringing of children, the parents ought to have a general knowledge of the care and nursing of babies". In fact, it is believed that the development of the child begins in the conception stage of the fetus itself.

It is believed that the physical and mental states of the parents at the moment of conception have an effect an on the characteristics of the infant. And in fact thereafter the moods of the mother throughout the period of pregnancy, the desires and the temperament collectively have a strong developmental effect on the child's mental state.

Mahatma Gandhi considered character building as the highest form of learning that is to be imparted to a child. In his own words on the subject he states: "I had always given the first place to the culture of the heart or the building of character, and as I felt confident that moral training could be given to all alike, no matter how different their ages and their upbringing, I decided to live amongst my children all the 24 hours of the day as their father. I regarded character building as the proper foundation for their education and if the foundation was firmly laid, they would be able to face life in a much better way.

However, according to Gandhi character education of a child never equated to propagating to force one's viewpoint on the children. It was Gandhi who said, "It is idle to expect one's children and wards necessarily to follow the same course of evolution as oneself."

Mahatma Gandhi was born in Porbander, which is a small town in Gujarat. He was born into a family of humble origins. His father did not have more than an education of the third grade, and his mother was illiterate. Most of the other senior members of the Gandhi family also had very meager academic education.

Mohandas Karam Chand Gandhi was therefore the very first person from his family to obtain the degree of graduation from a high school. However, it is also to be noted that his academic achievement was below average. And in spite of such humble beginnings and a below average performance in the academic fields, Gandhi went on to become the most reckoned leaders of India who led India to achieve the state of freedom. This is because, though Gandhi's parents could not impart much of academic education, they ensured that they instilled in him a strong character education.

It is this very strength of character that later enabled Gandhi to educate himself and complete the London Matriculation as well as the London Bar examinations. It was this very strength of character that stood by Gandhi when he later went to South Africa.

His sound character proved to be his main strength in the difficult circumstances that prevailed there. It was with the help of this asset of character that Gandhi managed to overcome many seemingly insurmountable obstacles. Not only that, Gandhi also took it upon himself to impart character education to thousands of almost illiterate Indians in South Africa.

If the main element of Gandhi's success were to be traced back, then it would become clear that his strong sense of character was the unique asset that he possessed which assisted him during his crises in South Africa as well as later in India, with his unique weapon, 'Satyagraha', whose implementation primarily requires lesser academic education but a very strong dosage of character education.

In a particular presentation that was made by Dr. Shall Sinha, he discussed the techniques that were used by Gandhi to teach the value, acquisition and implementation of character education. According to

Gandhi, there were four vital elements of character education and these elements also help in academic performance.

One of the most memorable quotes by the Mahatma on education sums up aptly what he felt about the subject: "Education without courage is like a wax statue - beautiful to look at but bound to melt at the first touch of a hot stuff." - Mahatma Gandhi.

And although he had the largest and strongest following in terms of numbers, Mahatma Gandhi did not consider it his greatest strength, he believed more in the strength of character. The following quote by him sums up his view on the subject: "Strength of numbers is the delight of the timid." - Mahatma Gandhi.

Teaching Children Virtues and Values

Children are the pillars of our tomorrow is a statement that is repeated time and again. And it is an axiom; they are our pillars of the coming time. But then do we nurture them into becoming healthy human beings?

By healthy human beings here is not meant the physical well being, but the good human being. And how do you define a good human being? One with virtues and values that keeps them in the realm of working towards the benefit of humanity.

How can children imbibe within themselves the virtues and values? Well, this is the primary responsibility of parents and other immediate family members, followed by school authorities. The values and virtues of an individual is sown in their childhood and nurtured as they grow up. After all nobody is born a criminal, it is what they become as result of what they gain from their surroundings.

Depending on the way we bring up our children, we decide our own future. It is vital that in the formative years we give them quality time and attention. We teach them to discriminate between the good, bad and the ugly. WE have to inculcate into them positive emotions like love and compassion and teach them actions of kindness and generosity. At the same time we have to help them do way with the negatives of hatred, anger, jealousy, selfishness, etc.

Your child is like a plant. You sow the seeds and also reap the benefits of its growth and development. First and foremost you as a parent have to realize your responsibility in nurturing a child to growing into a good human being. And it is just not upto anyone of the parents, but both together to inculcate the values and virtues into your child.

Teaching your Child Honesty

Honesty is the virtue of being honest. And what is bring honest? Not being false; being truthful; bring frank and sincere. And honesty is one of the ingredients of a good human being. It is true that not anyone as a matter of fact can be hundred percent honest through their lifetime. There are times when harmless white lies need to be spoken to protect oneself and others. But harmful dishonesty could cause a lot of trouble.

Let us see firstly, why does one need to tell a lie at all. A person usually lies due to fear. The fear of telling the truth as that could get them into trouble. For instance, a child breaks a glass and his mother is very strict. When asked who broke it, the child would deny having broken it because he fears being shouted at or beaten. But, if the mother is understanding and not hot-tempered, the same child would fearlessly admit to his mistake.

The habit of lying begins with such small incidents and progresses into the more serious lies spoken. The more the child fears his parents, the more the lies he would continue to speak at every stage, only because he fears admitting what he has done wrong. And like each drop makes the ocean, each mistake amounts to the larger mistakes, till there maybe no turning back.

To be able to inculcate in your child the virtue of honesty in the first place you have to be more patient and understanding with your child. After all it is only human to err. If your child has made a certain mistake for the first or second time then patiently explain to them the wrong of it. However, if it is done the third time then strictly put across your viewpoint. In this way your child will consider you their best friend and confide in you no matter what it maybe. Remember respect and honesty from them does not come out of enforcing your authority as a parent, but your patience and understanding as a parent

Teaching your Child Trust

It has often been said that you can only trust others when you trust yourself completely. Only he you have high self esteem and self confidence. Otherwise trusting others is one of the most difficult things to do. Thus it is important to teach children to trust themselves. And for this as a parent you need to keep reassuring them.

Reward them & appreciate them for every right and punish them gently for every wrong. Sometimes as parents we are so driven by the need to bring out the best in our children that we overlook whatever right they do, but are extremely quick to reprimand their wrongs. And this is where they lose their confidence. This is where they are unable to bring up their levels of self esteem.

When you acknowledge their achievements, no matter how big or small, they have faith in you; simply because they know that you are with them at every step. They will develop faith in anyone who stands by them like a shadow. Be their to hold their hand.

There are certain incidents in childhood that work best to inculcate trust in your child. One for example is when your toddler is taking his first steps. The little one when walking looks towards you and what you must do is wait at such a distance that he makes every attempt the first couple of steps and yet in case he is about to fall you can catch him on time.

Like this even in other activities like cycling and swimming, you have to be there as a buffer for your child so that he knows that you will help him lest he falls or he feels he will drown and yet, he builds up the self confidence to cycle or swim without your help.

It is only in the formative years that we can teach our child how to trust others by teaching them how to trust us. And in all this lies the most important virtue of self trust.

Teaching your Child Love

Love moves the world and hate stagnates it. It is all to easy to look out of the window and complain about how much hate is dominating our lives today. But then, how much love do we spread in our lives? In the present stressful existence, we have forgotten how to love each other. Frustration, stress, anger, impatience, intolerance, reign supreme. And as a result we have children growing in an environment that is minus love and peace.

Love is the strongest emotion that brings happiness into ones lives. For us to nurture our children into becoming a good human beings we must inculcate in them the emotion called Love. And what is love? It maybe defined as affection, devotion, fondness, admiration, compassion, attachment, dedication, etc. When we learn to live by these emotions then we do away with all the negatives that cause our destruction.

We can bring into our children the emotion of love only when we create for ourselves a loving environment. As parents we firstly have to avoid bringing our bedroom fights into the drawing room. We have to have patience and tolerance and accept each other for each or our plusses and minuses. When we accept each other, then only can we teach our children the same.

Children growing up in a home where there is no love, grow into being insecure individuals. They are constantly disturbed by what happens between their parents. The constant fights and arguments instill in them fear and they do not trust the outside world. In fact these children seek attention from all over the place. They are always striving to be their best only out of insecurity. And this is a negative aspect, because at some point out of frustration they just want to stop short of everything and give up. A child not nurtured in love and affection grows into being a depressed emotional wreck who finds it difficult to adjust in society.

Remember, your childs well being, whether it is emotional, physical, psychological, mental or otherwise, depends on the environment you bring up your child in. If it is a loving one, then you are bringing up an adjusting human being. A terrorist after all is not born into a home of love and affection, but one shrouded by intense hate.

Teaching your Child Generosity

Selflessness is a virtue of humanity and selfishness is that of inhumanity. This can be further explained by drawing the difference between a patriot and a terrorism. A patriot sacrifices his life for the sake of his country. He gives up all he has for the sake of others. On the other hand the terrorist takes the lives of others for the sake of a cause. Selflessness in about giving and selfishness is about taking.

Generosity is an offshoot of selflessness. It is the virtue of bringing a smile onto other peoples faces. According to what the Spiritual Leaders profess, The more you give, the more you get. What does this mean? The connotation or meaning of this statement is simple; we can only fill what is always empty. How can we fill more water into a glass full of it. Obviously we have to fist empty it to fill it up again. Similarly in life we have to give out more in order to fill our coffers. And this is something we need to teach our children.

One way in which we can effectively teach our children the virtue of generosity is be making it a point to at visit home for underprivileged children and donating things. One effective practice could be to donate your kids old clothes and toys every year on his birthday. What you could do is sit down with your child and together sort out what can be given away, seeing that it is not the absolutely torn and tattered objects, but those that can still be used by the underprivileged children. Make your child distribute these himself. He will surely feel a sense of achievement and fulfillment having made these children happy. After doing that as a birthday treat take him shopping to purchase new clothes and toys.

In this way the child learns to give and even understands that in some form or the other there is a replacement for all that he give out from the smiles and gratefulness from the receivers to the gifts he receives in return. To teach him generosity it is vital to reimburse it with a sense of fulfillment not only in terms of material gains, but more so emotional.

Teaching your Child to Respect Elders

As you sow, so shall you reap. To gain respect from your children first you must respect your own elders in front of them. Not only that you have to respect each other too.

We tend to take for granted that respecting each other is about enslaving each other. WE consider that respect is what we give to an authority figure, because we need to be in their good books. However, that is not respect, but disrespect since it is not something genuine.

Respect towards elders or any person, as a matter of fact is about honoring or holding in esteem an individual. It implies regarding an individual as a person of value and virtue. We all expect respect from others. But then do we actually respect others? For instance, because we are adults we tend to take our parents for granted. We tend to get irritated by every suggestion they make simply because we think that we can never be wrong. We then admonish them or ignore them. We do not realize that our children copy or rather mimic us. They then treat us the same way.

Apart from this even the way we address the servants, is the way our children will address them too. While your servant is hired by you and you have every right to give them orders the way you want, realize that they are still elders for your children. When you ill-treat or talk with disrespect to your servant, your child does the same thing.

It is vital to teach your child how to respect each individual, in order for him or her to command his or her own respect. And it all begins with you as a parent. Another aspect we overlook is also the way we talk about people in front of our children. For instance, when we bad-mouth somebody in front of our children, they overhear our conversation, disrespect that person and put us into an embarrassing situation. So it is very vital that we watch our own actions and words in the presence of our children, otherwise it will spell trouble not only for us, but also for them, as there would be nothing beyond disrespect in the dictionary of upbringing.

5

Gandhi's *Nayee Talim*

By the middle of the nineteenth century a significant degree of awareness of their own identity had developed among the educated elite of the country. It was the dawn of the period of social reformation and growth of Indian nationalism. There were two distinct ways of looking at the issues of reconstructing the social fabric of the country at that point in time of the freedom struggle. Some of the leaders were of the opinion that to be able to rise to the level of the British rulers Indians must educate themselves in the English system. They established educational institutions which aimed at the particular goal. Although they too were interested in discovering their original roots, they probably felt that the British were able to rule India because of their superiority over us in many ways. On another level movements grew to motivate people to go back to their Vedic culture, in other words, to discover the classical roots of Indian civilisation. They founded *gurukul*s and other traditional institutions of learning and teaching. According to them India had become weak because she had drifted away from her classical way of life. Neither of these approaches faced the real issues, issues that were related to the question of real liberation and self-reliance.

India had been severely impoverished and her population demoralised. The Indian masses had lost the taste for freedom almost completely. Until the end of the first half of the nineteenth century, the military might of the whole country, if it could have been put together, was considerable. But during the period after the 1857 soldiers' mutiny, the morale of the people had fallen to a very low ebb. Moreover, the British rulers, having realised the tenacity of the Indian soldiers and realising that militarily they could not enslave India permanently, cunningly and systematically disarmed the nation. So much so that the simple farmer could not own an ordinary gun to protect his crops from the menace of wild and stray animals.

Industrially India, according to Romesh Dutt, was one of the leading countries of the world until the middle of the eighteenth century. But by the end of the nineteenth century Indian industry had been nearly totally destroyed. The country which supplied a great variety of textiles to many countries of the world, specially northern Europe, was now importing cloth from Britain for most of its needs.

Several nations used to get their ships built by Indian ship-builders. Richard Greg quotes in *White Sahebas in India* the factor of the East Indian Company, who wrote in 1670:

> Many English merchants, and others have their ships and vessels yearly built. Here is the best and well grown timber . . . best iron upon the coast. . . . They have an excellent way of making shrouds, stays and any other rigging for the ships.

Lord Wellesley wrote in 1800:

> The port of Calcutta contains about 10,000 tons of shipping, built in India of a description calculated for the conveyance of cargo to England.

Taylor, in his *History of India,* quoted from Mrs Besant's *India Bond or Free*:

> the arrival in the Port of London of Indian produce in Indian-built ships created a sensation among the monopolists which could not have been exceeded if a hostile fleet had appeared in the Thames. The ship-builders of the Port of London took the lead in raising the cry of alarm . . . . An obliging Government saw to it that the Indian industry perished.

The creation of the worst kind of landlordism damaged human relationships and divided society into strata which were completely alien to the Indian experience. The planned destruction of the *panchayat,* the system of local government and administration, including the judiciary, had even a worse effect on social relationships.

The colonial rulers could not have been satisfied only by destroying India's industry, agriculture, administrative and legal institutions and their national defence system. They were hoping to enslave India permanently. The British knew that only material enslavement was not sufficient. Psychological enslavement was the most important and effective mechanism to reach that goal. Thus education became the biggest prey for the Raj.

The colonisers took immediate steps to build a long-term strategy based on 'educational reforms'. They took every possible step to weaken the educational traditions which were deeply ingrained in the culture of the people and were the most powerful instruments that had retained cultural values among the masses for such a long period.

We should also note the attitude of the colonisers to the literature of Asian countries. In his famous minutes Lord Macaulay wrote:

> I have no knowledge either of Sanskrit or Arabic, but I have done what I could to form a correct estimate of their value. I have read translations of the more celebrated Arabic and Sanskrit works. I have conversed both here and at home with men distinguished by their proficiency

> in the Eastern tongues. I am quite ready to take Oriental learning at the valuation of the orientalists themselves. I have never found one among them who could deny that a single shelf of a good European library was worth the whole native literature of India and Arabia.

He added:

> We must at present do our best to form a class who may be interpreters between us and the millions whom we govern — a class of persons Indian in blood and colour, but English in tastes, in opinions, in morals and in intellect.

The Governor General, Lord Bentinck, said:

> I give my entire concurrence to the sentiments expressed in minutes.

In spite of such a calculated onslaught on Indian culture, specially its educational traditions, a significant proportion of institutions had survived until at least 1835. Adams, who was an officer in the Education Department of Bengal, conducted an inquiry into the number of schools in that region at that time. According to his calculations there was a school for every thirty-two boys and these schools were provided to most of the 150,000 villages. Writing about the Indian educational system of that time, Max-M¥uller said:

> There is such a thing as social education and education outside the books; and this education is distinctly higher in India than in any part of Christendom. It is an education not in the so-called three R's, but in humanity.

There are documents prepared by some British officials of that period to show that in several regions of the country literacy was very high — 100 per cent among the male population and not very much lower among females. It is the same country in which literacy had fallen to less than 10 per cent by the end of the last century. By and large, India then was considered an illiterate nation!

National Awakening

The end of the last century saw the re-emergence of movements for national awakening, but this time of a different kind — very different from the wars of Tipu Sultan and the Sepoy Mutiny. The emergence of the Arya Samaj, the Prarthana Samaj and the Brahmo Samaj brought about much awareness among the people of their cultural heritage, which gave them a sense of self-identity.

The Indian National Congress, which had a political character, was formed in 1885. Although it started talking of Indian self-rule, Indians' participation in the administrative services, etc., the majority of its leadership was English educated and did not speak the language of the people, who did not understand what the Congress leadership was talking about. As these leaders had no contact with the masses, the Congress could not command a popular following.

During the beginning of the growth of the Indian National Congress the British took advantage of the situation and, to some extent, were able to co-opt some of its leadership to neutralise their effect, if any, on the masses. But this time they could not stop the tide of liberation. They could only slow it down by their classical technique of divide and rule.

Educational Work in South Africa

Before going into Gandhiji's educational experiments in India we should briefly discuss his educational experiences in South Africa.

While mobilising the Indians living in South Africa for the struggle for self-dignity, Gandhiji had gone through various experiences and had conducted experiments to find an alternative approach to conflict resolution and re-structuring social relationships through non-violence. Among these experiments those on education are the most important for us here.

After reading *Unto This Last* he said:

> I believe that I discovered some of my deepest convictions reflected in this great book of Ruskin, that is why it so captured me and made me transform my life.

The teachings of the book as he grasped them were: (a) that the good of the individual is contained in the good of all; (b) that a lawyer's work has the same value as the barber's, inasmuch as all have the same right of earning their livelihood from their work; (c) that a life of labour, i.e., the life of the tiller of the soil and the handicraftsman, is the life worth living. This experience put him on to a new track more intensely and with greater commitment to search for a better life.

Gandhiji was also editing and publishing *Indian Opinion* from Durban, which he thought should be moved to a farm, on which everyone should labour, drawing the same living wage, and attending to press work in their spare time. After a discussion with his colleagues about his ideas, with which they all agreed, *Indian Opinion* was moved to Phoenix, fourteen miles from Durban. Thus the Phoenix Settlement was started in 1904. It became a well-knit family of committed people trying to live their lives under the guidance of Gandhiji.

He was very conscious about the need for the education of the members of the Phoenix Farm, specially of children. He wrote in his autobiography:

> As the Farm grew, it was found necessary to make some provision for the education of its boys and girls. There were among these, Hindu, Musalman, Parsi and Christian boys and some Hindu girls. It was not possible, and I did not think necessary, to engage a special teacher for them. It was not possible, for qualified Indian teachers were scarce, and even when available, none would be ready to

> go to a place 21 miles distant from Johannesburg on a small salary . . . .I did not believe in the existing system of education, and I had a mind to [find] by experience and experiment the true system.

Gandhiji wrote in his autobiography:

> When I landed at Durban in January 1897, I had three children with me. My sister's son aged 10, and my own sons aged 9 and 6. Where was I to educate them? I could have sent them to the school for European children, but only as a matter of favour and exception. For no other Indian children would be allowed. For these there were schools established by Christian missions, but I was not prepared to send my children there, as I did not like the education imparted in those schools. For one thing, the medium of instruction there would be only English, or perhaps incorrect Tamil or Hindi, which too could be arranged not without difficulty. I could not possibly put up with this and other disadvantages. I was making my own attempt to teach them but that was at best irregular and I could not get hold of a suitable Gujrati teacher . . . . I was at my wits' end. . . .

Gandhiji's struggle continued. On the one hand he totally rejected the existing system of education, but on the other he did not have a clear alternative to replace it. He had no idea of how to go about the task of educating the children of his extended family. However, he was deeply convinced that only that education is desirable which develops a healthy self-image and inculcates certain values in the individual. He wrote:

> Had I been blind to a sense of self-respect, and allowed myself to be satisfied by having for my children the education that other children could not get, I should have deprived them of the object-lesson in liberty and self-respect that I gave them at the cost of literary training. And where a choice has to be made between liberty and learning, who will not say that the former has to be preferred a thousand times to the latter.

After getting the journal well settled he wanted to start a school for Indian children. On 13 January 1905 he wrote a letter to Professor Gokhale asking for his support. Following are a few sentences from it:

> It is also my intention, if my earnings continue, to open a school on the grounds, which would be second to none in South Africa, for the education primarily of Indian children who would be resident boarders and, secondly, of all who want to join the school but would also reside on the premises. For this too volunteer workers are required. It would be possible to induce one or two English men or English ladies here to give their lifetime to this work, but Indian teachers are absolutely necessary. Could you induce any graduates who have an aptitude for teaching, who bear a blameless character and who would be prepared to work for a mere living. Those who would come must be well-tried first-class men. I would want two or three at least but more could certainly be accommodated, and after the school is in working order, it is intended to add a sanatorium with open-air treatment on hygienic lines. . . .

The school eventually had fifty children. He was determined 'to find out by experience and experiment the true system'. He took some time to discover it, specially the kind that could be offered for wider application in a country so large as India, for he knew that his home was India and not South Africa.

Gandhiji in India

Gandhiji eventually realised that it was time for him to return to his home country. He reached Bombay with Kasturba on 9 January 1915.

Wise man that he was, Gandhiji decided not to straight away plunge into the politics of the country or even pass any judgement on the situation here. He gave a year to going around the country to see and acquaint himself with the life of the people and their feelings. He wanted to have first-hand knowledge of the rural as well as urban conditions in which the common man and woman lived. This was also the advice given to him by Gopal Krishna Gokhale, who was like a political *guru* to him. The question of discovering the right kind of educational system, however, remained his primary concern.

Within two or three years Gandhiji had to undertake three major *satyagraha* campaigns — the Ahmedabad Satyagraha related to the textile mill-hands' strike, the Kheda Satyagraha about the payment of land revenue by farmers, and the Champaran Satyagraha against the exploitation of the indigo farmers by the British plantation owners.

The Champaran Satyagraha was Gandhiji's first major non-violent struggle in India. It was aimed at uplifting the physical conditions and morale of the indigo farmers and liberating them from the grip of the British indigo plantation owners who were exploiting them in a most inhuman manner. This *satyagràha* proved to be the first profound victory of non-violent struggle against the exploitation of the helpless by the white plantation owners. However, when the *satyagraha* was still going on, he was thinking of improving the conditions of the poor of Champaran district.

In *Satyagràha in Champaran* Rajendra Prasad wrote:

> He [Gandhiji] was convinced from the very beginning that it was impossible for any outside agency to improve their lot unless their mental and moral condition was improved. This applies to the whole of India but it can be demonstrated beyond contradiction in Champaran . . . . Mahatmaji had accordingly decided that arrangement for spread of education was as necessary among them as the redress of their grievances. Some time before the Enquiry Committee commenced its work Mahatmaji had written to some friends about it and told them what sorts of volunteers he needed for social work.

He did get some of the most educated people from various parts of India to run the schools which he had managed to start. Unfortunately very few educated people from Bihar joined him. Describing the plan he wrote to a Government official:

> In the schools I am opening, children under the age of 12 only are admitted. The idea is to get hold of as many children as possible and to give them an all round education, i.e. a good knowledge of Hindi or Urdu, [and] through that medium, of arithmetic and the rudiments of history and geography, a knowledge of simple scientific principles and some industrial training. No cut and dried syllabus has yet been prepared because I am going on an unbeaten track. I look upon our present system with horror and distrust. Instead of developing the moral and mental faculties of the little children it dwarfs them. . . .

Five schools started functioning in the area. Some of his closest companions were with him to carry out the plans, about which he wrote:

> I shall endeavour to avoid the defects of the present system. The chief thing aimed at is contact of children with men and women of culture and unimpeachable moral character. That to me is education. Literary training is to be useful merely as a means to that end. . . .

The Champaran Satyagraha came to a successful end. In his autobiography Gandhiji wrote:

> The *ryots* [tenants], who had all along remained crushed, now somewhat came to their own, and the superstition that the stain of indigo could never be washed out was exploded . . . . It was my desire to continue the constructive work for some years, to establish more schools and to penetrate the villages more effectively. The ground had been prepared, but it did not please God, as often before, to allow my plans to be fulfilled. Fate decided otherwise and drove me to take up work elsewhere.

Those schools functioned for a while but were then closed for lack of workers and the vision required for such a pioneering work.

Satyagraha Ashram, Sabarmati

When leaving South Africa Gandhiji had an important question in his mind. Where should the Phoenix family settle in India? At the suggestion of C.F. Andrews the whole group went to Santiniketan, the *ashram* poet Rabindranath Tagore had set up in Bengal.

Tagore had a comprehensive educational programme, which, to put it briefly, had a precise philosophy and was built around creative activities. He was firm in his conviction that the medium of instruction at all levels should be the mother tongue. Second, for him Nature was the richest centre of learning; and third, creative activities ought to play a central role in the processes of education. Gandhiji admired and respected Tagore's educational system, but it has to be admitted that his goal was somewhat different, particularly his short-term goal.

The Phoenix 'settlement' shifted to Santiniketan. After a few days Gandhiji also joined them. He tried various experiments with the help of the poet and the teachers, specially about the way of life educational institutions should develop. No doubt he must have drawn some creative ideas from his and his colleagues' experience in Santiniketan. There is not much left of those experiments except that every year a day is observed to recall Gandhiji's stay and the programme of self-help.

Santiniketan was not the place for Gandhiji to make a home and conduct his own experiments. His need was to experiment with the perspective he had developed for the future of India. The 'family' went to Gujarat, first to Kochrab and finally to Sabarmati, a place just outside Ahmedabad.

In addition to his preoccupation with national politics there was one subject which occupied his mind all the time. It was education for the masses of India. He knew what 'education' meant in pre-British India. At a conference in Allahabad on 23 December 1916 he gave a talk which was reported in *The Leader* (27.12.1916). Following are a few sentences from that report:

> Mr Gandhi then described the ancient system of education . . . even elementary education imparted by the village teacher taught the students all that was necessary for their occupation. Those who went in for higher education became fully conversant with the science of wealth, *Artha Shastra*, ethics and religion, *Dharma Shastra*. In ancient times, there were no restrictions on education . . . . It was due to such a system of education that Indian civilization had outlived so many vicissitudes through thousands of years . . . . No doubt the wave of a new civilization had been passing through India. But he was sure that it was transitory, it would soon pass away and Indian civilization would be revivified.

Gandhiji was steadily getting closer to his ideal educational system. But he had yet to try many more experiments before he discovered **the true system.**

National Education

After the Sabarmati Ashram was well settled, Gandhiji began planning for a national school. Describing its basic principles in the prospectus he wrote:

> The education will be physical, intellectual and religious. For physical education there will be training in agriculture and hand-weaving and in the use of carpenter's and blacksmith's tools . . . In addition, they will be given drill, . . . and as part of this, they will be taught how to march in squads and how each one may work with quiet efficiency in case of accidents such as fire. . . . They will have instructions on how to preserve health and on home remedies for ordinary ailments, with as much of physiology and botany as may be necessary for the purpose . . . . For intellectual training, they will study Gujarati, Marathi, Hindi and Sanskrit as compulsory subjects . . . . There will be no teaching of English during the first three years".

The medium of instruction was to be Gujarati (the mother tongue and local language) right up to the highest stage. The syllabus included the usual subjects such as mathematics, book-keeping, history, geography, chemistry and astronomy. By way of instruction in religion, general ethical principles were to be taught. The aim of that education was that after a few years the student's equipment would approximate to that of a well-informed graduate.

It is obvious that although he was more or less clear about the objectives of his ideal education, he had not yet reached the stage when he could put forward a concrete plan of his system which, by definition, had to be entirely different from the existing one with the structure the British had created.

He was firm about education being imparted through the mother tongue at all its stages. In a speech at the Second Gujarat Educational Conference in October, 1917, he said:

It should be obvious to everyone that the first thing to do in this connection is to come to a definite decision about the medium of instruction. Unless that is done, all other efforts, I fear, are likely to prove fruitless.

He put equally great stress on the desirability of having a common language for the whole country. He enumerated five requirements of a national language. It should be:

(a) easy to learn for government officials;

(b) capable of serving as a medium of religious, economic and political contact between all parts of the country;

(c) the speech of a large number of Indians;

(d) easy for everyone to learn; and

(e) chosen without consideration of temporary or passing circumstances.

It was evident that English did not fulfil any of these requirements. Gandhiji considered Hindi, eventually Hindustani, to be the language that fulfilled all the requirements.

Gandhiji emphasised the building of character as the major task of education. The third item on which he put emphasis was music and the fourth was physical training. He strongly pleaded for the education of women.

We think our entire life depends on success at examinations. Gandhiji said:

> India never knew the institution of examination. The method is of recent introduction . . . . The system has lent itself to serious abuse, every subject being taught with an eye on the examination and the conviction firmly planted in the pupil's mind that passing the examination was all that was necessary.

In his scheme it was stated:

> Having regard to the view that examinations are quite undesirable, pupils in this institution will be tested periodically from two points of view — whether the teacher has made the right effort and whether the pupil has followed. The pupil will be freed from the fear of examinations. . . .

National Universities

After the First World War India waited for a change of heart on the part of the British. Instead she received the Rowlatt Act. The people as a whole resented it. In April 1919 more than a thousand innocent unarmed people were massacred in Jallianwalla Bagh, Amritsar, by the army. This outrage wounded India's pride and she rose in revolt against foreign domination. Gandhiji said that Jallianwalla Bagh was only the beginning:

> We must be prepared to contemplate with equanimity not a thousand murders of innocent men and women, but many thousands before we attain a status in the world that shall not be surpassed by any nation. We hope, therefore, that all concerned will take rather than lose heart and treat hanging as an ordinary affair of life.

On 1 August 1920 he wrote to the Viceroy: "I can retain neither respect nor affection for a government which has been moving from wrong to wrong in order to defend its immorality". The Congress and Gandhiji declared total non-cooperation with the British Government. The call included a total boycott of legislative bodies, Government schools and law courts.

The Gujarat Political Conference held on 27-29 August passed a resolution which meant that title-holders and persons holding medals should renounce the titles and return the medals; lawyers should try to settle disputes privately and should give up practice in law courts; parents should withdraw their children from any school that had any connection with the Government; college students should give up colleges on their own; voters should refuse to vote for any one seeking election to a council and candidates should withdraw their candidature; and every man, woman and child should follow the rule of perfect *swadeshi* and should spin cotton.

Although it was a solely political campaign, it had a profound impact on the educational scene in the country. With the call for boycotting schools and colleges having any connection with the government, it was necessary to have some alternative institutions. That was the beginning of the establishment of *vidyapeeths* — national schools and colleges all over the country. In November Gandhiji founded the National University of Gujarat, Gujarat Vidyapeeth. Such national institutions also came up in Calcutta, Patna, Aligarh, Bombay, Banaras and Delhi. The Jamia Millia Islamia — the National Muslim University — was founded through the joint efforts of Gandhiji and Md. Ali.

These institutions made a significant contribution in the fields of both political awakening and educational awareness. Establishing these centres of learning was a step towards the growth of a new approach to education.

They created the spirit of freedom, an element essential for the development of a healthy personality. Second, they prepared a cadre of freedom-fighters for the next 'battle for liberation'. More important, as experimental centres they were useful for Gandhiji to explore the structural side of his educational scheme, *buniyadi talim* (basic education), which was started in 1937. By that time institutions like Gujarat Vidyapeeth and Jamia Millia Islamia had fully developed their systemic structures in a way that was favourable for giving a trial to the new scheme.

Concept of Education and Nayee Talim

Between 1920 and 1937 a lot happened in the country. People's awareness of their cultural foundation, their knowledge of the damage done to it by the colonial rulers, and an understanding of the socio-political conditions of the country made it imperative that for building a healthy India mass education in general and education of the individual along with the struggle for freedom were the most important elements. Gandhiji also believed that without gaining freedom, building a new and independent educational programme was not possible.

Most of the revivalist institutions, barring some exceptions, such as Santiniketan and *vidyapeeths*, had lost their original relevance or had become dependent on government recognition. Some continued catering for the needs of the elite, who looked for government patronage. Santiniketan was deliberately kept apolitical by Tagore, except that some individuals occasionally took active part in the freedom struggle. Without going into a discussion on the why of these issues I shall try to see the relationship between the Tagorean concept of education and *nayee talim* as developed under the guidance of Gandhiji.

According to Tagore's scheme there are three centres of education: the mother tongue, not only as the medium of instruction but also as the major means of communication between people; creative activities; and Nature, of which we are an inseparable part.

Gandhiji's scheme as presented to the nation in 1937 also had three similar elements. He was convinced that the medium of instruction in schools and colleges must be the mother tongue or the language of the area. He also insisted that the language of communication between people of various regions ought to be that which most people understood or could easily learn.

In other words, it should be an effective tool for community relationships. For most of its needs, physical as well as spiritual, human society depended on Nature. *Nayee talim,* as envisaged by Gandhiji, gave top priority to our relationship with Nature. According to Tagore Nature was the most important source of knowledge, human creativity and livelihood. The highest education is that which does not merely impart information but puts life in harmony with all existence.

The third element is meaningful manual work according to Gandhiji, and creative activities according to Tagore. There is very little difference in the two approaches. Tagore did not talk of the economic side of creative activities. For him it was art, something that caters for all human needs, physical, emotional and spiritual. Gandhiji, on the other hand, placed emphasis on it as a vocation for livelihood and a way of gaining knowledge.

I do not think the difference between the two is crucial. While Gandhiji's approach is obviously egalitarian, Tagore's sounds elitist. Taking into account the time factor, Gandhiji had the advantage of drawing from Gurudev's educational experience. He did not only learn something but he also improved on it.

Basic Education Starts in Seven Provinces

The fruit which Gandhiji had nurtured for two decades was now nearly ripe. The political situation in India had changed. After the elections for Legislative Assemblies the British Government had to accept the formation of Congress ministries in nine provinces. In addition to whatsoever these Congress Governments were hoping to do, Gandhiji offered them an educational plan to replace the current system of education. He had written an article, 'Education', in the 31-7-1937 issue of *Harijan*.

> How to solve the problem of education is the problem unfortunately mixed up with the disappearance of the drink revenue. . . .

Until then the expenditure on education came from excise (alcohol) revenue. Gandhiji wrote:

> . . . as a nation we are so backward in education that we cannot hope to fulfil our obligation to the nation in this respect in a given time during this generation, if the programme is to depend on money. I have therefore made bold, even at the risk of losing a reputation for constructive ability, to suggest that education should be self-supporting. By education I mean all-round drawing out of the best in child and man — body, mind and spirit . . . .

He suggested that the money required for education could be raised by taxing the rich.

This is not a fanciful picture. If we would but shed our mental laziness, it would appear to be an eminently reasonable and practical solution of the problem of education that faces the Congress Ministers and therefore the Congress.

In October 1937 Gandhiji called a conference which was attended by many eminent education experts of the country and the Education Ministers of several provinces. He presented his scheme to them. The conference passed a resolution which agreed that free and compulsory education should be provided to every child of seven to fourteen years of age; the medium of instruction should be the mother tongue; the process of education throughout this period should centre around some form of manual productive work, and all the other abilities to be developed should be integrally related to the central handicraft chosen, with due regard to the environment of the child; and this system of education would gradually be able to cover the remuneration of the teachers.

A little later the Hindustani Talimi Sangh, an all-India organisation, was formed to develop the Basic Education programme all over the country and run experimental schools. The first such school was set up in Sevagram, Gandhiji's *ashram*, which also became the central office of the Sangh with Shri E.W. Aryanayakam as General Secretary. Gandhiji chose Dr Zakir Hussain, the head of Jamia Millia Islamia, as the Chairman of the Sangh.

A wave of educational reconstruction seemed to pass over the country. Some provinces appointed education reorganization committees, teacher training and refresher training centres. Some basic schools were opened and some primary schools were converted into basic schools. New literature on Basic Education was published for the use of teachers. A seven-year syllabus was prepared by some of the most experienced teachers of their subjects.

In his report of two years of work Aryanayakam wrote that

> basic education was being carried out as an educational experiment by the Governments of C.P., U.P., Bihar, Orissa, Bombay, and Kashmir and a few non-Government institutions. In all there were twelve training schools and two training colleges, seven Refreshers Training Centres and over five thousand schools carrying out the experiment of basic education.

There was so much enthusiasm that even when the Orissa Government closed its basic schools in the second year of the experiment, the people of the province continued the work on their own. Out of the fifteen basic schools, seven continued functioning, which indicates that the system had attracted the interest of the people.

After about two years the Congress Ministries resigned, resulting in the closure of basic schools run by the governments in all the seven provinces. But the ones run by voluntary bodies continued until the launch of the Quit India struggle in 1942, the consequence of which was the arrest of most of the active workers, including those engaged in Gandhiji's constructive programmes. He was the first to be arrested.

The resolution passed by the Second Basic Education Conference held on the campus of Jamia Millia Islamia gives an idea of the results attained by the basic schools during the short period of a little over two years.

> This conference records with satisfaction that the reports on the working of basic schools run by the Governments, local bodies and by private enterprise are almost unanimous that general standards of health or behaviour as well as intellectual attainment, are very encouraging. The children in basic schools are more active, cheerful, self-reliant, their power of self-expression is well-developed, they are developing habits of cooperative work, and social prejudices are breaking down. Considering the difficulties inherent in the initial stages of a new scheme of education, involving a new ideology and a new technique, the progress reported holds out the promise that even better results can be expected in future.

The Quit India movement of 1942 proved a very intense experience for the country, specially in regard to looking back and reviewing the achievements and difficulties faced by the freedom struggle led by Gandhiji. Within a very few days most of the cadres of the freedom movement had been arrested. Only those remained outside who either went underground or were co-opted

— willingly or otherwise — by the State machinery. Members of political parties which were not in favour of the Quit India Call also remained out of prisons.

Gandhiji was in prison for nearly two years. That was probably the hardest period in his life. His two closest life companions died in the same prison — his wife Kasturba and Mahadev Desai, his right hand. During that period he must have introspected and reviewed almost everything he did in his life or wanted to do. His life-long *tapasya* as a teacher must have made him ask why he had not yet been able to find **the right way**, which he had been seeking since he started teaching the children of his large family in South Africa. He must have asked himself many questions including some regarding his experiment of basic education and its future.

When he came out of prison, two of his major concerns were (a) to see the British rule over India end at the earliest, and (b) to plan an educational programme for the people of India which would prepare them for using that freedom to lift themselves up from the conditions they had been pushed into during colonial rule, such as stark poverty, pessimism, ignorance and helplessness.

For the last quarter of a century Gandhiji had led the non-violent war of freedom on political as well as socio-economic grounds. He went on encouraging the people to build alternatives for nearly all aspects of life. The eighteen-point Constructive Programme was for replacing the existing systems and institutions. For instance, development of indigenous industries — textiles, housing, food, basic education, health and sanitation, social equality and cooperative living.

Whenever a suggestion came to him for improving or changing some aspect of Indian life, if he felt that the suggestion warranted attention, he found people, or people came to him to take up the responsibility to organise that particular activity. The building of the leprosy campaign is a remarkable example of that kind. Traditionally leprosy was a most misunderstood disease. Someone with that disease was considered lower than an untouchable.

Gandhiji had always been working against such traditions on both medical and socio-economic grounds. In 1946 a man who had the disease and who had cured himself went and told Gandhiji his story. I remember having heard him say to this gentleman: "You have been sent to me by God with the plan that you will organise and lead an all-India movement against this most inhuman attitude towards leprosy". It inspired the man so much that he built an all-India leprosy campaign. Thus it became one of the eighteen items of the Constructive Programme.

Gandhiji's Constructive Programme was built to provide the country with alternative techniques and institutions to replace the ones imposed by the colonial rulers, and with which the country did not wish to continue after attaining freedom. He had hoped that once India became free she would have a fully tested pattern of political, economic and social structures to run the country on a sound non-violent basis.

His internment in the Aga Khan Palace, as has been said before, was a time of introspection for Gandhiji. After coming out of prison he said: "I have been thinking hard during the detention over the possibilities of Nayee Talim until my mind became restive". He also said:

> We must not rest content with our present achievements. We must penetrate the homes of the children. We must educate their parents. Basic education must become literally education for life. . . . It had become clear to me that the scope of basic education has to be extended. . . . A basic school teacher must consider himself a universal teacher. His village is his universe . . . .

A *nayee talim* conference was called in the month of January 1945. In his inaugural speech Gandhiji introduced an entirely revised and enlarged map of the system. Addressing the basic education workers he said:

> Although we have been working for Nayee Talim all these years, we have so far been, as it were, sailing in an inland sea which is comparatively safe. We are now leaving the shoals and heading for the open sea. So far our course was mapped out. We have now before us uncharted waters with the Pole Star as our only guide and protection. That Pole Star is village handicrafts.
>
> Our sphere of work now is not confined to Nayee Talim of children from seven and fourteen years; it is to cover the whole of life from the moment of conception to the moment of death. This means that our work has increased tremendously. Yet workers remain the same. But that should not worry us. Our guide and companion is Truth which is God. He will never betray us. But Truth will be our help only if we stand by it regardless of everything. There can be in it no room for hypocrisy, camouflage, pride, attachment or anger.
>
> We have to become teachers of villagers; that is to say, we have to become their servants in the true sense. Our reward, if any, has to come from within and not from without. It should make no difference to us whether in our quest for Truth we have any human company or not. Nor does Nayee Talim depend on outside financial help. It must proceed on its own way, whatever critics might say. I know that true education must be self-supporting. There is nothing to feel ashamed of in this. It may be a novel idea if we can make good our claim and demonstrate that ours is the only method for the true development of the mind. Those who scoff at Nayee Talim today will become our ardent admirers in the end and Nayee Talim will find universal acceptance.
>
> Whether this is a mere dream or a practical reality, this is the goal of Nayee Talim and nothing short of it. May the God of Truth help us to realise it.
>
> I want to draw your attention also to another thing. I consider the Sevagram centre to be an ideal centre for conducting the central experiment in Nayee Talim, as it is here that the Charkha Sangh (All Indian Spinners'

> Association) is carrying out its main experiment. Wardha is the centre for the other village industries . . . . Sevagram does not stand alone; there are nearly 20 villages lying about it in close proximity. Therefore if experiments in Nayee Talim in its most natural form can be carried out anywhere, it is here.

The plan he put forward was for the education of everybody in the community. It was divided as follows: (i) Adult education — of the whole community, including the parents of unborn babies; (ii) pre-basic — education of children between two and a half to seven years; (iii) basic education — for children between seven and fourteen years; (iv) post-basic education — fourteen to eighteen years; (v) university level education — beyond eighteen years of age.

The most significant statement from Gandhiji at that time was that after the launching of the new perspective of *nayee talim* every constructive programme must have its orientation. To put it the other way round, it would mean that all those activities should be considered a part of *nayee talim.* In other words, all the work that was being done for the attainment of freedom for the country and for the reconstruction of the Indian polity should be educationally oriented.

NAYEE TALIM AT SEVAGRAM

Several organisations which had been engaged in basic education earlier restarted their work. The main centre in this regard was Sevagram. I was fortunate to have been offered a position as art instructor for the first six-month teachers' training camp with a very active basic school as the practising school for the teacher trainees and a model school for the country wide *nayee talim* work. It feels strange that instead of six months I continued with *nayee talim* at Sevagram for eighteen years! When I reached Sevagram in November 1944 I remember noticing the enthusiasm of the teachers and the lively faces of the children. The Teachers' Training Camp had more that sixty trainees from almost every part of the country. It was indeed a bright and active group of people of ages between twenty and fifty.

After the prayer at six in the morning and then breakfast, we divided ourselves into groups to do the cleaning of every place on the campus, including the lavatories. In fact cleaning of lavatories had the first priority. It is particularly important in India, because cleaning of lavatories has been considered the work of untouchables. When I experienced that aspect of *nayee talim* I was reminded of Pestalozzi, who said that he descended down to their level (of the poor uneducated) so that he could lift them up with him. A very moving and uplifting experience indeed it was.

Actually, all the staff of the school and other members of the Sevagram community had made cleanliness a science as well as an art, developing its technique thoroughly. It became a separate subject in the school and the community. After those forty-five minutes of community cleaning everybody went to his or her work — some to the farm in which we tried to produce all the grains, vegetables and fruits needed for the community, others to their spinning and weaving workshops, and yet others to other activities, which included lunch for the community. We all took turns preparing dinner everyday. The number of workshops gradually increased according to the needs of the community and the growing educational programme.

After a couple of hours' break at midday all the children went to their studies related to the day's work and to other aspects of their life, such as health, culture, etc. In the afternoon there were music and art classes for all the children. Some of the time in the afternoon was also devoted to practice and rehearsals for the celebration of festivals and special occasions. Children and class teachers along with the art teacher decorated the places of celebrations and festivals with *alpana,* flowers and textiles. Stage craft and management was an important part of *nayee talim.* We had arrangements for simple sports and games — mostly games that needed no equipment.

Yet another feature that ought to be mentioned here is the character of festivals celebrated and the daily prayer conducted in *nayee talim* schools. Festivals of all religions were celebrated in as good a way as possible. School prayers were the same as those of Gandhiji's *ashram,* i.e., inclusive of all religions. It had a very positive impact on the children about the equality of all religions.

At the end it may be useful to mention here something about self-evaluation by students. A list of headings of paragraphs from the annual self-evaluation by a post-basic student would give an idea of the content of the education he received. Instead of the usual type of examinations the Sevagram school considered self-evaluation — along with evaluation by teachers — a more effective and creative method of judging the all-round progress of a student.

Some of the sub-titles from it were: My health; Social Life; Kitchen work; Community cleanliness; Prayers; Looking after guests; Looking after the sick; Festivals; Cooperative store; My behaviour in the hostel and in my family; Village work; Craft and self-sufficiency; Spinning and self-sufficiency in clothing; Building work; Gardening; Work in the printing press; Language and literature; Mother tongue; National language; Other languages (English); Industrial and agricultural science; Social science; Self study; My aptitude and future studies/work.

There is much to tell and explain about the experiment of *nayee talim*. It is impossible to put even a tenth of it in such a small space. There is much, though not sufficient, material that is available for further study about the subject. What is lacking is an analytical study of *nayee talim*. For example, a question is often asked: In spite of *nayee talim* being such an ideal and practical system of education, why did it not spread as it should have? One day a thorough study on this question will have to be done. For the present purpose, I hope the above should suffice.

6

Gandhi's Social Theory

Two master narratives dominate the sociological thinking about present-day India. Dumont's well known study conceived Indian society on the principles of hierarchy and totality. He gave the Brahmanic world view the status of objective truth and created a master narrative of Indian society as hierarchically based on the caste system. Thereafter, sociologists either actively rejected his model or tamely imitated his thesis. Another master narrative was fabricated by the colonial state and spoke of the eternal conflict between Hindus and Muslims, and the neutral mediator role of the British. Any instance of social conflict is seen as the inevitable repetition of this phenomenon.

These two master narratives are the creations of the West, as part of their attempt to comprehend intellectually other cultures. In post-independent India, this discourse has been inherited by the nation-state. Today's political agenda cannot get beyond these stereotyped understandings. Any discourse about Indian society begins and ends on these two master narratives, and nation-state claims to be the sole authority to mediate on social problems. In the recent past, with the emergence of the Hindu revivalist party on the national political scene, the nation-state is increasingly claiming to be the sole authority to speak on Indian society, attempting to relegate all other agencies to the background.4 All agencies, including religion, are defined in a manner entirely consistent with the needs of the nation-state.

In the background of these two master narratives and the claim of the nation-state to be the sole guardian of society, we would like to examine the concept of civil society, especially in the context of multi?cultures and religions. A sociological rather than a strictly philosophical approach is in order at this stage when we try to understand the nature of society as such. Community spatially bound, face-to-face with the sphere of human relationships, is based on an innate moral order.

The most natural communities, like the family, have intimate human relationships and are bound morally. However, in modern times we have many more communities which do not fall into the natural community category. Sociologists speak of 'imagined' or constructed community when talking about communities other than the natural ones. A constructed or imagined community ". . . consists of members who do not know each other in their concrete existence and yet, in each member, there lived an image of a larger communion." Such communities demand allegiance from people who have no concrete relations with each other. It fosters relations by creating images of communion and oneness.

In traditional societies like that of India, communities with multiple levels of relationships and moral agencies exist. However, the creation of a nation-state at the arrival of colonialism, and later by the independent India, led to increasing standardization of relationships. The nation-state, with its ideologies of nationalism and secularism and through its agencies of bureaucracy, legislation and judiciary, is encroaching upon and claiming the intimate loyalties of peoples.

The increasing violence implied in the nation-state has led people to search for 'identity groups,' and they nostalgically long for traditional models of communities. Indian sociologists are critiquing the pathologies of the nation-state and modernity, and are engaged in developing a concept of society that is more normal and healthy. In this search, they fall back on primordial identities. Gandhian social vision can be seen as one such primordial model for taking care of plural identities.10 Hence, An enquiry into Gandhi's social theory and vision might be a useful exercise as part of our enquiry into the nature of the pluralist Indian social fabric.

Gandhi's social theory evolved out of his engagement with life-issues and problems and also from his "experiments with truth" at the personal level. His social theory was not the result of philosophical analysis of social concepts, but the consequence of his engagements with the historical social forces of his time.

The development of his social theory had two phases: one of deconstruction, the other of reconstruction. The particular socio-political situation in which he lived and with which he struggled demanded a deconstructionive approach. It included deconstructing its colonial entrenchment from the fundamentalist forces.

This was not simply an attempt at political freedom from the colonial masters, but at deconstructing the understanding of Indianness and Indian society from the colonial constructions. The colonial construct of Indianness and Indian society had deeply affected the Indian psyche. The cultural deconstruction of India from the colonial construct occupied much of Gandhi's struggle.

In the popular presentation of Gandhi, it is the political aspect of deconstruction in the narrow sense which is highlighted. However, the reconstruction of

India formed the essential dimension of his program. In this attempt, he appealed to the 'primordial traditions' of India. This 'primordial appeal' should immediately be distinguished from the 'primordialist approach' of the nationalist Hindus of his and also of our time. Their primordialism consisted of a 'strategic' reference to a golden age in order to revive Hinduism; at the same time they are 'syncretic' in adopting elements from Western developmental models and from organizational factors of Christianity.

Gandhi's approach was different. He appealed to the mythological persons, cultural symbols and social systems of India's past to reconstruct India's present, not a past that is idealized but a past that embodies the essential and the ultimate values of life. His primordialism involved a faith-epistemic in constructing a society that is holistic, and that cares for the self-realization of the individuals. The master symbol of his social theory was 'swaraj'.

Concept of Swaraj

Gandhi's social theories were already formed in 1908 when he wrote Hind Swaraj, during his return voyage from London to South Africa, in answer to the Indian anarchists whom he had met in London. Apart from its repudiation of modern civilization as based on power and wealth (greed), Gandhi elaborated his social theory based on 'Truth and Non-violence'. That his social-manifesto was written as early as 1908 may prompt us to think that he would have changed much of it in the course of his life. However, he endorsed his theory as late as 1921 when he wrote: "The booklet was written in 1908. My conviction is deeper today than ever"; and again later in 1938 saying: ". . . after the stormy thirty years through which I have since passes, I have seen nothing to make me alter the views expounded in it [Hind Swaraj]." The two pillars of his ideal society are: genuine freedom, based on truth and non-violence, and selfless-action through suffering to achieve that freedom. Quoting James Allen, he said:

For ages the oppressed have cried for freedom and yet a thousand manmade statutes have failed to give it to them. 'They can give it only to themselves; they shall find it only in obedience to the Divine Statutes which are inscribed upon their hearts. Let them resort to the inward freedom, and the shadow of repression shall no more darken the earth.

Let us elaborate on these two notions in swaraj. Swaraj consists of striving for total freedom on a national scale that will guarantee real self-dependence and genuine interdependence. Gandhi's concept of swaraj meant that every village would be a republic or panchayat, having full powers as a self-sustained and self-dependent body, having the individual as the ultimate unit who would render his cooperation freely and willingly. The ultimate basis of the individual and the village-society is truth which is both a transcendent and immanent concept having non-violence as it operational principle.

In this structure composed of innumerable villages, there will be ever-widening, never-ascending circles. Life will not be a pyramid with the apex sustained by the bottom. But it will be an oceanic circle whose center will be the individual, always ready to perish for the village, the latter ready to perish for the circle of villages, till at last the whole becomes one life composed of individuals, never aggressive in their arrogance but ever humble, sharing the majesty of the oceanic circle for which they are integral units.

The outermost circumference in this design would not wield power to crush the inner circle, but would give strength to all within and derive its own strength from it. Machinery would not displace human labor, nor would there be concentration of power in a few hands.

Gandhi preferred the Sanskrit word swaraj to the English expression 'independence'. Swaraj meant rule of the self, where the self is a related entity: related to the nature, to others and to the ultimate. Here self is understood not as an isolated monad subsisting in itself and for itself. Here self is self of the Self which is the transcendent-immanent reality. It has immediately a transcendent reference which is the basis for its horizontal relatedness.

The truth of the individual is the presence of the ultimate Truth. It is the realization of ultimate Truth that is the goal of the individual. Since all individuals are in the quest after Truth, they are related to one another in this search. This transcendent referentiality of all individuals gives them an axis and teleos that binds them freely and non-competitively. Swaraj presupposes the interdependence of the individual on others, nature and the ultimate. This inter-dependent nature of realities, this inter-relatedness and being-with-others constitutes the very core of the individual. Hence inter-relatedness is not an additional quality of the individual arrived at through a social contrast for the sake of socialization.

The individual is related. This inter-relatedness presupposes pluralism which is not simply a philosophical concept in the Gandhian system, but an operational principle which immediately gives non-violence its legitimacy. The individual should not violate the Truth in others. This respect for the truth in others, and this relatedness with others non-violently is the path of self-rule or swaraj. It is the very striving after swaraj that takes care of swaraj.

In Gandhi's vision, this freedom or liberation is not an individualist affair. Freedom is a political reality: freedom from every kind of foreign domination; it is an economic program: freedom from oppressive and exploitative market-system; and it is more as well: freedom from every kind of inner compulsion and self-alienating desires.

Swaraj and Sarvodaya

For Gandhi, swaraj or freedom is not an anthropocentric project where human beings devise ways and means to achieve the highest social good through social contract and a manipulation of nature. It is based on the very nature of self, understood in its relatedness.

The ultimate goal is mukti: the realization of the self. If so, in this search for liberation/freedom, how are we related to one another? The relationship is understood in terms of Swadeshi. Swaraj implies swadeshi, i.e., at homeness. This means being rooted in one?s immediate surroundings. As the entire creation is linked together, the correct mode of relating is to remain true to one's immediate surroundings. Fidelity to one's own earth and water will eventually prepare one for final emancipation and for reaching out to all, and thus achieving oneness with the entire creation.

At the social level swadeshi amounts to self-reliance and self-sufficiency. One does not become a burden to society, but relies on one?s own resources for subsistence. Swadeshi means:

> . . . that spirit in us which restricts us to the use and service of our immediate surroundings, to the exclusion of the more remote. I restrict myself to my ancestral religion; if defective, I purge it from within. In politics, I use indigenous institutions; if defective, I improve upon them; in economics, I use the immediate surroundings.17

Swaraj as total freedom is true home-coming. Gandhi's vision of swadeshi is better expressed in the words of Edward Carpenter who also advocated the return to nature. He said:

> In such new human life then — its fields, its farms, its worships, its cities ? always the work of man perfecting and beautifying the lands, aiding the efforts of the sun and soil, giving voice to the desire of the mute earth — in such new communal life near to nature, so far from any asceticism or inhospitality, we see far more humanity and sociability than ever before; an infinite helpfulness and sympathy as between the children of a common mother.

SWARAJ AND SARVODAYA

Swaraj also means sarvodaya: the welfare of all. Gandhi's social theory envisages well-being for all, well-being that is oriented to self-realization of one and all. In this new society economic relations are not controlled by market-forces, but by social affections. Political economy gives way to 'affective economy'; a mother, though hungry, may go starving in order to feed her son.

Accordingly, Gandhi argued that affective resources could enter into all economic equations, and produce the maximum. If the spirit of the worker is brought to its greatest strength by the motivating forces of affection, it can produce more. Labor, with stable wages and constancy of numbers in employment, functions in terms of service, not in terms of profit, the wages being a necessary adjunct, not the object of life. But political economy is interested in production, preservation and distribution at the proper place and time of things that are useful and pleasurable, and the merchandising economy is interested in the accumulation of wealth in the hands of a few, with legal claims and power over the labor of others.

Their vested interests create poverty and debt, on the one hand, and riches and power, on the other hand. Here riches or money means power over others, and this in direct proportion to the poverty of the men over whom power is exercised. The disgraceful record in human history is "Buy in the cheapest market and sell in the dearest." The chief value of money seems to be "having power over human beings". But power over human beings is available by other means than by money.

In the ultimate analysis, we learn that persons are wealth, not silver and gold. If persons are wealth, then modern economics is the systematic disobedience of the first principles of religion. Swaraj really means self-control, and the right perception of what genuine richness is: Sarvodaya does not accept the utilitarian formula of the greatest good of the greatest number, but the greatest good of all and the readiness to die for it. It is possible on the basis of bread-labor and trusteeship whereby hoarding is avoided.

In the construction of a civil society, Gandhi introduces the quest for liberation or self-realization as the basic component. Search for liberation gives all the members a transcendent reference point and enables them to relativize everything else, and, at the same time, to be related to one another on a basis that is above themselves. By introducing a transcendent referentiality in the construction of civil society, Gandhi visualizes a civil society that is eco-friendly and theandric, not narrowly anthropocentric. It gives civil society a primordial character.

Pedagogy of Swaraj

Swaraj is a primordial vision of a civil society. Such a social vision is realized through relentless search after Truth, through continuous action. Resisting untruth while holding on to Truth becomes imperative in the very formation of a civil society. In this engagement Gandhi's innovative reading of the Gita provides the key. The Gita in Gandhi's interpretation says: "No one has attained his goal without action. If we were to cease working, the world would perish. People need to engage in action." All actions do not lead to freedom.

The uniqueness of the Gita consisted in providing the matchless remedy for attaining freedom — the renunciation of fruits of action. Here renunciation means absence of hankering after the fruit. The renunciation in the Gita is the acid test of faith. Gandhi believed that he who brooded over the results was like someone given to objects of the senses, ever distracted and resorting to means fair and foul. When there is no desire for fruit, there is no temptation for untruth or himsa.

Take any instance of untruth or violence, and it will be found that at its source was the desire to attain the cherished end. Such renunciation gives rise to fearlessness of action. "If we are unmanly today, we are so, not because we do not know how to strike, but because we fear to die. He is no follower of Mahavira, the apostle of Jainism, or of Buddha or of the Vedas who being afraid to die, takes flight before any danger, real or imaginary, all the while wishing that somebody else would remove the danger by destroying the person causing it." Alluding to Chapter XVI of the Gita, where fearlessness heads the list of the divine virtues. Gandhi said:

Fearlessness connotes freedom from all external fear, fear of disease, bodily injury and death, of dispossession, of losing one's nearest and dearest, of losing reputation or giving offence, and so on. . . . Some of us do not fear death, but flee from the minor illness of life. The seeker after Truth must conquer all these fears.

Selfless and fearless action requires and results in suffering, Gandhi was less interested in solving philosophically the riddle of suffering than in involving himself in suffering in order to counter the manifold and engulfing violence. Differences, multiplicities and pluralists bring about violence when relationships are not for 'liberation' and when actions are 'result'-oriented. The single-mindedness of purpose in 'liberation' and selfless action form the basis of civil society. Pain and suffering are not negative categories in the Gandhian vision, but agents in the formation of civil society.

In the context of satyagraha, Gandhi had spoken about the function of suffering in creating a moral community. Suffering is best understood in its historical and political context. However, without elaborating on the context, we shall dwell upon the function of suffering undertaken in the Gandhian vision.

(1) Suffering undertaken in the form of fast or self-discipline purifies the heart and makes one unattached: "Without inward purification, work cannot be done in a spirit of non-attachment".

(2) In satyagraha, suffering would convince the agent of the power of injustice against which the struggle is undertaken and of the earnestness of the demand.28

(3) Suffering is the dynamics of human love. "Love does not burn others, it burns itself".

(4) "Non-violence in its dynamic condition means conscious suffering. It does not mean meek submission to the will of the evil-doer, but it means putting one's whole soul against the will of the tyrant." Suffering is a program of transformation of relationship.

(5) Suffering is a more efficacious and more manly method of representation. "My faith in the efficacy of quiet but continued suffering is much greater than

in negotiation and public agitation, though I am aware that both are part of the struggle, in so far as the struggle represents strong and weak parties alike."31

(6) The fearless self-suffering for a righteous cause overflows into infinite compassion (karuna) and benevolent friendship (maitri), doing good even to evil-doers and reaching out to all in love.

(7) Fasting, as a protest against an injustice, awakens the sleeping conscience either of the loved ones, of the society or of the ruler (tapas = heat produced from single-minded devotion). Fasting is not a means to force someone into action. A genuine fast is a direct act of resistance to untruth; it is an immediate appeal to the conscience of the wrong-doer; it relies on one's inner spiritual strength. In this sense fasting epitomizes the meaning of suffering in non-violent resistance as an eminently "transformative pedagogic act."

In the immediate context of Gandhi's struggle against colonial power, suffering was aimed at convincing the imperial power of the earnestness of the struggle and the immensity of the injustice. However, already at that time Gandhi had employed suffering in bringing about a moral community out of the society shattered by immense oppression and communal violence. As Lord Mountbatten remarked at the instance of the immense communal violence and massacre following the partition of India, Gandhi and his fast was the 'one man army' between the warring communities and the nation.

In the reconstruction of village communities, in the context of the many poor and the many religions, self-suffering love played the important role. For Gandhi, this suffering is not simply theoretical, but practical, and is undertaken in simple bodily actions or by undergoing physical pain. The body plays an important role in creating and forging communities. The violated bodies of satyagrahis during the salt march, or his own body during the Delhi fast played an important role increasing a moral community of the masses of India.

Moreover, in this non-violent, selfless suffering, Gandhi attributed a greater role to women in Satyagraha. Gandhi believed that women had a greater capacity for suffering and therefore a greater role to play in the forming of societies.

In talking about freedom and selfless action and suffering, body and women as the components of a civil society specially in the context of many cultures and religions Gandhi introduced non-academic categories into academic discussion. That was Gandhi's strength and weakness: his strength because he introduced "human categories and affections" into academic discussion; his weakness because he was dismissed by the academicians as too moralistic and utopian. However, more and more anthropological studies on modern societies affirm the role and function of suffering and pain in forging communities.

Gandhian Model of Pluralist Society

In her study of the critical events in recent Indian history, Veena Das holds that the voice of the victims is not heard through the language of the professional and of the state. They do not have the conceptual structures to hear the voice of the victims.

In the memory of an event, as it is organized and consecrated by the State, only the voice of the expert is embodied. From her analysis, Veena Das draws two important conclusions: pain often destroys the capacity to communicate, and pain creates a moral community out of those who suffer. What is interesting for our purpose is the way in which anthropologists are bringing the categories of pain and suffering into their discourse.

From a sociological point of view, it has been stated that pain is the medium through which society establishes its ownership over individuals, and pain is the medium available to an individual through which historical wrong done to a person can be represented either by describing individual symptoms or in the form of a memory inscribed on the body. Initiation rituals of various communities represent the former, while inflicted pain during a riot or suffering self-undertaken in a struggle exemplify the latter.

What is further interesting is the point that pain is experienced in and carried by the body. In the initiation rituals, through inflicting pain, the society integrates its members into a single moral community. It tests the capacity of the members to resist, and thus the quality of the members is reassured. The body becomes the memory of initiation.

The societal law is written on the body. Pain inscribed in the body is the medium by which the individual is linked with society. Pain, as in the case of the totem, is the price for belonging. Pain in other cases can be the somatized form of social criticism. It is the condensed expression of the trauma of the individual and is read as a "bodily criticism" of injustice. Somatic signs are signs of historical wrongs. Through these, the individual resists total incorporation into an "unjust" society.

In the case of the partition riots, names of the new nations were tattooed on the secrets of women — where women's bodies were considered another territory. The Hindus for polluting the purity of Islam; Muslims for introducing foreign elements into the Bharat; each punishes the other by inflicting pain on women, so that the memory of the indignities would haunt the future as well. Torture claims their most precious possession, i.e., violent dialogue is conducted through the bodies of women. Bodies of women marked by rape, or victims of industrial disaster — all are evidence that the "body is the surface on which the political program of both the state and industrial capital are described."

According to Veena Das, the partition discourse in the Constituent Assembly did not create public space (neither real nor theatrical) where victims could narrate the experience; acknowledge their suffering, or hear exemplary instances of altruism with redemptive possibilities. No therapeutic space was created to let the private experiences of pain move out into the realm of publicly articulated experiences of pain.

Durkheim spoke of creating a moral community through the sharing of pain, where the individual pain is collectively experienced. Pain and suffering have the sociological function of inscribing memories in the body, of sharing the pain and forming a moral community. Pain can be communicated, and one can locate pain outside one?s body. Wittgenstein's analysis of 'pain discourse' contends that by relating pain to others, we create relationships with people, giving birth to moral communities.

Through the sharing of pain, they create one body. When another consents to form one body, even if it is with an ill body, this exerts a healing force. The experience of suffering (if not done to consolidate authority or discipline) can be the occasion for forming one body and voice. Construing memory through the common sharing of pain can be healing and integrating.

Pain and suffering, as experienced and communicated by the victims, contribute towards creating and healing communities. At the deconstructive phase of Gandhian struggle, this was evident. Besides, Gandhi in his body 'symbolized' the suffering of the colonized people and carved a 'moral force' out of the unorganized and dispersed millions of people of India. What is significant for us is to reflect upon the role and function of pain and suffering in the construction of civil communities.

In Gandhian social theory, suffering and pain are agents in constructing civil society. Suffering is not a negative category nor is it glorified in an unhealthy way. It is seen as an anthropological phenomenon in the relentless process of engagement with a life of action that is oriented towards liberation.

In short, proceeding from a sociological starting point, we argued that in its search for identities in the wake of the emergence of a powerful and homogenizing nation-state, people are looking for 'primordial identities' where there is space for their transcendental aspirations and living pluralities. The Gandhian model was one such primordial vision. Its basic components were a search for total liberation and selfless action, leading to self-suffering love. Gandhi brings two non-academic categories into the discussion of the formation of pluralist societies.

7

Gandhi on Educational Issues

India's recorded and unrecorded culture and civilization are rare features in the course of world history. Today, along with modernization, it is very much a part of our living culture, at every level of the society, as well as a documented testimony to the greatest strength of education, which catapulted the Indian Civilisation to its zenith. Perhaps few other cultures and civilizations have produced such courageous, saintly and visionary role models such as Radhakrishnan, Sri Aurobindo, Swami Vivekananda, Mira Bai, Rani of Jhansi, Netaji Subas Chandra Bose, Rabindra Nath Tagore, Sant Kabir, Sant Ram Das, Mahatma Gandhi, to name a few.

Gandhiji influenced the lives of our countrymen for more than half a century. His approach to most issues was down-to-earth and holistic-be it social, cultural, economic, health or education. His philosophies were pragmatic and farsighted. The villager was the centre of his economic thought. His warnings against the British Education system were prophetic. Today, when Indian illiteracy rate stands at 34.62%, crime, violence and corruption are at its zenith, and more than one third of our population lives below the poverty line, it is indeed tempting to muse over the relevance of Gandhiji's contribution to education as well as his model of basic education, incorporating his philosophy, approach and strategy.

Gandhiji's model was not only holistic and practical, it was highly decentralized and integrated, with a demonstrated capacity to motivate the entire community and place responsibility and accountability at the community level versus the State.

Gandhiji's views on various educational issues are described in this chapter in his own words. It will provide an insight into the vastness of his vision on education and development.

Infant Education

We should try to draw all the children towards us. We should admit that it is our fault if some do not come to us. They should all want to come to us.

We should treat those children who come to us as our own children. If their body and mind become sound and they acquire normal discipline, we should be satisfied that our purpose has been served.

I have taught many boys. I never allowed them to indulge in mischief. If they were under my care, I would educate them in such a way that they would learn from their very childhood that the desire to destroy was a very bad thing. Whatever they do, they should create something, produce something. There is an art in making anything and whatever they make should be artistic.

I do not believe that children are either good or bad from their very birth. Some tendency is there, but we have to mould them. This means that an infant starts learning right from the time of conception. At that time I would teach the mother. That would be a part of adult education. The training of the infant begins from that stage. We have to train the future generation on these lines. Till the child is separated from the mother, I would teach the mother. The infant is ever moving its hands and feet and is able to do something. If we are able to take under our care children of two or two and a half years of age and if they learn to move their hands and feet according to our method, I cannot set any limits to their progress.

If the child is put under our care, he will not destroy anything. He will feel hurt in doing so.

Whatever education we give to the children, it should be constructive and creative but never destructive.

When the child starts speaking, he starts learning a language. First you should teach him to distinguish different colours. Begin teaching him the letters of the alphabet only with the help of the pictures. Don't you have charts showing 1-2, A-B and so on? Reading, writing and arithmetic will come in due course of time and the child will not be overstrained. His education should be a form of play.

Whatever thing he makes should be useful. In this way his mind and hands and feet develop in co-ordination.

There are no distinctions between work and play in basic education. For a child everything is play. I would go so far as to say that thus his whole life becomes a kind of game. I have been doing this for many years now. I never feel that it is time for play and I should go and play. For me even writing is a game. Under basic education of my conception children will learn while playing.

Early Childhood Education

Educating children should be normally the easiest of things; but somehow it has become, or been made, the most difficult. Experience shows that the children are always learning one thing or another whether we notice it or not and whether what they learn is good or bad. This may seem strange to some readers. But if we would consider carefully—who is a child; what is education and who is best qualified to teach the children?—the observation made above would not seem strange and might even appear quite correct.

By children we mean young boys and girls not more than 10 years of age. Then, education does not mean simply the knowledge of letters—the capacity to read and write. The knowledge of letters is only one of the means to education. Really speaking, education consists in learning to use in the right way all one's sense-organs, including the mind. In other words, the child should know how to use his organs of action such as hands and feet etc. as also his organs of knowledge such as the nose, the eyes etc.

A boy who knows that he should not use his hands in stealing things or killing flies or beating the younger brothers, sisters and play-mates has already made a good beginning on his way to education. The same may be said of the boy who understands the need for keeping his teeth, tongue, ears, eyes, nails etc. clean and does so.

A boy who does not indulge in pranks while eating or drinking, who has learnt to eat and drink in the right manner whether alone or in company, who knows the distinction between wholesome and unwholesome food and chooses the former, who does not overeat, who does not ask for every new thing that he sees and who, when he asks for it and does not get it, remains quiet, may be said to have progressed quite a great deal in his education. Whose pronunciation is good, who can tell the history and geography of his region—even though he may not know these terms,—who knows what is meant by the motherland, he has traversed a fairly good distance on the road to education. Similarly with him who has learnt to distinguish between truth and untruth, between good and evil and who invariably chooses what is true and good, there is no need to further elaborate the point. The readers can fill in the picture themselves. Only I should make one thing clear: there is no need of the knowledge of reading and writing in order to learn the things I have spoken of above.

To make the boys to learn the alphabet is to put an undue burden on their young minds and to misuse their eyes and hands. A rightly educated boy gets to learn reading and writing almost without any effort and, what is more, gladly at the proper time. At the present time, however, this thing becomes a heavy burden upon him.

Much of the valuable time which could be put to better use goes to waste and in the end, instead of producing shapely letters or acquiring a finely articulated pronunciation, all that they succeed in doing is to produce mis-shapen letters and cultivate a bad handwriting. As for reading, they read much which had better been left unread and read it indifferently without any sense of pronunciation.

To call it education is to abuse that august term. The boy must first get elementary knowledge before learning to read and write. If this is done our poor country would be saved from much unnecessary expense incurred on various readers and children's books and many other evils. If children's readers are at all thought necessary they should be written for use by the teachers and not for boys of my conception. But for our drifting with the current vogue this thing should be as clear to us as daylight.

The boys can get the education I have spoken of only at home and that too only through the mother. In a way, all boys do get some sort of an education from the mother. But seeing that the home has disintegrated, so to say, and seeing that most parents are not equal to the task, the boys should be placed in surroundings where they will get the same atmosphere as they do at home. Since of all persons the mother is the most competent to undertake the duty of educating the children, this particular task should be entrusted only to women.

As a rule men are far behind women in respect of love and patience. If this is true the question of the education of children cannot be solved unless efforts are made simultaneously to solve the women's education. And I have no hesitation in saying that as long as we do not have real mother-teachers who can successfully impart true education to our children they will remain uneducated even though they may be going to schools.

Let me now set forth in brief an outline of the children's education. Suppose that a mother-teacher is entrusted with five children. These children have no training in manners. They do not speak distinctly. They do not know how to walk or even to sit in the right manner. The nose, eyes, ears, and nails are dirty. Asked to sit, they stretch out their legs and when they speak, they mumble. They have no knowledge of directions. The clothes are untidy and the pockets are filled with dirty tit-bits which they are always taking out and putting in their mouths.

The border of the cap on the head has turned black and sticky and it gives out a foul odour. Now the teacher in question can train them only if she has the heart of a mother. The first lesson she has to give them would be that of cleanliness. She will drench them with her love and amuse them in various ways as only mothers know how to do and as did Kaushalya her Rama and thus she will bind them to herself with the ties of love and so will be in a position to secure from them willing compliance to all that she wants. She will know no rest until these boys have learnt to keep neat and tidy, until their teeth, ears, hands and feet are clean, until they learn to take care of their clothes and have improved their pronunciation. Having accomplished this she will first teach them *Ramanama*—the name of Lord God. He has many names and it does not matter by which name He is called.

The next in order after *dharma* is *artha* i.e., the temporal knowledge. So she will now set out to teach them arithmetic. She will get them to learn the multiplication tables and teach them addition and subtraction—as much of it as can be managed orally. The boys must know the place where they live. So she will tell them of the rivers and rivulets, hills, buildings of interest etc. and in the process give them the knowledge of directions. She will improve her own knowledge for the sake of the children. History and geography are not to be treated as separate subjects in this method. Both will be taught by way of stories. She will not however be content with this.

A Hindu mother will recite Sanskrit verses to her children from their infancy, so that they get used to the pronunciation of Sanskrit words. She will get them to learn Sanskrit verses in praise of God. A patriotic mother will of course teach them Hindi too. She will therefore converse with them in Hindi. She will read out to them selected passages from Hindi books and thus make them bilingual. She will not teach them the alphabet yet, but she will certainly give them the brush. She will get them to trace the geometrical figures—to draw straight lines and circles. A boy who cannot draw a flower or a water-jug or a triangle cannot be said to be educated. Again, she will not but introduce them to good music. She will not tolerate the children being unable to sing in unison the national song or hymns etc. She will teach them to sing to the accompaniment of time. If possible, she will give them *ektara,* or *jhanjh.* To make them physically fit she will get them to do physical exercises, to practise running and jumping. Then, the boys should also be taught the love of service and various skills. She will therefore teach them spinning with all the ancillary processes beginning from the picking of cotton pods. And these boys will willingly spin for at least half an hour every day.

Most of the text-books which we have today are useless for this purpose. The mother-teacher therefore will find out or produce new ones and her love for the children will help her in this task. Every village has its own history and geography; naturally it will have its own history-book and geography-book. The arithmetical exercises too will be new. The mother-teacher will prepare the lessons she wants to teach the children herself everyday. She will produce new sums and will always have many new things to say to the boys—which she will note down in her note-book when she prepares the lesson. Her lesson in the class will thus be not a mechanical performance but something lively and creative.

The syllabus will vary according to the progress of the children. It should therefore be drawn up after every three months. The children constituting the class come from different homes—each has his own different background of nurture. We cannot therefore have the same syllabus for all of them. At times it may be necessary even to induce them to unlearn what they have learnt. For example, if a six or seven year old child has learnt to trace letters in a slovenly way or has picked up the habit of reading without trying to understand what he reads, the mother-teacher will see that he unlearns all that. She must cast out the illusion that the child can acquire knowledge only through reading. It is easy enough to understand that even one who never had any training in reading can be wise.

I have not used the word teacher in this article; I have throughout used the word 'mother-teacher' in its place. Because the teacher must really be a mother to the children she teaches. One who cannot take the place of a mother cannot be a teacher. The child should never feel that he is being taught. Let her simply keep her eye upon him and guide him. A child who spends six hours in the school will possibly be wasting his time while the former will be learning something or the other all the time in terms of real education.

It is likely that we may not get good women-teachers in the existing conditions. That being so we may make use of men for the purpose. In that case these men-teachers will have to fill the place of the mother. But eventually it is the mother who will have to undertake the task. But if I am right any mother who has love for children can easily prepare herself for it. And she can also prepare the children at the same time that she is preparing herself.

Montessori Education

I have no difficulty in agreeing with the scientific views of Madame Montessori. However, if they are propagated in their Western garb in Indian villages they are more likely to prove useless and might even prove harmful, because in that garb they will be too expensive for Indian villages and ill-adapted to the village atmosphere. It is possible the cities may not feel the expense so much and women influenced by Western ways may be receptive to the ideas presented in Western garb; but even so it will be of no use because India lives not in cities but in its seven lakh villages. Besides, scientific education with Western trappings might prove poisonous to the city dwellers because here education begins the moment the child is conceived and ends no one knows when. These days the cities are created by the foreigners to serve their ends and so they do not represent the villages. They do not protect the interests of the villagers but are becoming their exploiters.

NURSERY EDUCATION

I saw the work done by teachers trained under Madame Montessori, and carefully observed the working of the Nursery School. Of course the things were foreign and the poor teacher had not digested what she had been taught. What to speak of the children? They could not even observe normal discipline. I am not criticising anyone. I have given the gist of my experience just for your information.

Imbibe whatever you find useful and discard the rest. The conclusion I have drawn from this experience is that we shall be able to propagate scientific knowledge of child education only when our teachers are competent. They should have the will to become one with children. I am afraid I am not saying anything new in this. These things are certainly not beyond your range of experience but since I have come to know you and also love you I hope you will not find fault with me for saying the things you already know.

PRIMARY EDUCATION

After a great deal of reflection and experimentation I have come to the conclusion that primary education should be given for at least a year without books and even after that the use of books should be restricted to the minimum.

If books are introduced from the very start and the children made to master the alphabet, the development of their various abilities are arrested and their intelligence stunted, although this is the time when it should grow rapidly. A child begins to learn immediately after its birth, but mostly through the eyes and ears or through the senses. And, as soon as he has learnt to speak, i.e., to imitate the sound of words, he begins rapidly to acquire the use of language.

Naturally he picks up the same language as that of his parents. If the parents have taste and refinement, he also develops those qualities. He pronounces the words correctly and copies their good manners and conduct. This is his real education. And if our culture and traditions had not fallen apart, children would still be receiving the best kind of education in their homes.

But looking at the deplorable conditions in which we are living at present this cannot be and there is no alternative save to send our boys to schools. But if the child has to go to a school, we must see that it looks like a home to him and the teachers like parents, and the education provided should be such as would be provided in a cultured home. This means that all preliminary teaching should be oral. A child educated in this way would learn in a year ten times more than the boy taught in the other way, i.e., through the alphabet.

Oral teaching would enable the children to know the usual rudiments of history and geography much in the same way as they get to know stories, quite easily, in the very first year. They would commit to memory a fairly good number of poems; and they would learn the counting of numbers almost automatically without any effort. And because they would not be subjected to the burden of recognizing and learning the alphabet, the growth of their minds would not be stopped and their eyes would not be misused.

They would use their hands not in tracing different letters—a practice which spoils their handwriting for good—but in drawing the figures of geometry and simple pictures. This would be good preliminary training for the hand, as it would develop both co-ordination and skill.

And if we want to provide education to the crores of children of Gujarat and of India, this is the only way in which primary education should be imparted to them.

Under the conditions existing in the country it is impossible to give books to children. I admit that if it is necessary to give books to children in the primary stage also, then attempts must be made to do so whatever the expenditure, but if they are considered unnecessary and even harmful then this plea for stopping the use of books in the initial years. The idea should be given a fair trial. A thing which is unnecessary from the moral point of view is always found to be impermissible also from the practical point of view. In an ideal civilization morality and what is called practical policy are not two contradictory things.

Lastly, it is clear that the present group of teachers cannot be expected to give effect to the scheme of education presented here. They may manage to teach the boys the alphabet and also simple arithmetic. But they themselves are ignorant of the type of knowledge which, according to the scheme I have sketched, should be made available to the boys in the very first year of the school. Since they themselves do not speak correctly, how can they then help the boys to form the habit of correct speech?

Secondary Education

A system of education has to be so conceived as to be an instrument of protection of the freedom of a nation.

Hence, we must make our own experiments in education. It may well be that in the course of these experiments we get to know the experiences which Europe has had; but we should never give credence to the idea that everything European is good, or that what is good for Europe under the conditions obtaining there will also be good for us here in India.

Granting that this line of reasoning is correct, one of the conclusions it leads us to is that we should evaluate what goes on in the Government schools critically. Knowing as we do that Government education is detrimental to Swaraj and destructive of our civilization, we are likely to get at the right solution for us if we do just the opposite of what is done in the Government schools. Let us now study examples:

There, the medium of education is English. We should know from this that it should never be permitted in national education.

There, they have big expensive buildings. We should know that this is undesirable. The buildings of our school should be simple— as befit the poor.

There, they concentrate on mere literacy and the study of language and literature and neglect the indigenous crafts. Evidently this is not right.

There they leave out the teaching of religion—I mean the basic principles common to all religions and not any particular creed. We know that this has the effect of nullifying the good that the rest of the education might ordinarily do to students.

History, as taught in Government schools, if not wholly untrue, is presented essentially from the point of view of the British Government. German, French and American historians would treat and interpret the same material in a different way. Even recent events, as for example, the Punjab Massacre is presented by Government writers in one way and by nationalist writers in quite another light.

Economics, as taught in Government schools, approves of the policies of the Government, while we look at them from a totally different point of view.

While in Government primary schools, the teachers are appointed without any consideration of their character, in our schools they must be men of the highest character. The former have only the minimum qualifications for the work they are expected to do and are paid the lowest salaries. The latter, on the other hand, should be highly qualified men and though they will also be paid low salaries, the reason would be their selflessness and not their helplessness. This, I think, should give you some idea of the type of education which should be given in our city schools.

Our students should be men who will work for the stabilization and revitalization of our rural civilization. They would study the needs of the villagers, try to remove the defects they may discover in them and train their children to become good farmers and good villagers and not to be lured by the dazzle of the cities. Thus, as long as we do not set about to make a radical change in the form and content of the education now going on in the cities, we cannot fulfil one of the important aims of the Vidyapith. Take only one example: We are running three institutions in Ahmedabad—the Mahavidyalaya or the college, the New Gujarati Pathashala, and the Vinaya Mandir or the secondary school. We have the right to run these institutions only if we mean to try to make good villagers of the students studying in them. They should have a thorough knowledge of village life and develop a love for it. Eventually, those of them who pass out of the Mahavidyalaya or the Vinaya Mandir, after having completed their studies, should spread out in the villages and immerse themselves in the service of the people there.

Rural Education

The problem of primary education, i.e., of rural education, can be tackled and solved only if the teachers appreciate and accept the point of view presented by me, and we agree to overhaul and change the curriculum in the Vinaya Mandir and Mahavidyalaya.

Today, we hesitate to make any changes out of fear for what people might say, or because the number of students might go down and the institution may suffer in the estimate of the people. But if we could make bold and introduce the necessary changes there would pass out from these schools a group of workers pledged to the service of the villages who would atone in some degree at least for the sin of the cities.

The students passing out of these schools should be first class carders, spinners and weavers. They should be experts in the cultivation of cotton. They should know enough carpentry for the purposes of the village, that is, they should be able to manufacture good Charkhas and should be able if not to manufacture at least to repair the carts and ploughs etc.

Then they should know enough sewing for village-life. Their handwriting must be good, and they should be able to write good simple prose, as also to work out simple arithmetical problems They should be intimately conversant with old religious books like the *Ramayana* and *Mahabharata,* and have the ability to interpret them in terms of today.

They should know village games and the rules of health. They should be able to recognize simple diseases and cure them through simple home remedies. They should know the art of cleaning the village-wells, tanks and dust-heaps. I could recount many other things. But the point is that our schools should provide such training to the boys as would enable them to serve the villages in every way. And the expenditure incurred on this training should be regarded as having been incurred on education. Such training alone would qualify us to enter and reform village-life.

I am aware that some of you fear that as soon as we introduce these changes and clarify our aim as above our schools would be empty. But even if this fear proves true I would be ready to face it for the sake of truth. But as long as it is the object of the Vidyapith to work out a suitable system of education for the villages, it will be a betrayal of our trust not to do so.

But it is my experience and conviction that if we stick to our aims with undivided loyalty, the people will come to recognize their importance in the end and co-operate with us in their propagation. If we try to discover the reasons of this real or supposed failure we will find that the workers were either not loyal to their aims or only half-hearted in carrying them out. A man who wavers in his faith, as says the *Gita*, is doomed to failure.

It is my firm belief that if there were in our schools teachers who have faith and the spirit of sacrifice, they would be filled with students. People do recognize and appreciate fundamental values. It may seem that this takes an unusually long time to come about in many cases. But this is merely an illusion. The fact is that the right path is also always the shortest.

How does it profit anyone if a school which encourages the desire for sensual pleasures and panders to the weaknesses of people attracts large numbers? Mere numbers do not prove the usefulness of an institution or its success in its chosen task. I am aware that the acceptance of my scheme may lead to but one result, i.e, the students who have come here in the hope of getting the same sort of education as they do in Government school or of acquiring the equipment for a comfortable city-life, will leave our schools. But that would be good. It will save both us and them from an undesirable situation and enable both to serve each other in a disinterested way.

I think I have said enough to have explained my viewpoint in regard to the problem of primary education which was the purpose in writing the present series. I have to add only a little more and then I will close it.

And then I hope to discuss a few questions put to me on the subject.

If the idea of not introducing the teaching of the alphabet in the first year of primary education is correct, some of its good result should also be visible in our Vinaya Mandirs or secondary schools and the Mahavidyalaya.

There is a great increase in the number of books being brought out today. Books are being published daily. Whoever has or thinks he has a certain command of the language or believes to have studied or reflected a little over a certain thing, becomes impatient to express his ideas in writing and have them printed, and actually thinks that he thereby serves the country.

The result is that there is a great strain on the minds of the students and the pockets of the parents! The intellectual growth of the students is paralyzed. The minds become store-houses of strange and unrelated facts and there is no room left in them for original ideas. And those facts too do not fall each into its right place as in a well-arranged plan but lie scattered as the things in the house of a lazy man. Neither can they make any worthwhile use of them nor do they yield any good to the people.

Therefore, if I could have my way, I would not put the large number of books that are being published today into the hands of the people. Even the students who know reading and writing receive most of what they get to learn from the teacher's mouth. So I would advise the students to read only a few selected books. But they should think over what they read and put into practice what appears worthwhile. If they do so, it will make their lives beautiful and pure as also full of strength and energy. They will have learnt to think and discriminate—the hall-mark of real education. This is the education which will suit and profit our poor people. It will do good to both the students and the people.

The solution of the difficult problem which faces Vidyapith depends upon the capacity of its present teachers to sincerely reflect upon and accept the aims of the Vidyapith and to try to implement them in practice.

Teacher–Taught Relationship

I believe in *guru-bhakti*. But every teacher cannot be a *guru*. The *guru–shishya*—the teacher–disciple—relation in this sense is something spiritual and springs up spontaneously. In any case it is not an artificial thing or a product of pressure from without. Such teachers still exist in India. (It should not be necessary to sound the warning that I am not speaking here of spiritual teachers who have the power to lead the aspirants to liberation.) Such teachers have no use for flattery. Respect for them must be natural and so is the love of the teacher for his pupil. That being so, the teacher is ever ready to give, and the pupil equally ready to receive.

Some Related Questions

Having written the previous three articles about primary education, it is now somewhat easy to answer the following questions:

You once wrote that if the burden of English were lightened it will save a few precious years in the life of the students which are now wasted. What is your estimate of this wastage in terms of years and of the loss it means to society?

Let me first explain what I mean by lightening the burden of English. I do not mean that the students should stop learning English altogether. We may learn it and use it but only as a Frenchman knows and uses English; that is, we should learn and know it as one does a foreign language. If we try to limit our learning of English to this extend, we would not be required to think in English and speak it correctly with the right pronunciation and to write it with the mastery of an Englishman. I am inclined to think that every student wastes at least five years of his life in this useless endeavour. Not only that, this forced labour over a thing for which he feels no genuine attraction cripples his power of original thinking. His body weakens and he becomes almost a blotting-paper—a blind imitator of superfluities. How much more a man can acquire if he spends five years in acquiring knowledge through his mother tongue? How much time and energy would he save? He will easily get to know the best thought through his own language and yet be saved from the great trouble in mastering the difficult pronunciation of a foreign language.

Child education at one end and college education at the other are both very expensive. Are both these to be included in national education? Have you a scheme to provide both and an equally high type of education at a cheaper cost?

I have tried to show in the three previous articles how the education of the children can be made cheaper, even, almost self-supporting. If we could bring the same approach to bear on college education, it too could be made cheaper, and the students well enabled to acquire such knowledge which will strengthen the nation. If by the expression—'an equally high type of education' the correspondent means an education resembling that to be found in Government institution, the question does not arise, because I do not consider Government type of education to be desirable at all. The education offered in national colleges or national schools is different from the former and often original in many ways. Therefore, it is good in its own way.

Do you think that teachers have the right to impart religious instruction to the boys in their charge in whatever way they like?

Teachers have to conform to the policy or policies laid down by the organization to which they belong; they cannot, therefore, claim the right to give religious education in the way they would like to do it. As in other subject so also in the matter of religious instruction the teacher must carry out the policy decided upon by those in charge of the organization. Of course, the teacher should be free to choose his method of teaching, but what he teaches will have to be in conformity with the ideals accepted by the organization in the matter of religion. It is true that while one may teach other subjects by reading a few selected books on those subjects, this is not possible in the case of religious education.

In fact, it cannot be imparted through books at all. While instruction in other subjects is mostly through the intellect, in religious education it has to be from the heart to the heart. Therefore, a teacher should not undertake to teach religion unless he is himself deeply religious. It is also necessary to exercise a certain discrimination. For example, nothing that is likely to promote violence should be taught in a school which accepts non-violence as the highest form of religion.

Similarly, there should be no room for any propaganda against any of the other religions in a school which has adopted for itself the ideal of love, charity and tolerance in regard to all religions. In short, if a school accepts the need for providing religious education, it must also clearly define the content of such education, and not leave it to the whims of the teachers concerned as this would result in chaos.

If it is considered necessary for every student to know at least three to four languages don't you think it is equally necessary to introduce students to the basic tenets, rites, dogmas and superstitions of all the existing religions?

If we want to create a feeling of respect and love among the students towards every religion—which is religion in the true sense of the word and not an irreligion, we must surely provide them a knowledge of its main tenets. I do not think it is necessary to know the superstitions which have crept in into different religions and the special rites pertaining to each of them.

In a country like India everyone who keeps his eyes and ears open can easily see for himself what these rites and superstitions are. If we would become seekers of good—wherever we find it, as we must, we should not want to know the rites and superstitions of every religion. They are quite unnecessary. It should be enough to know the rites and superstitions of our own religion and to impress upon the boys the need to reform them wherever necessary. That would itself take up enough of their time.

Since you believe in the *varna,* i.e, the four-fold division of society, do you accept, or not accept, that education provided to students should differ according to the *varna*?

I do not think that education should differ according to *varna*. There is much that is common between the different *varnas* and the education provided to them should be the same. The chief aim of education is to make of the students decent men and women. And he who would become a decent man would easily learn the laws of conduct governing human society—the laws which add to the glory of men.

My conception of *varna* is that since the *varna* division rests on the difference in vocations, and every *varna* has to earn its livelihood through its appointed vocation, it would be found that men belonging to a particular *varna* generally inherit the characteristics of their class. I do not mean that a particular *varna* does not or cannot have the characteristics of the other three *varnas*. A Brahman would not earn his bread by working for others on hire-purchase basis, but if he does not know the art of service or is ashamed of it, he is not a *Brahman* at all. In the same way, though a *Shudra* may not teach the *Vedas* etc. and has to live on alms voluntarily given, he would surely have been given a sufficient grounding in the *Vedas* etc. in a well-organized society.

Is it true that training in useful crafts automatically includes all other education and that intellectual education is no more than a superficial decoration? If it is true, why do you approve and support the education given by the Mahavidyalaya?

This view is as true as it is false. Where people have idolized intellectual education I say that training in crafts includes all other education, for there is no insurmountable barrier between what is called intellectual education and the crafts. They are not like two water-tight compartments without any relation with each other. On the contrary, training in arts and crafts offers full scope for the development of the intellect. And I venture to claim that without it the development of intellect is impossible. If a mason knows just enough to earn his bread, he cannot be said to have had any education.

The education of a mason should therefore include: the place of this craft in social life, the science of brick-laying, the need of housing, the requisites of a good house, and the close relation between civilization and houses for human habitation. To think that intellectual education means no more than a knowledge of certain facts is a gross misapprehension. Development of intellect is fully possible without any such knowledge.

A teacher who turns the mind of students into a cupboard for storing all manner of facts has himself not learnt even the first lesson in teaching. The reader must, by now, have gathered from the above why I have called the view stated by the correspondent both true and false. It is false if my view about the training in crafts and intellectual training is accepted. But it is true if the question has been framed keeping in view the misunderstanding which springs from regarding intellectual education and training in useful crafts as two different things. It should be easy to see now why, and on what conditions, I approve and support the Mahvidyalaya and the education provided by it.

In the institution of my conception the mason, the carpenter and the weaver will be intelligent social workers and not mere bread-earners who know only as much of their job as may be sufficient for the purpose. I hope for Kabir, Bhoja Bhagat, Akha and Guru Govind springing up respectively from the weavers, cobblers, goldsmiths and peasants studying at the Maha-vidyalaya. Who would say that Kabir, Bhoja Bhagat, Akha and Guru Govind were not men with an intellectual education?

If training in crafts be the essence of education why shouldn't you entrust the Vidyapith to a committee composed of carpenters, blacksmiths and weavers? Let them then engage the services of teachers having to do with intellectual education if they so choose.

I think the answer to this question is already covered before. If I had weavers like Kabir I would certainly place the direction of the Vidyapith in their charge, and I am sure 'the teachers having to do with intellectual education' would consider it an honour to work as servants under them. That we did not consider arts and crafts fit to be included in the content of education is the reason why our craftsmen are relegated today to an inferior status in society and we cannot get any help from them in our endeavour to serve society.

It is mentioned in the statement of the aims and objects of Vidyapith that the progress of the country depends on the villages and not on the cities. If it is so, why do you spoil our city boys? Give village education to the village boys, if you must. But the city boys desire to live a city life. Why not arrange to give them an education which would suit them? And don't you get all the money for the Vidyapith from the cities? Of course, we will have nothing to say if you would transfer the Vidyapith to some ideal village and collect the necessary money, grain and cotton locally from the village itself.

Fortunately, this question does not arise in the mind of many city people or city students. How can the city people who have expressed their readiness to atone for the wrong done to the villages ask for the village education to be given to the village boys at their own expense? The Vidyapith has come into existence as a result of the city people's attention being drawn to the villages. It is the city people who decided to start the Vidyapith after they had their eyes opened. How could the villagers be called upon to pay its bill if it aims specially at the uplift of the villages? It is up to the city people to provide the wherewithal for the education even in the villages for the time being at least.

The villagers can bring against us the same charge as we do against the Government. They may well say: "You city people have exploited us and are still exploiting us. Please stop it now. We will forget the past. Some of us realized the reality of the situation and woke up to our duty. We saw the wrong we have done to the villagers and resolved to make amends for it. The first part of this process was to non-co-operate with the Government under whose protection and with whose help we could and still can drain out the sap of life from them.

The next was that as we learnt the deeper implications of non-co-operation, we also learnt to reject the illegitimate gains of that co-operation. If, after launching out on non-co-operation, we had simply sat quietly, it could justly be said against us that we had not grasped the meaning of non-co-operation. Supposing somebody started plundering our house, then it would not be enough not to help him. We must also step in to stop him from his nefarious business as also desist from sharing the spoils. Then only can it be called true non-co-operation with the plunderer. This non-co-operation can either be violent or non-violent, riotous or peaceful, based on brute-force or on soul-force. We have chosen to practise non-violent and peaceful non-co-operation based on soul-force. And we have come to realize in the process that as an expiation for the exploitation of the wealth of the villages which many city people indulge in, we should render some service at least to the villagers.

The Vidyapith had its birth as a result of this realization on our part. And as some of us are wakeful and persistent in our efforts to know the truth, we are realizing the secret of non-co-operation more clearly every day, and to that extent trying to give a truer shape to the Vidyapith. This is sufficient reason why a major portion of the money donated by the city people should be spent on bringing education to the villagers. And the education for time being should be carried to them only through the students from the cities trained by the Vidyapith?

I am of the opinion that any other use of the money received by the Vidyapith will be a betrayal of the assurance given to the people. The donors have given the money in the belief that it will be used in providing education which will be of a different kind from the present one and conform to my conception of it.

The Vidyapith has consistently followed a policy of the removal of untouchability for the past eight years. How many *vinitas* and *snatakas* from among the untouchables has it turned out during this period?

The question appears strange, and suggests ignorance to me. The removal of untouchability does not and should not mean that we are to make the so-called "untouchable" boys *vinitas* and *snatakas*. It is quite possible that in the course of time some of them may become *vinitas* and *snatakas*. And that would be welcome. It is also right that the Vidyapith should be ready to help such boys. But to turn out *snatakas* from among the untouchables is in no way a part of the campaign for the removal of untouchability. The Vidyapith has demonstrated its love for the cause of the removal of untouchability by refusing thousands, if not lakhs, of rupees offered to it, by staking its very existence and by foregoing the valuable help of quite a few who were otherwise very able men in organizing its work.

We see quite clearly that in the absence of *brahmacharya* the nation has become both physically and mentally weak and its capacity for adventure, enterprise and perseverance has gone down. How is it then that you have not included *brahmacharya* in the last article of the constitution dealing with its aims and objects?

It is a good question. It cannot be proved that the physical and mental weakness afflicting the nation and the slackening of its capacity for adventure and enterprise are all due directly to the absence of *brahmacharya*. Nor can it be proved that *brahmacharya* will always result in physical strength. It is not therefore proper to connect *brahmacharya* with physical strength or weakness—which is after all an ephemeral good—and thus to detract from the importance of that celestial virtue.

The people of the West are not *brahmacharis,* but they are not physically or mentally weak. Their capacity for sustained work and enterprise are excellent and exemplary. It may be said that the Gurkhas, Pathans, Sikhs, Dogras, and the English among the soldiers are not *brahmacharis,* but they have strongly built bodies. They will easily beat the student of our *vyayamshala* in a physical contest. It can thus be proved that it is not quite correct to maintain that physical strength, even a kind of mental energy, capacity for persistent effort and enterprise are impossible to achieve except through *brahmacharya.* The *brahmacharya* of my conception—the *brahmacharya* which leads one to the realization of *Brahma* is beyond physical and mental fitness. It is itself both the end and the means. I will, therefore, be willing to sacrifice the body to be able to observe it and achieve it. He who is attached to the body can hardly observe unbroken *brahmacharya.*

Examples of its observance by Bhishma and others are likely to misdirect us in this case. Literal acceptance of things mentioned in the *Mahabharata* and *Ramayana* will lead us astray. What is required is to grasp their inner meaning which we should then put into practice. If we do that in the spirit of true inquiry and experimentation we would surely march forward.

The body is not a thing to be carelessly thrown away. It has to be preserved. The body, if it is at times the abode of Ravana, is also the Ayodhya of Rama. If it is *kurukshetra*—the field of action, it is also *dharmakshetra*—the field of duty. Hence, it cannot be ignored. It has to be kept fit and strong.

Physical exercise is therefore necessary. But this is as far as we can go to praise physical exercise and this should be enough to popularize it among the students. We cannot insist on an unbreakable relation between physical exercise and *brahmacharya.* It will not only be an exaggeration; there is in it the further danger of a person abandoning *brahmacharya* when he finds himself lagging behind in physical strength in the erroneous belief that the reason for his failure lies in his practice of *brahmacharya.*

Brahmacharya does not need the support of physical strength. Its importance and need lie elsewhere. The West may have physical strength and mental energy, but they do not have soul-force. How can we entertain any feeling of envy for their physical strength and mental energy when we see that they succumb to inferior passions at every moment, cannot put up with the least opposition to their will, and spend all their energy, industry and enterprise in plundering and destroying other races? How can we think of copying them? Their strength and energy, shows lack of *brahmacharya;* this is why it has proved disastrous to the real progress of the world, and that is why I have called it satanic. I am not condemning the West, nor belittling it.

There are many in the West who are votaries of truth and other moral principles. There are also many *brahmacharis* there. They understand these undesirable features of Western life I am referring to here. And so we can, in spite of our love and respect for the West, speak of all the sad results its furious endeavours have led to. If the civilization of the West had been raised on the secure foundations of the *brahmacharya* ideal, the world today would have been a different place. It would not then be the sorry mess it is, but a happy and beautiful habitation of noble men and women.

Knowing thus the evil consequences of the non-observance of *brahmacharya,* we should put forward the ideal of *brahmacharya* before the people. Full development of the soul is impossible without it. A man may behave like an unbridled wild horse without *brahmacharya,* but he cannot achieve refinement and purity which is the mark of culture. There can be no *sattwik,* i.e., pure and enlightened endeavour and enterprise without *brahmacharya.* One may seem to have a strong and energetic mind even without *brahmacharya,* but then it will be a prey to a thousand passions and lures. Similarly, one may have a well-built and strong body even without *brahmacharya,* but it will not be a truly healthy body. It is not necessary for health to strengthen the muscles and put on fat.

A body which, though lean and thin like a chip of wood, can bear cold and sun and rain and yet remain healthy—such a healthy body is impossible to have without *brahmacharya.* This is not a belief which I have come to hold today; it is an old belief and is moreover based on experience. I can give you numerous examples from my life and from the life of my friends and co-workers as to how every single impure thought wastes man's energy and destroys his soul. I will say, therefore, that those who seek self-realization should preserve their *brahmacharya* even though the body may decline.

The reason for the weakness of the body and the mind to be found in our students lies elsewhere. The reasons are: child-marriage, the burden of the family, the lack of good food due to poverty, etc. Let not the readers make the mistake of regarding child-marriage as just non-*brahmacharya*. Great and persistent efforts are necessary in order to eradicate these evil habits.

The harmful customs prevailing in society have to be reformed, and the burden of the present artificial type of education should be lightened. This is however a different subject; I will therefore not dwell on it here. I will merely state that our students cannot have a strong and healthy body merely by taking physical exercise. Efforts will have to be made in all directions; only then may we hope to achieve the results we desire.

Ever since you made your entry into the public life of this country, there has been a tendency to approach you and get your view of a problem whenever a person or persons have been in doubt and have thus failed to reach a clear-cut conclusion. People are eager to know from you whether a certain thing on a certain occasion is right or not. I am only describing the situation as it really is. It shows that all your activity is basically of a religious nature. Would it be right that when you are no more, these decisions be delivered by a body of persons by a majority vote if necessary? If not, is it not necessary to create what may prove to be continuous line of knowledgeable men, versed in the precepts of *dharma*?

I do not deem it worthy that people should approach me and ask me to pronounce judgment on disputable points. It is true that all my activities, whatever their outer form, are fundamentally religious. But the fact that I am asked to pronounce judgments on every disputed matter shows that people have either not understood the principles which I follow in shaping my conduct, or they have doubts about them.

And because I am known as the Mahatma or respected as a good man, our people are credulous and not given to thinking for themselves, they continue to put all forms of questions to me. This may gratify my sense of pride or even help me up to a point in doing my work, but it does not appear to me if it helps in any appreciable way either the people or questioners. Indeed, I have often felt how nice it would be if I stopped making any pronouncements and did whatever suggested itself to me silently.

But in that case I must first stop this weekly that I am now conducting, as also severely cut down much of my present correspondence. That, however, would need a courage which I do not feel within myself. But, there is the great friend of man, the Lord of Death, who can extend his invitation to me at any time and put a stop to all this chatter on my part whether I agree or not.

I do not see any wrong in bodies or associations of men following my principles and giving their opinions on disputed questions by a majority vote when I am no more, or even now whilst I am alive. But as in the case of individuals so also in that of groups they must be inspired by the ideal of *dharma*.

The education in the Vidyapith is divided into three distinct stages: the primary, the secondary and the higher. How far would it be right to name these respectively as the education for the village, education for the city, and the education for those who would take up social service work?

I do not like the meanings suggested here by the correspondent to the primary, the secondary and the higher education respectively. Why should we want village people to be satisfied merely with primary education? They too have a right to receive secondary and higher education—those of them at least who want it. And the boys in the cities cannot do without primary education. The object of all the three should be the prosperity of the villages.

Why do you always attach so much importance to music?

It is said that the study of music is generally neglected in our country today. Without it, the entire educational system seems to me to be incomplete. Music brings sweetness to the individual and to the social life of the people. Even as *pranayam* is necessary for the regulation of breath, so is music for disciplining the voice. A dissemination of the knowledge of music among the people will greatly help in controlling and stopping the noise which is an usual feature of public meetings in this country. Music pacifies anger and its judicious use is highly helpful in leading a man to the vision of God. It does not mean shouting and shrieking a tune anyhow like a rigmarole, nor does it mean the singing of film songs. I have already referred to its ordinary meaning above, but its deeper meaning is that our whole life should be sweet and musical like a song. It goes without saying that life cannot be made like that without the practice of virtues such as truth, honesty etc. To make life musical means to make it one with God, to merge it into Him. He who has not rid himself of *raga* and *dwesha*, i.e., likes and dislike, who has not tasted of the joy of service, cannot have any understanding of celestial music. A study of music, which does not take account of this deeper aspect of this divine art, has little or no value for me.

The art of painting means an expression of the emotions of the artist through line and colour. If this definition of painting were to be accepted, would you include painting as an essential part of the scheme of national education which should be universally taught to all?

I have never disparaged drawing and painting, though I have certainly deprecated the blots of ink and colour passing under its name. I doubt if painting as defined by the artist could be made universal. There is this difference between music and painting: While painting can be learnt only by a few who have a natural aptitude for it, music must be and can be learnt by all. In painting too, drawing of straight lines and the figures of animate and inanimate objects can be taught to all. It is certainly useful and necessary and I want it to be taught to every boy before he is taught the alphabet.

Some people are of the view that such subjects as grammar, compound interest, higher geometry etc, which the learners are apt to forget in after years should not be included in the courses to be framed for purposes of national education. Do you agree to this? If you do, why should not Urdu also be put in the same category? When Hindus and Muslims feel the urge to come into close contact with each other and to understand each other's cultures, then only will the knowledge of Sanskrit and Urdu prove useful and lasting. Knowledge of Urdu will be put to active use and hence increase only when there is respect for and a desire to learn the culture of which Urdu is the vehicle. Until then it is bound to remain no more than a religious rite like the worship of Ganesh—a formal affair without any practical value.

I do not understand why grammar, compound interest and higher geometry have all been classed together. I have always believed that grammar is absolutely necessary for the mastery of a language, and that grammar and higher geometry are highly interesting subjects. Both provide innocent intellectual entertainment. Besides, grammar is indispensable for the study of philology. I will, therefore, accord a place to both these subjects in the courses of study for national education.

In the same way, he who wants to be good at accounts cannot do so without learning compound interest. Therefore, all the three things mentioned by the correspondent in the question will have their due place in the syllabus for national education. The point is that there are things which are common to all schemes of education. Today, we have to differentiate between Government education and National education because the former is detrimental to national development. But there are many things in Government schools which will and must also be in our schools. Thus, though there are points of similarity between the two, the atmosphere in Government schools strengthens the bonds of slavery and is used at critical moments to suppress us. Therefore, such schools are to be renounced. Besides, as we have already seen, a portion, at least, of the education imparted there is wholly unnecessary; it is just a burden and nothing more. But I am moving away from the subject under discussion. I have thought it fit to offer this clarification under the impression that I might not have grasped the point behind this question.

Urdu stands apart from the above-mentioned subjects: the question of its study must be considered separately. Hindus and Muslims will ultimately unite but in our national schools we must continue to strive unremittingly to bring them closer together. For this, we must acquaint ourselves with each other's religion. If the students forget whatever little of Urdu they learn, evidently they are not serious about its study and must be learning it only because they must. But this can also be said about Hindi. Only God knows how interest in Hindi or Urdu can be created among the students, but there is no doubt in my mind that its knowledge is necessary for the progress of the nation.

Students should have full freedom; there should be nothing which will obstruct their free growth; to achieve this objective the teachers should have no prejudices for or against anything; while they teach they should so conduct themselves as though they have no partiality for any particular rule or habit or principle: This ideal for a teacher is coming to be accepted in many places. Do you accept it?

What has been said above can be supported as well as opposed. If it does not help in preserving the real essence, is should be opposed, and if it does help, the students may well be allowed full freedom and the teachers remain as detached and neutral as they like. They may do what they wish with a view to securing the independence of the students, the only condition being that they must mix with the students to the extent of being one of them. In the language of Akha, I will say to them:

"Live in the world as you like, but keep constantly before your mind the aim of attaining to God at any cost."

An ideal teacher never had nor should he ever have any other aim before him.

National University

The National University stands today as a protest against British injustice, and as a vindication of national honour. But it has come to stay. It draws its inspiration from the national ideals of a united India. It stands for a religion which is the Dharma of the Hindus and Islam of Mohammedans. It wants to rescue the Indian vernaculars from unmerited oblivion and make them the fountains of national regeneration and Indian culture. It holds that a systematic study of Asiatic cultures is no less essential than the study of Western sciences for a complete education for life.

The vast treasures of Sanskrit and Arabic, Persian and Pali, and Magadhi have to be ransacked in order to discover wherein lies the source of strength for the nation. It does not propose merely to feed on, or repeat, the ancient cultures. It rather hopes to build a new culture based on the traditions of the past, enriched by the experience of later times. It stands for the synthesis of the different cultures that have come to stay in India, that have influenced Indian life and that in their turn, have themselves been influenced by the spirit of the soil. This synthesis will naturally be of the Swadeshi type where each culture is assured its legitimate place, and not of American pattern, where one dominant culture absorbs the rest, and where the aim is not towards harmony, but towards an artificial and forced unity. That is why the University has desired a study of all the Indian religions by its students.

The Hindus may thus have an opportunity of studying the Koran and the Muslims of knowing what the Hindus Shastras contain. If the University has excluded anything, it is the spirit of exclusion that regards any section of humanity as permanently untouchable. The study of Hindustani, which is a national blend of Sanskrit, Hindi and Persianized Urdu, has been made compulsory.

The spirit of independence will be fostered not only through Religion, Politics and History but through vocational training also, which alone can give the youths of the country economic independence and a backbone that comes out of a sense of self-respect. The University hopes to organize higher schools throughout the mofussil towns, so that education may be spread broadcast and filtered down to the masses as early as possible.

The use of Gujarati as the medium of education will facilitate this process and, ere long, the suicidal cleavage between the educated and the non-educated will be bridged. And as an effect of industrial education to the genteel folks, and literary education for the industrial classes, the unequal distribution of wealth and the consequent social discontent will be considerably checked. The greatest defect of the Government Universities has been their alien control and the false values they have created as regards 'careers'. The Gujarat Universities by non-co-operating with the Government has automatically eradicated both these evils from its own system. If the founders and promoters stick to this resolve till the Government becomes nationalized, it will help them to cultivate a clear perception of national ideals and national needs.

College Education

I would revolutionize college education and relate it to national necessities. There would be degrees for mechanical and other engineers. They would be attached to the different industries which should pay for the training of the graduates they need. Thus the Tatas would be expected to run a college for training engineers under the supervision of the State, the mill associations would run among them a college for training graduates whom they need.

Similary for the other industries that may be named. Commerce will have its college. There remain arts, medicine and agriculture. Several private arts colleges are today self-supporting. The State would, therefore, cease to run its own. Medical colleges would be attached to certified hospitals. As they are popular among moneyed men they may be expected by voluntary contributions to support medical colleges. And agricultural colleges to be worthy of the name must be self-supporting. I have a painful experience of some agricultural graduates. Their knowledge is superficial. They lack practical experience. But if they had their apprenticeship on farms which are self-sustained and answer the requirements of the country, they would not have to gain experience after getting their degrees and at the expense of their employers.

State Universities

Higher education should be left to private enterprise and for meeting national requirements whether in the various industries, technical arts, belles-letters or fine arts.

The State Universities should be purely examining bodies, self-supporting through the fees charged for examinations.

Universities will look after the whole of the field of education and will prepare and approve courses of studies in the various departments of education. No private school should be run without the previous sanction of the respective Universities. University charters should be given liberally to any body of persons of proved worth and integrity, it being always understood that the Universities will not cost the State anything except that it will bear the cost of running a Central Education Department.

The foregoing scheme does not absolve the State from running such seminaries as may be required for supplying State needs.

Higher Education

1. I am not opposed to education even of the highest type attainable in the world.
2. The State must pay for it wherever it has definite use for it.
3. I am opposed to all higher education being paid for from the general revenue.
4. It is my firm conviction that the vast amount of the so-called education in arts, given in our colleges, is sheer waste and has resulted in unemployment among the educated classes. What is more, it has destroyed the health, both mental and physical, of the boys and girls who have the misfortune to go through the grind in our colleges.
5. The medium of a foreign language through which higher education has been imparted in India has caused incalculable intellectual and moral injury to the nation. We are too near our own times to judge the enormity of the damage done. And we who have received such education have both to be victims and judges—an almost impossible feat.

Thus I claim that I am not an enemy of Higher Education. But I am an enemy of Higher Education as it is given in this country. Under my scheme there will be more and better libraries, more and better laboratories, more and better research institutes. Under it we should have an army of chemists, engineers and other experts who will be real servants of the nation, and answer the varied and growing requirements of a people who are becoming increasingly conscious of their rights and wants. And all these experts will speak, not a foreign language, but the language of the people. The knowledge gained by them will be the common property of the people. There will be truly original work instead of mere imitation. And the cost will be evenly and justly distributed.

SELF-SUPPORTING UNIVERSITITES

Your third conclusion about general revenue and claims of Higher Education and its corollary, viz. that Universities should be self-supporting, has left me unconvinced. I believe that every country to be a progressive country must have sufficient facilities for the pursuit of *all* branches of knowledge—not merely chemistry, medicine and engineering, but every kind of knowledge, literature, philosophy, history, sociology, both abstract and applied.

All higher pursuits require many facilities which cannot be had without State support. A country depending *only* on voluntary effort for such pursuits is sure to fall behind and suffer. It can never hope to be free and be able to maintain that freedom. The State must be jealously watchful over the position of higher education in *all* fields. Voluntary effort must be there and we must have our Nuffields and Rockfellers. But the State cannot and must not be allowed to remain a silent spectator. It must actively come forward to organize, help and direct. I wish you to clarify this aspect of the question.

You say at the end of your article: 'Under my scheme there will be more and better libraries.' I do not find *The Scheme* you speak of in your article, nor am I able to make out how 'more and better libraries and laboratories' will come into being thereunder. I am of opinion that such libraries and laboratories must be maintained, and so long as donors and voluntary agencies are not coming forward in sufficient numbers, the State cannot divest itself of this responsibility.1

My article is clear enough if the expression 'definite use' mentioned in it is given its extensive meaning. I have not pictured a poverty-stricken India containing ignorant millions. I have pictured to myself an India continually progressing along the lines best suited to her genius. I do not, however, picture it as a third class or even a first class copy of the dying civilization of the West. If my dream is fulfilled and every one of the seven lakhs of villages becomes a well-living republic in which there are no illiterates, in which no one is idle for want of work, in which everyone is usefully occupied and has nourishing food, well-ventilated dwellings, and sufficient Khadi for covering the body, and in which all the villagers know and observe the laws of hygiene and sanitation, such a State must have varied and increasing needs, which it must supply unless it would stagnate. I can therefore well imagine the State financing all the education my correspondent mentions and much more that I could add. And if the State has such requirements, surely it will have corresponding libraries.

What, however, according to my view the State will not have is an army of B.A.'s and M.A.'s with their brains sapped with too much cramming and minds almost paralyzed by the impossible attempt to speak and write English like Englishmen. The majority of these have no work, no employment. And when they have the latter, it is usually clerkships at which most of the knowledge gained during their twelve years of High Schools and Colleges is of no use whatsoever to them.

University training becomes self-supporting when it is utilized by the State. It is criminal to pay for a training which benefits neither the nation nor the individual. In my opinion there is no such thing as individual benefit which cannot be proved to be also national benefit. And since most of my critics seem to be agreed that the existing Higher Education, and for that matter both Primary and Secondary, are not connected with realities, it cannot be of benefit to the State. When it is directly based on realities and is wholly given through the mother tongue, I shall perhaps have nothing to say against it. To be based on realities is to be based on national, i.e., State, requirements. And the State will pay for it.

Even when that happy time comes, we shall find that many institutions will be conducted by voluntary contributions. They may or may not benefit the State. Much of what passes for education today in India belongs to that category and would therefore not be paid for from the general revenue, if I had the way.

Reorientation of University Education

Gandhiji remarked at the Conference of Education Ministers in Poona that what he had said about adult education applied to University education. It must be originally related to the Indian scene. It must therefore be an extension and continuation of the Basic Education course. That was the central point. If they did not see eye to eye with him on that point, he was afraid they would have little use for his advice. If, on the other hand, they agreed with him that the present University education did not fit them for independence but only enslaved them, they would be as impatient as he was to completely overhaul and scrap that system and remodel it on new lines consonant with the national requirement.

Today the youth educated in our universities either ran after the Government jobs or fell into devious ways and sought outlet for their frustration by fomenting unrest. They were not even ashamed to beg or sponge upon others. Such was their sad plight. The aim of University education should be to turn out true servants of the people, who would live and die for the country's freedom. He was therefore of opinion that University education should be co-ordinated and brought into line with Basic Education, by taking in teachers from the Talimi Sangh.

Harijan, 25 August 1946

New Universities

There seems to be a mania for establishing new universities in the provinces. Gujarat wants one for Gujarati, Maharashtra for Marathi, Karnatic for Kannad, Orissa for Uriya, Assam for Assami and what not. I do believe that there should be such universities if these rich provincial languages and the people who speak them are to attain their full height.

At the same time I fear that we betray ourselves into undue haste in accomplishing the object. The first step should be linguistic political redistribution of provinces. Their separate administration will naturally lead to the establishment of universities where there are none.

The province of Bombay absorbs three languages: Gujarati, Marathi and Kannad and, therefore, stunts their growth. Madras absorbs four: Tamil, Telugu, Malayalam and Kannad. Thus there is overlapping also. That Andradesh has an Andhra University is true. In my opinion it does not occupy the place it would, if Andhra was a separate administrative unit, free from foreign control. India attained that freedom only two months ago. The same thing can be said of the Annamalai University.

Who can say that Tamil has come to its own in that University?

There should be a proper background for new universities. They should have feeders in the shape of schools and colleges which will impart instruction through the medium of their respective provincial languages. Then only can there be a proper milieu. University is at the top. A majestic top can only be sustained if there is a sound foundation.

Though we are politically free, we are hardly free from the subtle domination of the West. I have nothing to say to that school of politicians who believe that knowledge can only come from the West. Nor do I subscribe to the belief that nothing good can come out of the West. I do fear, however, that we are unable as yet to come to a correct decision in the matter. It is to be hoped that no one contends that because we seem to be politically free from foreign domination, the mere fact gives us freedom from the more subtle influence of the foreign language and foreign thought. Is it not wisdom, does not duty to the country dictate, that before we embark on new universities we should stop and fill our own lungs first with the ozone of our newly got freedom? A university never needs a pile of majestic buildings and treasures of gold and silver. What it does need most of all is the intelligent backing of public opinion. It should have a large reservoir of teachers to draw upon. Its founders should be farseeing.

In my opinion it is not for a democratic State to find money for founding universities. If the people want them they will supply the funds. Universities so founded will adorn the country which they represent. Where administration is in foreign hands, whatever comes to the people comes from the top and thus they become more and more dependent. Where it is broad-based on popular will, everything goes from bottom upward and hence it lasts. It is good looking and strengthens the people. In such a democratic scheme money invested in the promotion of learning gives a tenfold return to the people even as a seed sown in good soil returns a luxuriant crop. Universities founded under foreign domination have run in the reverse direction. Any other result was perhaps impossible. Therefore, there is every reason for being cautious about founding new universities till India has digested the newly-acquired freedom.

Then take the Hindu–Muslim question. The poison has assumed dangerous proportions, such that it is difficult to forecast where it will land us. Assume that the unthinkable has happened and that not a single Muslim can remain in the Union safely and honourably and that neither Hindu nor Sikh can do likewise in Pakistan. Our education will then wear a poisonous form. If, on the other hand, Hindus, Muslims and all the others who may belong to different faiths can live in either dominion with perfect safety and honour, then in the nature of things our education will take a shape altogether pleasing. Either people of different faiths having lived together in friendship have produced a beautiful blend of cultures, which we shall strive to perpetuate and increasingly strengthen and shape, or we shall cast about for the day when there was only one religion represented in Hindustan and retrace our steps to that exclusive culture.

It is just possible that we might not be able to find any such historical date and if we do and we retrace our steps, we shall throw our culture back to that ugly period and deservedly earn the execration of the universe. By way of example, if we make the vain attempt to obliterate the Muslim period, we shall have to forget that there was a mighty Juma Masjid in Delhi second to none in the world, or that there was a Muslim University in Aligarh, or that there was the Taj in Agra, one of the seven wonders of the world, or that there were the great forts of Delhi and Agra built during the Moghul period.

We shall then have to rewrite our history with that end in view. Surely, today we have not the atmosphere whch will enable us to come to a right conclusion about the conflicting choices. Our two months' old freedom is struggling to get itself shaped. We do not know what shape it will ultimately take. Until we know this definitely, it should be enough if we make such changes as are possible in the existing universities and breathe in our existing educational institutions the quickening spirit of freedom. The experience we will thus gain will be helpful when the time is ripe for founding new universities.

8

Gandhi on Language Education

Gandhiji's ideas on language education are described in this chapter in his own words. It will provide an insight into the vastness of his vision and the expanse of his thought-process.

Mother Tongue Fundamental

I must cling to my mother tongue as to my mother's breast, in spite of its shortcomings. It alone can give me the life-giving milk.

Medium of Instruction

I am hoping that this University1 will see to it that the youths who come to it will receive their instruction through the medium of their vernaculars. Our language is the reflection of ourselves, and if you tell me that our languages are too poor to express the best thought, then I say that the sooner we are wiped out of existence the better for us. Is there a man who dreams that English can ever become the national language of India? (Cries of 'Never') Why this handicap on the nation? Just consider for one moment what an unequal race our lads have to run with every English lad.

I had the privilege of a close conversation with some Poona professors. They assured me that every Indian youth, because he reached his knowledge through the English language, lost at least six precious years of life. Multiply that by the number of students turned out by our schools and colleges and find out for yourselves how many thousand years have been lost to the nation. The charge against us is, that we have no initiative. How can we have any if we are to devote the precious years of our life to the mastery of a foreign tongue? We fail in this attempt also. . . . I have heard it said that after all it is English-educated India which is leading and which is doing everything for the nation.

It would be monstrous if it were otherwise. The only education we receive is English education. Surely we must show something for it. But suppose that we had been receiving during the past fifty years education through our vernaculars, what should we have today? We should have today a free India, we should have our educated men, not as if they were foreigners in their own land, but speaking to the heart of the nation; they would be working amongst the poorest of the poor, and whatever they would have gained during the past fifty years would be a heritage for the nation (Applause). Today even our wives are not sharers in our best thought. Look at Professor Bose and Professor Ray and their brilliant researches. Is it not a shame that their researches are not the common property of the masses?

Foreign Medium

The foreign medium has caused brain fag, put an undue strain upon the nerves of our children, made them crammers and imitators, unfitted them for original work and thought, and disabled them for filtrating their learning to the family or the masses. The foreign medium has made our children practically foreigners in their own land. It is the greatest tragedy of the existing system. The foreign medium has prevented the growth of our vernaculars. If I had the powers of a despot, I would today stop the tuition of our boys and girls through a foreign medium, and require all the teachers and professors on pain of dismissal to introduce the change forthwith. I would not wait for the preparation of text-books. They will follow the change. It is an evil that needs a summary remedy.

Vernacular versus Foreign Medium

But for the fact that the only higher education, the only education worth the name has been received by us through the English medium, there would be no need to prove such a self-evident proposition that the youth of a nation to remain a nation must receive all instruction including the highest in its own vernacular or vernaculars.

Surely, it is a self-demonstrated proposition that the youth of a nation cannot keep or establish a living contact with the masses unless their knowledge is received and assimilated through a medium understood by the people. Who can calculate the immeasurable loss sustained by the nation owing to thousands of its young men having been obliged to waste years in mastering a foreign language and its idiom of which in their daily life they have the least use and in learning which they had to neglect their own mother tongue and their own literature? There never was a greater superstition than that a particular language can be incapable of expansion or expressing abstruse or scientific ideas. A language is an exact reflection of the character and growth of its speakers.

Among the many evils of foreign rule this blighting imposition of a foreign medium upon the youth of the country will be counted by history as one of the greatest. It has sapped the energy of the nation, it has shortened the lives of the pupils, it has estranged them from the masses, it has made education unnecessarily expensive. If this process is still persisted in, it bids fair to rob the nation of its soul. The sooner therefore educated India shakes itself free from the hypnotic spell of the foreign medium, the better it would be for them and the people.

De-Indianizing Education

I find daily proof of the increasing and continuing wrong being done to the millions by our false de-Indianizing education. These graduates who are my valued associates themselves flounder when they have to give expression to their innermost thoughts. They are strangers in their own homes. Their vocabulary in the mother tongue is so limited that they cannot always finish their speech without having recourse to English words and even sentences. Nor can they exist without English books. They often write to one another in English. I cite the case of my companions to show how deep the evil has gone. For we have made a conscious effort to mend ourselves.

It has been argued that the wastage that occurs in our colleges need not worry us if, out of the collegians, one Jagadish Bose can be produced by them. I should freely subscribe to the argument, if the wastage was unavoidable. I hope I have shown that it was and is even now avoidable. Moreover the creation of a Bose does not help the argument. For Bose was not a product of the present education. He rose in spite of the terrible handicaps under which he had to labour.

And his knowledge became almost intrans-missible to the masses. We seem to have come to think that no one can hope to be like a Bose unless he knows English. I cannot conceive a grosser superstition than this. No Japanese feels so helpless as we seem to do.

The medium of instruction should be altered at once and at any cost, the provincial languages being given their rightful place. I would prefer temporary chaos in higher education to the criminal waste that is daily accumulating.

In order to enhance the status and the market-value of the provincial languages, I would have the language of the law courts to be the language of the province where the court is situated. The proceedings of the provincial legislatures must be in the language, or even the languages of the province where a province has more than one language within its borders. I suggest to the legislators that they could, by enough application, inside of a month understand the languages of their provinces. There is nothing to prevent a Tamilian from easily learning the simple grammar and a few hundred words of Telugu, Malayalam, and Kanarese all allied to Tamil. At the centre Hindustani must rule supreme.

In my opinion this is not a question to be decided by aca-demicians. They cannot decide through what language the boys and girls of a place are to be educated. That question is already decided for them in every free country. Nor can they decide the subjects to be taught. That depends upon the wants of the country to which they belong. Theirs is a privilege of enforcing the nation's will in the best manner possible. When this country becomes really free the question of medium will be settled only one way.

The academicians will frame the syllabus and prepare text-books accordingly. And the products of the education of a free India will answer the requirements of the country as today they answer those of the foreign ruler. So long as we the educated classes play with this question, I very much fear we shall not produce the free and healthy India of our dream. We have to grow by strenuous effort out of our bondage, whether it is

Educational, Economical, Social or Political. The effort itself is three-fourths of the battle.

State Languages

If the medium is changed at once and not gradually, in an incredibly short time we shall find text-books and teachers coming into being to supply the want. And if we mean business, in a year's time we shall find that we need never have been party to the tragic waste of the nation's time and energy in trying to learn the essentials of culture through a foreign medium. The condition of success is undoubtedly that provincial languages are introduced at once in Government offices and courts, if the Provincial Governments have the power or the influence over the courts. If we believe in the necessity of the reform, we can achieve it in no time.

Richness of Dialects

Gandhiji deprecated the suggestion that it would need a lot of research and preparation to enable them to impart technical education through the medium of the mother tongue. Those who argued like that, were unaware of the rich treasure of expressions and idioms that were buried in the dialects of our villages. In Gandhiji's opinion there was no need to go to Sanskrit or Persian in search for many expressions. He had been in Champaran and he had found that the village folk there, could fully express themselves with ease and without the help of a single foreign expression or idiom. As an illustration of their resourcefulness, he mentioned the word *hava gadi* which they had coined to denote a motor car.

National Language

It behoves us to devote attention to a consideration of a national language, as we have done to that of the medium of instruction. If English is to become a national language, it ought to be treated as a compulsory subject. Can English become the national language? Some learned patriots contend that even to raise the question betrays ignorance. In their opinion, English already occupies that place. His Excellency the Viceroy in his recent utterance has merely expressed a hope that English will occupy that place. His enthusiasm does not take him as far as that of the former. His Excellency believes that English will day after day command a larger place, will permeate the family circle, and at last rise to the status of a national language.

A superficial consideration will support the viceregal contention. The condition of our educated classes gives one the impression that all our activities would come to a stand-still if we stop the use of English. And yet deeper thought will show that English can never and ought not to become the national language of India. What is the test of national language?

1. For the official class it should be easy to learn.
2. The religious, commercial and political activity throughout India should be possible in that language.
3. It should be the speech of the majority of the inhabitants of India.
4. For the whole of the country it should be easy to learn.
5. In considering the question, weight ought not to be put upon momentary of shortlived conditions.

The English language does not fulfil any of the conditions above-named. The first ought to have been the last, but I have purposely given it the first place, because that condition alone gives it the appearance of being applicable to the English language. But upon further consideration we should find that for the officials even at the present moment it is not an easy language to learn.

In our scheme of administration, it is assumed that the number of English officials will progressively decrease, so that in the end only the Viceroy and others whom one may count on one's finger-tips will be English. The majority are of Indian nationality today, and their number must increase.

And every one will admit that for them, English is more difficult to be learnt than any Indian language. Upon an examination of the second condition, we find that until the public at large can speak English, religious activity through that tongue is an impossibility. And a spread of English to that extent among the masses seems also impossible.

English cannot satisfy the third condition, because the majority in India do not speak it.

The fourth, too, cannot be satisfied by English, because it is not an easy language to learn for the whole of India.

Considering the last condition we observe that the position that English occupies today is momentary. The permanent condition is that there will be little necessity for English in national affairs. It will certainly be required for imperial affairs. That, therefore, it will be an imperial language, the language of diplomacy, is a different question. For that purpose its knowledge is a necessity. We are not jealous of English. All that is contended for is, that it ought not to be allowed to go beyond its proper sphere. And as it will be the imperial language, we shall compel our Malaviyajis, our Shastriars and our Banerjees to learn it. And we shall feel assured that they will advertise the greatness of India in other parts of the world. But English cannot become the national language of India. To give it that place is like an attempt to introduce Esperanto. In my opinion, it is unmanly even to think that English can become our national language. The attempt to introduce Esperanto merely betrays ignorance. Then which is the language that satisfies all the five conditions? We shall be obliged to admit that Hindi satisfies all those conditions.

I call that language Hindi which Hindus and Mohammedans in the North speak and write, either in the Devanagari or the Urdu character. Exception has been taken to this definition. It seems to be argued that Hindi and Urdu are different languages. This is not a valid argument. In the Northern parts of India, Mussalmans and Hindus speak the same language. The literate classes have created a division.

The learned Hindus have Sanskritized Hindi. The Mussalmans, therefore, cannot understand it. The Moslems of Lucknow have Persianized their speech and made it unintelligible to the Hindus. These represent two excesses of the same language. They find no common place in the speech of the masses. I have lived in the North. I have freely mixed with Hindus and Mohammedans and although I have but a poor knowledge of Hindi, I have never found any difficulty in holding communion with them. Call the language of the North what you will, Urdu or Hindi, it is the same. If you write it in the Urdu character, you may know it as Urdu. Write the same thing in the Nagari character and it is Hindi.

There, therefore, remains a difference about the script. For the time being Mohammedan children will certainly write in the Urdu character, and Hindus will mostly write in the Devanagari. I say mostly, because thousands of Hindus use the Urdu character, and some do not even know the Nagari character. But when Hindus and Mohammedans come to regard one another without suspicion, when the causes begetting suspicion are removed, that script which has greater vitality will be more universally used, and therefore, become the national script. Meanwhile those Hindus and Mohammedans who desire to write their petitions in the Urdu character, should be free to do so and should have the right of having them accepted at the seat of the National Government.

There is not another language capable of competing with Hindi in satisfying the five conditions. Bengali comes next to Hindi. But the Bengalis themselves make use of Hindi outside Bengal. No one wonders to see a Hindi-speaking man making use of Hindi, no matter where he goes. Hindu preachers and Mohammedan Moulvis deliver their religious discourses throughout India in Hindi and Urdu and even the illiterate masses follow them.

Even the unlettered Gujarati going to the North, attempts to use a few Hindi words whereas a gate-keeper from the North declines to speak in Gujarati even to his employer, who has on that account to speak to him in broken Hindi. I have heard Hindi spoken even in the Dravid country. It is not true to say that in Madras one can go on with English. Even there I have employed Hindi with effect. In the trains I have heard Madras passengers undoubtedly use Hindi. It is worthy of note that Mohammedans throughout India speak Urdu and they are to be found in large numbers in every Province. Thus Hindi is destined to be the national language. We have made use of it as such in times gone by. The rise of Urdu itself is due to that fact.

The Mohammedan kings were unable to make Persian or Arabic the national language. They accepted the Hindi grammar but employed the Urdu character and Persian words in their speeches. They could not, however, carry on their intercourse with the masses through a foreign tongue. All this is not unknown to the English. Those who know anything of the sepoys, know that for them military terms have had to be prepared in Hindi or Urdu.

Thus we see that Hindi alone can become the national language. It presents some difficulty in the case of the learned classes in Madras. For men from the Deccan, Gujarat, Sind and Bengal it is easy enough. In a few months they can acquire sufficient command over Hindi to enable them to carry on national intercourse in that tongue. It is not so for the Tamils.

The Dravidian languages are distinct from their Sanskrit sister in structure and grammar. The only thing common to the two groups is their Sanskrit vocabulary to an extent. But the difficulty is confined to the learned class alone. We have a right to appeal to their patriotic spirit and expect them to put forth sufficient effort in order to learn Hindi. For in future when Hindi has received State recognition, it will be introduced as a compulsory language in Madras as in other Provinces, and intercourse between Madras and them will then increase. English has not permeated the Dravidian masses. Hindi, however, will take no time.

Hindustani

Do not consider for one moment that you can possibly make English a common medium of expression between the masses. Twenty-two crores of Indians know Hindustani—they do not know any other language. And if you want to steal into their hearts Hindustani is the only language open to you.

Richness of the Hindi Language

You talk of the poverty of Hindi literature—you talk of the poverty of today's Hindi, but if you dive deep into the pages of Tulsidas, probably you will share my opinion that there is no other book that stands equal to it in the literature of the world in modern languages. That one book has given me faith and hope which no other book has given. I think that it is a book which can stand any criticism and any scrutiny, alike in literary grace, in metaphor and in religious fervour.

National Languages versus State Languages

A fear had been expressed, observed Gandhiji, that the propagation of Rashtrabhasha or the national tongue would prove inimical to the provincial languages. That fear was rooted in ignorance. Provincial tongues provided the sure foundation on which the edifice of the national tongue should rest. The two were intended to complement, not supplant each other.

Place of English

I do not dislike English; its riches are infinite. It is the language of administration and is rich with the wealth of knowledge. All this notwithstanding, I hold that it is not necessary for every Indian to learn it. But of this, I do not wish to speak more here. Students have been learning English and they have no option but to do so till some other system is devised and the present schools undergo a revolution. I shall, therefore, end this all-important subject of the mother tongue here, merely saying in conclusion that in their dealings with one another, and whenever possible, people should use only their mother tongue and that others, besides students, who are present here should strive their utmost to make the mother tongue the medium of education.

English versus Mother Tongue

English is a language of international commerce, it is the

language of diplomacy, and it contains many a rich literary treasure, it gives us an introduction to Western thought and culture. For a few of us, therefore, a knowledge of English is necessary. They can carry on the departments of national commerce and international diplomacy, and for giving to the nation the best of Western literature, thought, and science. That would be the legitimate use of English, whereas today English has usurped the dearest place in our hearts and dethroned our mother tongues. It is an unnatural place due to our unequal relations with Englishmen.

The highest development of the Indian mind must be possible without a knowledge of English. It is doing violence to the manhood and specially the womanhood of India to encourage our boys and girls to think that an entry into the best society is impossible without a knowledge of English. It is too humiliating a thought to be bearable. To get rid of the infatuation for English is one of the essentials of Swaraj.

English: Language and Culture

My uncompromising opposition to the foreign medium has resulted in an unwarranted charge being levelled against me of being hostile to foreign culture or the learning of the English language. No reader of *Young India* could have missed the statement often made by me in these pages, that I regard English as the language of international commerce and diplomacy and therefore consider its knowledge on the part of some of us as essential. As it contains some of the richest treasures of thought and literature, I would certainly encourage its careful study among them who have linguistic talents and expect them to translate those treasures for the nation in its vernaculars.

English versus Hindi

I know this tussle between English and Hindi is almost an eternal tussle. Whenever I have addressed student audiences, I have been surprised by the demand for English. You know, or ought to know, that I am a lover of the English language. But I do believe that the students of India, who are expected to throw in their lot with the teeming millions and to serve them, will be better qualified if they pay more attention to Hindi than to English. I do not say that you should not learn English; learn it by all means. But, so far as I can see, it cannot be the language of the millions of Indian homes. It will be confined to thousands or tens of thousands, but it will not reach the millions.

Literary Treasure in English

I must not be understood to decry English or its noble literature. The columns of the *Harijan* are sufficient evidence of my love of English. But the nobility of its literature cannot avail the Indian nation any more than the temperate climate or the scenery of England can avail her. India has to flourish in her own climate, and scenery, and her own literature, even though all the three may be inferior to the English climate, scenery and literature. We and our children must build on our own heritage.

If we borrow another, we impoverish our own. We can never grow on foreign victuals. I want the nation to have the treasures contained in that language and, for that matter, in other languages of the world, through its own vernaculars. I do not need to learn Bengali in order to know the beauties of Rabindranath's matchless productions. I get them through good translations. Gujarati boys and girls do not need to learn Russian to appreciate Tolstoy's short stories. They learn them through good translations. It is the boast of Englishmen that the best of the world's literary output is in the hands of that nation in simple English inside of a week of its publication. Why need I learn English to get at the best of what Shakespeare and Milton thought and wrote?

English as an Optional Language

English is today admittedly the world language. I would therefore accord it a place as a second, optional language, not in the school but in the university course. That can only be for the select few—not for the millions. Today when we have not the means to introduce even free compulsory primary education, how can we make provision for teaching English? Russia has achieved all her scientific progress without English. It is our mental slavery that makes us feel that we cannot do without English. I can never subscribe to that defeatist creed.

Sanskrit and Education

For the purpose of marriage ceremonies, *sandhya*1, *yajna* rituals and prayers, Sanskrit verses are used in our age. The verses are recited by the person officiating on these occasions and those who have engaged him join him in reciting the verses without understanding their meaning. Sanskrit is no longer our mother tongue.

Many institutions ask the people to use that language for prayers, *sandhya, yajna* rituals, etc. But the people do not understand the language. How, then, can they concentrate attention on what is being recited? Sanskrit, moreover, is a difficult language. Learning the verses by heart and remembering their meanings seems to me, therefore, a double burden. When Sanskrit was people's mother tongue, all their work was done in it and that was but right. That is no longer the position now. It helps people to use their mother tongue for all their work, but our present practice is different. The religious ceremonies mentioned above are performed in Sanskrit among the general public.

My view is that Sanskrit should be used in all Hindu religious ceremonies. However good a translation, it cannot give us the meaning which lies in the sounds of certain words in the original. Moreover, by translating into regional languages, and remaining content with such translations, verses which belong to a language which has acquired a certain refinement over thousands of years and in which those verses have always been recited, we diminish the air of solemnity which attaches to them. But I have no doubt at all in my mind that the meaning of every verse and every step in the ceremony should be explained in their own language to the people for whose benefit they are being recited or performed. It is also my view that the education of every Hindu is incomplete without an elementary knowledge of Sanskrit. I simply cannot conceive the continued existence of Hinduism without a widespread knowledge of Sanskrit. The language has been made difficult by the type of curriculum we follow in teaching it, in itself it is not difficult at all. Even if it is, the practice of dharma is still more difficult and, therefore, to those who wish to follow it in life the means of doing so should seem easy, however difficult they may actually be.

Sanskrit and Other Languages

"It is the duty of every Indian student to learn Sanskrit—the duty not only of the Hindus but also of the Muslims, because, after all, Rama and Krishna were as much their ancestors as of the Hindus, and to understand them they must learn Sanskrit. But it is equally the duty of the Hindus to learn the language of the Muslims in order to keep in touch and communicate with them. Today we run away from each other's language because we have turned mad. Be sure that an institution which preaches hate and fear is not, cannot be, national."

Sanskrit Scriptures

And remember that since you are in a vast majority, the responsi-bility rests on your shoulders to make Jaffna, and through Jaffna Ceylon also perfectly dry. Hinduism does not permit you to drink. And if the board of education will do its duty, you will encourage Sanskrit study in your schools. I regard the education of any Hindu child as incomplete unless he has some knowledge of Sanskrit. And so far as I have been able to see we have in Hinduism no book so compact and so acceptable all round as the *Bhagavad Gita*. If you will, therefore, saturate your children and yourselves with the spirit of Hinduism, you will endeavour to understand the spirit of the teachings of the *Gita*. You should also cultivate a common knowledge of the *Mahabharata* and the *Ramayana*.

Sanskrit versus State Languages

Do you know that the Patna University has practically tabooed the study of Sanskrit? Do you approve of the step? If you do not, will you express your opinion in *Harijan*?

I do not know what the Patna University has done. But I quite agree with you that the study of Sanskrit is being sadly neglected. I belong to a generation which believed in the study of the ancient languages. I do not believe that such a study is a waste of time and effort. I believe it is an aid to the study of modern languages.

This is truer of Sanskrit than of any other ancient language so far as India is concerned, and every nationalist should study it because it makes a study of the provincial languages easier than otherwise. It is the language in which our forefathers thought and wrote. No

Hindu boy or girl should be without a knowledge of the rudiments of Sanskrit, if he will imbibe the spirit of his religion. Thus the Gayatri is untranslatable. No translation can give the music of the original which I hold has a meaning all its own. The Gayatri is but one example of what I have said.

Pronunciation

By all means study Sanskrit. The effort made for learning correct pronunciation will not be wasted. Chaste pronunciation is a requisite for [learning] any language. But perhaps for Sanskrit accuracy of pronunciation is imperative. It is not at all necessary for you to study English. Assimilate the knowledge you already have and add to it.

Languages versus Composite Culture

Every cultured Indian should know in addition to his own provincial language, if a Hindu, Sanskrit; if a Mohammedan, Arabic; if a Parsee, Persian; and all, Hindi. Some Hindus should know Arabic and Persian; some Mohammedans and Parsees, Sanskrit. Several Northerners and Westerners should learn Tamil. A universal language for India should be Hindi, with the option of writing it in Persian or Nagari characters. In order that the Hindus and Mohammedans may have closer relations, it is necessary to know both the characters.

Language Chasm

Our love of the English language in preference to our own mother tongue has caused a deep chasm between the educated and politically-minded classes and the masses. The languages of India have suffered impoverishment. We flounder when we make the vain attempt to express abstruse thought in the mother tongue. There are no equivalents for scientific terms. The result has been disastrous. The masses remain cut off from the modern mind. We are too near our own times correctly to measure the disservice caused to India by this neglect of its great languages. It is easy enough to understand that unless we undo the mischief the mass mind must remain imprisoned.

The masses can make no solid contribution to the construction of swaraj. It is inherent in swaraj based on non-violence that every individual makes his own direct contribution to the Independence movement. The masses cannot do this fully unless they understand every step with all its implications. This is impossible unless every step is explained in their own languages.

Place for Languages in Curriculum

It is now my opinion that in all Indian curricula of higher education there should be a place for Hindi, Sanskrit, Persian, Arabic and English, besides of course the vernacular. This big list need not frighten anyone. If our education were more systematic, and the boys free from the burden of having to learn their subjects through a foreign medium, I am sure learning all these languages would not be an irksome task, but a perfect pleasure. A scientific knowledge of one language makes a knowledge of other languages comparatively easy.

Multiplicity of Scripts

If we are to make good our claim as one nation, we must have several things common. We have a common culture running through a variety of creeds and sub-creeds. We have common disabilities. I am endeavouring to show that a common material for our dress is not only desirable but necessary. We need also a common language not in supersession of the vernaculars, but in addition to them. It is generally agreed that that medium should be Hindustani—a resultant of Hindi and Urdu, neither highly Sanskritized, nor highly Persianized or Arabianized. The greatest obstacle in the way are the numerous scripts we have for the vernaculars. If it is possible to adopt a common script, we should remove a great hindrance in the way of realizing the dream, which at present it is, of having a common language.

A variety of scripts is an obstacle in more ways than one. It constitutes an effectual barrier against the acquisition of knowledge. The Aryan languages have so much in common that, if a great deal of time had not to be wasted in mastering the different scripts, we should all know several languages without much difficulty; for instance, most people who have a little knowledge of Sanskrit would have no difficulty in understanding the matchless creation of Rabindranath Tagore, if it was all printed in Devanagari script. But the Bengalee script is a notice to the non-Bengalis—"hands off".

Conversely, if the Bengalis knew the Devanagari script, they would at once be able to enjoy the marvellous beauty and spirituality of Tulsidas and a host of other Hindustani writers. When I returned to India in 1905, I had a communication from a society whose headquarters were, I believe, in Calcutta, and whose object was to advocate a common script for all India. I do not know the activities of that society, but its object is worthy, and a great deal of substantial work can be done by a few earnest workers in this direction. There are obvious limitations.

A common script for all India is a distant ideal. A common script for all those who speak the Indo-Sanskrit languages, including the Southern stock, is a practical ideal, if we can but shed our provincialisms. There is little virtue, for instance, in a Gujarati clinging to the Gujarati script. A provincial patriotism is good where it feeds the larger stream of all-India patriotism, as the latter is good to the extent that it serves the still larger end of the universe. But a provincial patriotism that says "India is nothing, Gujarat is all", is wickedness. I have selected Gujarat because it is the half-way house, and because I am myself a Gujarati.

In Gujarat, somewhat fortunately those who settled the principles of primary education, decided to make Devanagari script compulsory. Every Gujarati boy or girl, who has passed through a school, therefore knows both the Gujarati and the Devanagari scripts. If the committee had decided upon purely Devanagari script, it would have been better still. No doubt, the research scholars would still have learnt the Gujarati script for deciphering old manuscripts, but the Gujarati boy's energy would have been spared for more useful labour, if he had to learn only one instead of two scripts.

The committee that settled the education scheme for Maharashtra, was more enlightened, and it simply required the Devanagari script. The result is that a Mahratta reads, so far as mere reading is concerned, Tulsidas with as much facility as he reads Tukaram, and Gujaratis and Hindustanis read Tukaram with equal facility. The committee in Bengal, on the other hand, ruled otherwise, with the result we all know and many of us deplore. The treasures of the richest Indian vernacular have been rendered most difficult of access as if by design. That Devanagari should be the common script, I suppose, does not need any demonstration—the deciding factor being that it is the script known to the largest part of India.

These reflections arise, because, I was called upon to solve, during my visit to Cuttack, a practical question.

There is a tribe wedged between the Hindi-speaking people in Bihar and Uriya-speaking people of Orissa. What was to be done for the education of its children? Were they to be taught through Uriya or through Hindi? Or were they to be taught their own dialect, and if they were, was the script to be Devanagari or a new invention? The first thought of the Utkal Friends was to absorb the tribe amongst the Uriyas.

The Biharis would think of absorbing them in Bihar, and if the elders of the tribe were consulted, they would most probably and naturally say that their dialect was just as good as the Uriya or the Bihari, and that it should be reduced to writing. And for them it would be a toss whether the script to be adopted should be Devanagari or Uriya, if not even a newly invented script, as has happened in modern times in at least two instances I know. Endeavouring to think in terms of all-India I suggested to my friends that, whilst it was proper for them to strengthen the Uriya language among the Uriya-speaking people, the children of this tribe should be taught Hindi and naturally the script should be Devanagari.

A spirit that is so exclusive and narrow as to want every form of speech to be perpetuated and developed, is anti-national and anti-universal. All undeveloped and unwritten dialects should, in my humble opinion, be sacrificed and merged in the great Hindustani stream. It would be a sacrifice only to be nobler, not a suicide. If we are to have a common language for cultured India, we must arrest the growth of any process of disintegration or multiplication of languages and scripts. We must promote a common language.

The beginning must naturally be made with the script, and until the Hindu–Muslim question is solved, confined perhaps to Hindu India. If I could have my way,

I would make the learning of Devanagari script and Urdu script, in addition to the established provincial script, compulsory in all the provinces and I would print in Devanagari chief books in the different vernaculars with a literal translation in Hindustani.

ONE SCRIPT, MANY LANGUAGES

Although it is my firm conviction that there should be one script for all the Indian languages, and that script can only be Devanagari, I could not follow the correspondent's advice for the reasons stated in my note in *Navajivan*, and which I need not reiterate here. But there is no doubt that we ought to seize the opportunity that the great national awakening gives us, of not merely popularizing the idea but of doing something concrete in that direction.

The Hindu–Muslim madness no doubt stands in the way of a thorough reform. But before the acceptance of Devanagari script becomes a universal fact in India, Hindu India has got to be converted to the idea of one script for all the languages derived from Sanskrit and the Dravidian stock. At the present moment we have Bengali script in Bengal, Gurmukhi in the Punjab, Sindhi in Sind, Oriya in Utkal, Gujarati in Gujarat, Telugu in Andhradesha, Tamil in Tamilnad, Malayalam in Kerala, Kanarese in Karnatak, not to speak of Kaithi in Bihar and Modi in the Deccan. If all these scripts could be replaced by Devanagari for all practical and national purposes, it would mean a tremendous step forward. It will help to solidify Hindu India and bring the different provinces in closer touch.

Anyone who has any knowledge of the different Indian languages and scripts knows to his cost what time it takes to master a new script. For the love of his country, no doubt, nothing is difficult, and time spent in mastering the different scripts, some of which are very beautiful, is in no way idly spent. But this spirit of abandon is not to be expected of millions.

National leaders have to make things easy for them. Therefore, we must have an easily adaptable universal script for all India, and there is nothing so adaptable and readymade as Devanagari script. There is, or there used to be, an all-India organization for this very purpose. I do not know what its activities are at present. But if the work has to be done, either the original association should be strengthened, or a new one formed for this purpose. The movement should in no way be confused with the spread of Hindi or Hindustani as the lingua franca.

The latter work is going on very slowly, but steadily. Use of one script will facilitate the spread of one language. But the functions of the two run parallel only up to a point. Hindi or Hindustani is not designed to replace the provincial languages, but is intended to supplement them, and to be used for inter-provincial contact. And till the Hindu–Muslim tension lasts it takes the form either of Urdu written in the Persian script, and containing preponderance of Persian or Arabic words, or Hindi written in Devanagari and containing a preponderance of Sanskrit words. When the hearts of the two meet, the two forms of the same language will be fused together, and we shall have a resultant of the two, containing as many Sanskrit, Persians, Arabic or other words as may be necessary for its full growth and full expression.

But one script is undoubtedly designed to displace all the different scripts so as to render it easy for people belonging to different provinces to learn provincial languages. The best way of achieving the purpose is first to make the learning of Devanagari script compulsory at least for Hindus in all the schools, as it is in Gujarat, and secondly to print the important literature in different Indian languages in Devanagari script. Such effort has already been made to a certain extent. I have seen *Gitanjali* printed in Devanagari script. But the effort requires to be made on a large scale, and there should be propaganda carried on for the spread of such books.

Devanagari and National Unity

The object of this conference is to collect gems from all provincial literatures and to make them available through Hindi. For this purpose I would make an appeal to you. Of course everyone must know his own language thoroughly well, and he should also know the great literature of other Indian languages through Hindi. But it is also the object of this conference to stimulate in our people the desire to know languages of other provinces, e.g., Gujaratis should know Tamil, Bengalis should know Gujarati and so on. And I tell you from experience that it is not at all difficult to pick up another Indian language. But to this end a common script is quite essential. It is not difficult to achieve in Tamil Nad.

For look at this simple fact: over 90 per cent our people are illiterate. We have to start with a clean slate with them. Why should we not start making them literate by means of a common script? In Europe they have tried the experiment of a common script quite successfully. Some people even go the length of saying that we might adopt the Roman script from Europe. After a good deal of controversy there is a consensus of opinion that the common script can be Devanagari and none else. Urdu is claimed as a rival, but I think neither Urdu nor Roman has the perfection and phonetic capacity of Devanagari. Please remember that I say nothing against your languages. Tamil, Telugu, Malayalam, Kannada must be there and will be there. But why not teach the illiterate in these parts these languages through the Devanagari script. In the interest of the national unity we desire to achieve, the adoption of Devanagari as a common script is so essential. Here it is a question of just shedding our provincialism and narrowness, there are no difficulties at all.

UNIVERSALISING DEVANAGARI

I understand that some of the tribes in Assam are being taught to read and write through the Roman script instead of Devanagari. I have already expressed my opinion that the only script that is ever likely to be universal in India is Devanagari, either reformed or as it is. Urdu or Persian will go hand in hand unless Muslims, of their own free will, acknowledge the superiority of Devanagari from a purely scientific and national standpoint. But this is irrelevant to the present problem.

The Roman cannot go hand in hand with the other two scripts. Protagonists of the Roman script would displace both. But sentiment and science alike are against the Roman script. Its sole merit is its convenience for printing and typing purpose. But that is nothing compared to the strain its learning would put upon millions. It can be of no help to the millions who have to read their own literature either in their own provincial scripts or in Devanagari.

Devanagari is easier for the millions of Hindus and even Muslims to learn, because the provincial scripts are mostly derived from Devanagari. I have included Muslims advisedly. The mother tongue of Bengali Muslims, for instance, is Bengali as is Tamil of Tamil Muslims. The present movement for the propagation of Urdu will, as it should, result in Muslims all over India learning Urdu in addition to their mother tongue. They must, in any case, know Arabic for the purpose of learning the Holy Koran. But the millions whether

Hindus or Muslims will never need the Roman script except when they wish to learn English. Similarly, Hindus who want to read their scriptures in the original have to and do learn the Devanagari script. The movement for universalizing the Devanagari script has thus a sound basis.

The introduction of the Roman script is a superimposition which can never become popular. And all superimpositions will be swept out of existence when the true mass awakening comes, as it is coming, much sooner than anyone of us can expect from known causes. Yet the awakening of millions does take time. It cannot be manufactured. It comes or seems to come mysteriously. National workers can merely hasten the process by anticipating the mass mind.

One Script for Sister Languages

The question of having one script for the Indian languages which are daughters of Sanskrit by birth or adoption has been before the public for a number of years. Yet in these days of aggressive provincialism, perhaps, any plea for one script will be regarded as an impertinence. But the literacy campaigns raging all over the country should compel a hearing for the advocates of one script. I have been one such for years. I remember having even adopted in South Africa Devanagari script for my Indian correspondence with Gujaratis in select cases. Inter-provincial intercourse will be much facilitated by such adoption, and the learning of the various provincial languages will be made infinitely easier than it is today. If the educated people of the land were to put their heads together and decide upon one script, its universal adoption should be an easy thing.

To the millions who are illiterate it is a matter of indifference what script is prescribed to them. If the happy consummation comes to pass, there will be only two scripts in India—Devanagari and Urdu, and every nationalist will deem it his duty to master the two scripts. I am a lover of all Indian languages. I have tried to learn as many scripts as possible. And if only I had the time, even at the age of seventy I have energy enough to learn more Indian languages. That would be a recreation for me. But in spite of all my love for the languages I must confess that I have not learnt all the scripts.

But if the sister languages were written in one script, I should pick up a workable knowledge of the principal languages of the provinces in very little time. And Devanagari has nothing to be ashamed of in point of symmetry or beauty. I hope that those who are engaged in the literacy campaigns will give a passing thought to my suggestion. If they will adopt Devanagari script, they will save for the future generations tons of labour and time and earn their blessings.

National versus International Language

Where is the need for a national language? Will not the mother tongue and an international language suffice? And then why not the Roman script for both?

Your question surprises me. English no doubt is the inter-national language. But can it ever be our national language? The latter must be the common property of millions of our people. How can they sustain the burden of learning the English tongue? Hindustani is the natural national language, for it is already understood by 21 crores. The remainder of the population can also easily understand it. But English may be said to be the mother tongue of a mere handful—say, a lac at the most. If India is a nation, it must have a national language. English will appropriately remain the inter-national language with the Roman script. But the latter can never be the script of the national language.

9

Gandhi on Women Education

Gandhiji's ideas on women education are described in this chapter in his own words. It will provide an insight into the vastness of his vision and the expanse of his thought-process.

WOMEN'S EDUCATION

That India is very backward in the education of women is a fact that cannot be denied. But by admitting this, we do not mean to suggest that Indian women fail in their duty. We believe that, as there are in world few men of any class who can compete with the Indians considered from all points of view, so are there few women anywhere in the world who can compare with Indian women. But this position can no longer be kept up in the present squalid, low and helpless state of India.

The modern age is such that it does not allow anyone to remain in the same position. Those who do not want to go forward, or do not do so, must fall behind. In so far as this is true, we can see that Indian men have deliberately kept their women backward. Those who pose as reformers as also other well-to-do Indians, whether Hindu or Muslim, Parsi or Christian, either treat their women as if they were playthings or use them as they fancy for self-indulgence, with the result that they themselves become weak and help only to produce weaklings. And in this way they lead irreligious lives and still say, 'It is God's will that prevails.' If this state of affairs continues, India will remain in its present abominable condition even if she were to secure all her rights from the British Government.

In all countries where the people live a decent life, there is no disparity in the condition of men and women. It is easy to see how much the real wealth of India would be attenuated, if one half of her human beings remained ignorant and existed only as playthings of the others.

Equality of Rights for Women

We shall accept equality of rights for women, but I think their education should differ from men's as their nature and functions do. In progressive countries, women receive the very highest education but, after it is over, they do not have to perform the same duties as men and in our country women have never to compete with men for a livelihood.

Educated Women's Role

The women whom this message reaches are likely to have had some measure of education. I wish, therefore, to consider one thing. What should educated women do for their illiterate sisters? This is a very important issue. Beyond question, if women choose . . . they can attain a far greater measure of success in this field than men can ever do. At present, we do not find many women taking to this work. That is, I believe, not their fault but that of their education.

The first thing, therefore, which educated women must do is to try and see that their sisters do not fall a victim to it. Modern education fails utterly to prepare women for their distinctive role; this is not questioned by anyone. I do not wish here to examine the shortcomings of modern education or to bother you with the question how they may be overcome. All that I desire is that educated women should make this question their own and that those of them with some experience should dedicate their all to rouse Gujarat over it and focus attention on the right lines [of reform].

Educated women have no contact with those not educated; often, they don't welcome such contacts. This disease must be cured. It is necessary that educated women are made conscious of their most obvious duty. Men also are not free from faults of this kind, but women need not follow in their footsteps. They have the power, denied to men, of creating new ideals and translating them into action. By comparison, man is thoughtless, impatient and given to the pursuit of novelty.

Men versus Women's Education

The education of women is as faulty as that of men. They have not given any thought to the relations obtaining between men and women, or to the place woman occupies in India society.

It may be admitted that for the most part preliminary teaching of both boys and girls would be much the same. Barring that, there is great dissimilarity. There is need for similar distinction between the education of males and females as has been made between them by Mother Nature herself. True, they are equals. But there is a difference in the work they are ordained to do. It is woman's right to rule inside the home. Man is master outside it.

Man is the earner of livelihood, woman saves and spends. Woman brings up children. She is their mother. She is responsible for building up their character. She is their educator, and hence the *mother* of the race. Man is not, in that sense, the father of the race. After a certain age a father ceases to influence his son, but not so the mother. The son, even after attaining manhood, behaves like a child in the presence of his mother. He cannot, however, do this with his father.

If this arrangement is considered natural and right a woman should not have to earn her living. A society in which women have to work as telegraph clerks, typists or compositors is, I think, not well-organized. It is a symptom of moral and economic bankruptcy and is an indication that they, i.e., the people belonging to that society, have begun to live on their capital.

Hence, just as it is wrong to keep women in ignorance and under suppression on the one hand, it is wrong, on the other hand, to entrust them with the work which is ordinarily done by men; for this is a sign of weakness and is tantamount to oppression.

Therefore, after a certain age, there must be arrangements to provide women with a kind of education different to that of men. Women should be taught the management of the home, the things they should or should not do during pregnancy, and the nursing and care of children. It is difficult to make suitable arrangements for providing such teaching as the idea is a new one. The right course under the circumstances would be to constitute a committee of enlightened and experienced men and women of good character who would then explore the problem, come to the right decision, and produce a suitable plan for the purpose.

This committee should find out how best to impart the necessary education to girls after they have completed the period of childhood and enter on that of womanhood. But, unfortunately, there are a large number of girls in our country who get married even while they are in their childhood. Besides, the number goes on increasing. And once they are married, they just disappear from social life.

I have expressed my views about them fully in my foreword contributed to the first book of the "Bhagini Pustak-mala" series. I reproduce them here:

"We cannot achieve the education of women merely by educating girls. Claimed by the monster of child-marriage, thousands of girls disappear from view at the early age of twelve. From girls they change into house-wives at one stroke. As long as this wicked custom continues, the only alternative is that men must learn to act as teachers to women. A great many of our hopes in regard to the education of women rest on how men discharge their duty in this respect. Women must cease to be our servants and objects of enjoyment as they are at present, and become, instead, our life-companions, equal partners in the battle of life, sharers in our happiness and unhappiness. All our efforts seem utterly futile as long as this is not accomplished. There are some men who regard their women as beasts. For this sad state some of the Sanskrit sayings and the following well-known *doha* of Tulasidas may be held responsible. Tulasidas says at one place in his *Ramayana:* "The drum, the fool, the Shudra and the woman—all these are fit objects to beat." I hold Tulasidasji in high esteem, but my worship is not blind.

Either this couplet is an interpolation, or, if it is his, he must have written it without thought—as reflecting the prevailing views of the then society. As to the saying in Sanskrit, people seem to be labouring under the impression that every *shloka* written is, as it were, a scriptural precept. We must fight this impression and eradicate from its very root the custom of regarding women as inferior beings.

On the other hand, blinded by passion many among us adore women and decorate them with ornaments just as we decorate idols. We must keep away from this evil also. Our ultimate goal, however, will not be achieved until our women become to us what Parvati was to

Mahadeva, Sita to Rama, Damayanti to Nala. Then, they will participate in our discussions, argue things with us on an equal basis, understand through their wonderful insight born of sympathy, be partners in our fight for resolving them and become for us, when we need it, the givers of the most soothing peace. This goal cannot be achieved merely by starting girls' schools.

As long as we have around our necks the noose of child-marriage, men must be the teachers of their womenfolk. And this education which men will give to women will not be merely literacy; it will be extended to cover social reform and politics. Literacy must be only a preliminary to the teaching of the other subjects mentioned above. These may be taught even without it. A man who undertakes to teach his wife in this manner will have to change his attitude towards her. A man will himself be a student with his wife and will observe complete celibacy in his relation with her until she attains maturity. In no case will he subject a girl of twelve to fifteen years of age to the agony of bearing children to him. One ought to shudder at the very thought of it. If this is done we will not be crushed under the weight of inertia as we are at present.

"Classes are being started for married women and lecturers arranged for them. All this is good as far as it goes. Those who are engaged in this work are sacrificing their time and energy for a good cause. This is quite creditable. But simultaneously men must also undertake to discharge the duty indicated above, because in its absence all these efforts will not bear much result. On deeper reflection, I am sure that what I have said is self-evident."

Woman, like Man, Needs Education

Though much good and useful work can be done without

a knowledge of reading and writing, yet I believe that such knowledge is necessary, for one can hardly do without it these days. Reading of good books develops the intellect and that, in its turn, increases our capacity for service to our people and our country. I do not over-estimate the value of this knowledge, but I should like to give it its due place in the scheme of things. I have pointed out on several occasions that lack of education among women should not be made the reason for men to deprive them of their due human rights. But proper education is essential in order that they may use those rights well, adorn them and spread them amongst our masses. Without proper education and the knowledge acquired through such education, millions cannot acquire the true knowledge of the Self. Without education, the inexhaustible fund of innocent pleasure which lies in various books is also closed to us. It is no exaggeration but a statement of fact that a man without learning is not far removed from an animal. Thus, a woman, like man, needs education. Not that a woman should get the same kind of education as given to a man.

In the first place, the education that is being given us by the Government is, to a great extent, faulty and harmful. It should therefore be eschewed by both men and women. Even if its defects were removed I would not consider it proper for women. Men and women are equal in status, but they are not the same in physical or mental make-up. They are a unique pair. They complement each other and are absolutely necessary to each other, so much so that one cannot exist without the other. It follows as a corollary from these facts that anything that will impair the status of either of them will involve the ruin of both, in equal measure. Those who draw up plans for the education of women must remember this.

Man rules the outer circle of the life of a married pair. Therefore he must have the greater knowledge of all those activities of life which constitute his sphere. The woman, on the other hand, is dominant in the inner or domestic circle of their life. She must have special knowledge of the management of the home, care of children, their education etc. It is not suggested that either men or women should be forbidden from acquiring a knowledge of what belongs specially to the province of the other. But unless courses of instruction are based on a discriminating appreciation of these ideas, both men and women would be deprived of the opportunity of achieving perfection in their respective spheres.

A few words are also necessary about the question as to whether or not women need to know English. I feel that generally speaking, knowledge of English is not necessary either for men or for women. Men might require it for earning their livelihood or for taking part in political work. But I do not believe in women working for a living or undertaking commercial enterprises.

Therefore, only a few women would need to learn English. And those who want to may well learn it in the schools for men. Introducing English in all schools for women will only lead to a prolongation of the period of our helplessness. I have often heard people say that the rich treasures of English literature should be as easily available to women as they are to men. I humbly submit that this is an erroneous view even though the error may not be evident. No one says that the treasures of English literature should be open to men but closed to women. He who loves literature may well explore the literature of the whole world. None will, or can, stop him from doing so, if he has the necessary will. But, since we are concerned with formulating a plan to suit the needs of our people in general, we cannot attend to the special needs of a few lovers of literature.

For them there will have to be—when we are sufficiently advanced and prosperous—separate institutions for learning and research as there are in Europe. When there is a general spread of education, when most of our men and women start getting educated, we may be sure that numerous writers will rise from amongst us who will make available to us the joy of the literatures of other languages. If we continue to derive pleasure only from English literature alone, our language will always remain poor. This means that we as a people will also remain mentally poor. I would even say, if you will forgive me for the simile, that the habit of deriving joy from the literature of another language is like that of a thief who derives joy from stolen property. The English poet Pope presented to his people, in his beautiful English, whatever joy he tasted in *Iliad;* in the same way, Fitzgerald embodied the joy he derived from the poetry of Omar Khayyam in such attractive English that millions of Englishmen love and treasure his translation of the poetry of Khayyam like their own Bible.

Edwin Arnold tasted the nectar of our *Bhagavadgita.* He did not ask his people to learn Sanskrit to experience the joy that he had experienced in that book. On the other hand, he made it available to the people in English which is as beautiful as the original Sanskrit and in which besides he has succeeded in pouring out his very soul as it were. Seeing that we are still backward in this respect, we must pay more attention to the work of translating. But it will be possible only when we have made our plan of education along the lines I have indicated and implement it. If we give up being fascinated by English and our distrust of the power of our own language, this will not be difficult to achieve. It is not necessary for any man or woman to spend his or her time learning English in order to appreciate good literature. I do not say this merely to be a wet blanket.

But because I want the pleasure, which the English-educated people derive with great difficulty, made easily available to all of us through translations. The languages of the world are full of many a invaluable gem. And not all the gems of literature are in English. I want all these gems to be brought within the reach of our people. The only way to achieve this end is for those of us who have a flair for languages to learn them and then present the foreign literary classics in our own.

Higher Education for Women

After primary education, a girl gets another four to five years of secondary education. Expressing his views on the question as to whether in this period she should be taught through English or the mother tongue, Gandhiji said: "I feel that teaching English to them under the circumstances would be like killing them. It will never be possible for hundreds of thousands of women to think or express their thoughts in English; and even if it were possible, it would be undesirable.

"If the women for whom we are drawing up this plan are imparted higher education through the mother tongue, they could make their homes as bright and beautiful as gold. Not only that, they could also exert their good influence on their uneducated sisters and thus render valuable service to them as well."

Modern Girls' Education

I was really surprised to see the stride that education among girls had taken in the State of Travancore. It was a perfect eye-opener to me. The question has always occurred to me: "What will India do with its modern girls?" I call you modern girls of India. The education that we are receiving in these institutions, in my opinion, does not correspond with the life around us, and, when I say life around us, I do not mean the life around us in the cities but the life around us in the villages. Perhaps some of you girls, if not all of you, know that real India is to be found not here in the very few cities but in the seven hundred thousand villages covering a surface of 1,900 miles long and 1,500 miles broad. The question is whether you have any message for your sisters in the villages. Men do not need the message perhaps so much as the women, and I have long before come to the conclusion that unless women of India work side by side with men, there is no salvation for India, salvation in more senses than one. I mean political salvation in the broadest sense, and I mean economic salvation and spiritual salvation also.

Curriculum for Girls' Education

Women must learn as part of elementary education at least their own mother tongue, Hindi if it is not their mother tongue, enough Sanskrit to be able to understand the drift of the *Bhagavad Gita*, elementary arithmetic, elementary composition, elementary music and child-care. Along with this, I think they should know well the processes up to the weaving from cotton. When a woman receives this education she should have an environment that will shape her character and enable her to see clearly the evils in society and to avoid them. I have not mentioned religious education separately as it is acquired by practice and would be covered by general reading. Truly speaking, it is a part of the elevating company of a teacher. This is about girls. The education of a widow or a married woman is of course a different matter.

Education to Women

Today we have assembled for the opening of a girls' school. I have made a thorough study of child education. I could say the same thing about girls' education. But how can experts accepts this? Today, even I cannot make that claim. In the prevailing state of affairs it is not easy to talk about girls' education. Everyone may well claim that he is capable of giving education to girls. I will however ask him whether he has imparted true education to his daughter or his wife. How can he who has not observed his dharma towards his wife, sister, mother or mother-in-law, set out to teach the daughters or sisters of others? They may well become B.As. or M.As. but I shall put them to the same test. I should like to know what kind of husbands and fathers those who write books on girls' education are.

Co-education

In theory, we are quite in favour of boys and girls receiving education together. But, in practice, it is impossible to ignore deep-rooted habits or prejudices. Experience has shown that Indian parents, as a rule, will not allow their daughters to mingle with boys at a school or elsewhere. And, whenever a forcible mixture takes place, the result is ludicrous in the extreme. Both the boys and girls feel awkward. "Let them", shouts the unthinking reformer. "They will soon be at home, if left alone." But the parents will not wait for the process. They are not reformers and they will not allow experiments to be made at their children's expense.

Co-education not Compulsory

As for co-education, the Zakir Husain Committee has not made it compulsory. Where there is a demand for a separate school for girls, the State will have to make provision. The question of co-education has been left open. It will regulate itself according to the time-spirit. So far as I am aware the members of the Committee were not all of one mind. Personally I have an open mind. I think that there are just as valid reasons for as against co-education. And I would not oppose the experiment wherever it is made.

Co-education in Training Schools

Shri Avinashilingam, the Education Minister of Madras, felt that the co-education policy of the Talimi Sangh was not suitable to Madras. He had no objection to co-education among children and among grown-ups, when they knew their own minds. But he was not in favour of co-education at the impressionable age of 15 or 16 when most of the girls came to training schools. Gandhiji, however, disagreed. "If you keep co-education in your schools but not in your training-schools, the children will think there is something wrong somewhere, I should allow my children to run the risk. We shall have to rid ourselves one day of this sex mentality. We should not seek for examples from the West. Even in training-schools, if the teachers are intelligent, pure and filled with the spirit of Nayee Talim, there is no danger. Supposing if some accidents do take place, we should not be frightened by them. They would take place anywhere. Although I speak thus boldly, I am not unaware of the attendant risks. You, as a responsible Minister, should think for yourself and act accordingly."

Sex Education

May I invite you to discuss in the columns of *Harijanbandhu* a question which you have so far left more or less untouched, I mean the question of imparting sex instruction to young people?

Should sex education be included in the educational curricula of our children? Who should impart it? What would be the necessary qualification for the task? Should this subject be taught in a matter-of-fact manner to all and sundry just like geography or arithmetic? Or is there any limit? And if so, who is to draw the line and where? Again should the aim of sex education be to combat the onset of libido or simply to recognize it as an inevitable fact of nature which has to be accepted and submitted to?1

What place has instruction in sexual science in our educational system, or has it any place there at all? Sexual science is of two kinds, that which is used for controlling or overcoming the sexual passion and that which is used to stimulate and feed it. Instruction in the former is as necessary a part of a child's education as the latter is harmful and dangerous and fit therefore only to be shunned. All great religions have rightly regarded 'Kama' as the arch-enemy of man, anger or hatred coming only in the second place. According to the Gita, the latter is an offspring of the former. The Gita of course uses the word 'Kama' in its wider sense of desire. But the same holds good of the narrow sense in which it is used here.

This, however, still leaves unanswered the question, i.e., whether it is desirable to impart to young pupils a knowledge about the use and function of generative organs. It seems to me that it is necessary to impart such knowledge to a certain extent. At present they are often left to pick up such knowledge anyhow with the result that they are misled into abusive practices. We cannot properly control or conquer the sexual passion by turning a blind eye to it. I am therefore strongly in favour of teaching young boys and girls the significance and right use of their generative organs. And in my own way I have tried to impart this knowledge to young children of both sexes for whose training I was responsible.

But the sex education that I stand for must have for its object the conquest and sublimation of the sex passion. Such education should automatically serve to bring home to children the essential distinction between man and brute, to make them realize that it is man's special privilege and pride to be gifted with the faculties of head and heart both; that he is a thinking no less than a feeling animal, as the very derivation of the word YkTknaZk; (man) shows, and to renounce the sovereignty of reason over the blind instincts is therefore to renounce a man's estate. In man reason quickens and guides the feeling, in brute the soul lies ever dormant. To awaken the heart is to awaken the dormant soul, to awaken reason, to inculcate discrimination between good and evil.

Who should teach this true science of sex? Clearly, he who has attained mastery over his passions. To teach astronomy and kindred sciences we have teachers who have gone through a course of training in them and are masters of their art. Even so must we have as teachers of sexual science, i.e., the science of sex control, those who have studied it and have acquired mastery over self. Even a lofty utterance, that has not the backing of sincerity and experience, will be inert and lifeless, and will utterly fail to penetrate and quicken the hearts of men, while the speech that springs from self-realization and genuine experience is always fruitful.

Today our entire environment—our reading, our thinking, our social behaviour—is generally calculated to subserve and cater for the sex urge. To break through its coils is no easy task. But it is a task worthy of our highest endeavour. Even if there are a handful of teachers endowed with practical experience, who accept the ideal of attaining self-control as the highest duty of man, and are fired by a genuine and undying faith in their mission, and are sleeplessly vigilant and active, their labour will light the path of the children of Gujarat, save the unwary from falling into the mire of sexuality and rescue those who might be already engulfed in it.

10

Gandhi on Religious Education

Gandhiji's ideas on religious education are described in this chapter in his own words. It will provide an insight into the vastness of his vision and the expanse of his thought-process.

Religious Education

The question of religious education is very difficult. Yet we cannot do without it. India will never be godless. Rank atheism cannot flourish in this land. The task is indeed difficult. My head begins to turn as I think of religious education. Our religious teachers are hypocritical and selfish; they will have to be approached. The Mullas, the Dasturs and the Brahmins hold the key in their hands, but if they will not have the good sense, the energy that we have derived from English education will have to be devoted to religious education. This is not very difficult. Only the fringe of the ocean has been polluted, and it is those who are within the fringe who alone need cleaning. We who come under this category can even cleanse ourselves, because my remarks do not apply to the millions. In order to restore India to its pristine condition, we have to return to it.

Dharma and Scriptures

This brings me to the subject of dharma. Where there is

no dharma, there can be neither knowledge nor wealth, nor health, nor anything else. Where there is no dharma, life is devoid of all joy, is mere emptiness. We have had to go without instruction in dharma; we are in much the same position as the bridegroom's party at a wedding without the bridegroom. Students cannot have innocent joy without a knowledge of dharma. That they may have such joy, it is necessary for them to study the Shastras, to reflect over their teaching and bring their conduct in comformity with their ideals.

Smoking a cigarette the first thing in the morning or idle gossip does good to nobody. Nazir has said that, even the sparrows as they twitter, sing the name of the Lord morning and evening, when we are still lying in our beds full-length. It is the duty of every student to acquire the knowledge of dharma in any manner he can. Whether or not dharma is taught in schools, it is my prayer to students who have assembled here that they introduce its essential principles in their life. What exactly is dharma? In what manner can instruction in religion be imparted? This is not the place for a discussion of this subject. But I shall give you this practical advice, based on my own experience, that you should take to the *Ramacharitamanasa* [of Tulsidas] and the *Bhagavad Gita* in love and reverence. You have a real jewel in the latter; seize it. But see that you study these two books in order to learn the secret of dharma.

The seers who wrote these works did not set out to write history but only to teach dharma and morals. Millions of people read these books and lead pure lives. They read them with a guileless heart and live in this world full of innocent joy. It never occurs to them even in a dream to ask whether or not Ravana was a historical figure or whether they might not kill their enemies as Rama killed Ravana. Even when face to face with enemies, they pray for Ramachandra's protection and ramain unafraid. Tulsidas, the author of the *Ramayana*, had nothing but compassion by way of a weapon. He desired to kill none. He who creates, destroys. Rama was God; He had created Ravana and so had the right to kill him. When any of us becomes God; he may consider whether he is fit to have the power to destroy. I have ventured to say this by way of introduction to these great books. I was, myself, a sceptic once and lived in fear of being destroyed. I have grown out of that stage and become a believer. I have thought it fit here to describe the influence which these books have had on me. For Muslim students, the *Koran* is the best book in this respect. I would counsel them as well that they study this book in a spirit of devotion. They should understand its true message.

State versus Religious Instruction

If India is not to declare spiritual bankruptcy, religious instruction of its youth must be held to be at least as necessary as secular instruction. It is true that knowledge of religious books is no equivalent of that of religion. But if we cannot have religion, we must be satisfied with providing out boys and girls with what is next best. And whether there is such instruction given in the schools or not, grown-up students must cultivate the art of self-help about matters religious as about others. They may start their own class just as they have their debating, and now, spinners' clubs.

I do not believe that the State can concern itself or cope with religious education. I believe that religious education must be the sole concern of religious associations. Do not mix up religion and ethics. I believe that fundamental ethics is common to all religions. Teaching of fundamental ethics is undoubtedly a function of the State. By religion I have not in mind fundamental ethics but what goes by the name of denominationalism. We have suffered enough from State-aided religion and a State Church. A society or a group, which depends partly or wholly on State aid for the existence of its religion, does not deserve, or, better still, does not have any religion worth the name.

A curriculum of religious instruction should include a study of the tenets of faiths other than one's own. For this purpose the students should be trained to cultivate the habit of understanding and appreciating the doctrines of various great religions of the world in a spirit of reverence and broad-minded tolerance.

Religious Education and the Teacher

You have rightly found place for religious instruction. I have experimented with quite a number of boys in order to understand how best to impart religious instruction and whilst I found that book instruction was somewhat of an aid, by itself it was useless. Religious instruction, I discovered, was imparted by teachers living the religion themselves. I have found that boys imbibe more from the teachers' own lives than they do from the books that they read to them, or the lectures that they deliver to them with their lips. I have discovered to my great joy that boys and girls have unconsciously a faculty of penetration whereby they read the thoughts of their teachers. Woe to the teacher who teaches one thing with his lips, and carries another in his breast.

Liberal Education

I shall say to the 75 per cent Hindus receiving instruction in this College that your lives will be incomplete unless you reverently study the teaching of Jesus. I have come to the conclusion, in my own experience, that those who, no matter to what faith they belong, reverently study the teaching of other faiths broaden their own, instead of slackening their hearts. Personally, I do not regard any of the great religions of the world as false. All have served in embellishing mankind and are even now serving their purpose. A liberal education to all should include, as I have put it, a reverent study of other faiths, but I do not want to labour this point, nor have I the time to do so.

Religious Instruction

The other day, in the course of a conversation, a missionary friend asked me, if India was really a spiritually advanced country, why it was that he found only a few students having any knowledge of their own religion, even of the *Bhagavad Gita*. In support of the statement, the friend who is himself an educationist told me that he had made it a point to ask the students he met whether they had any knowledge of their religion or of the *Bhagavad Gita*. A vast majority of them were found to be innocent of any such knowledge.

I do not propose to take up at the present moment the inference that because certain students had no knowledge of their own religion, India was not a spiritually advanced country, beyond saying that the ignorance on the part of the students of religious books did not necessarily mean absence of all religious life or want of spirituality among the people to which the students belonged. But there is no doubt that the vast majority of students who pass through the Government educational institutions are devoid of any religious instruction.

The remark of the missionary had reference to the Mysore students, and I was somewhat pained to observe that even the students of Mysore had no religious instruction in the State schools. I know that there is a school of thought which believes in only secular instruction being given in public schools. I know also that in a country like India, where there are most religions of the world represented and where there are so many denominations in the same religion, there must be difficulty about making provision for religious instruction.

But if India is not to declare spiritual bankruptcy, religious instruction of its youth must be held to be at least as necessary as secular instruction. It is true that knowledge of religious books is no equivalent of that of religion. But if we cannot have religion we must be satisfied with providing our boys and girls with what is next best. And whether there is such instruction given in the schools or not, grown-up students must cultivate the art of self-help about matters religious as about other. They may start their own class just as they have their debating and now spinner's clubs.

Addressing the Collegiate High School students at Shimoga, I found upon enquiry at the meeting that out of a hundred or more Hindu boys, there were hardly eight who had read the *Bhagavad Gita*. None raised his hand in answer to the question, whether of the few who had read the *Gita* there was any who understood it.

Out of five or six Mussalman boys all raised their hands as having read the Koran. But only one could say that he knew its meaning. The *Gita* is, in my opinion, a very easy book to understand. It does present some fundamental problems which are no doubt difficult of solution. But the general trend of the *Gita* is in my opinion unmistakable. It is accepted by all Hindu sects as authoritative. It is free from any form of dogma. In a short compass it gives a complete reasoned moral code. It satisfies both the intellect and the heart. It is thus both philosophical and devotional. Its appeal is universal. The language is incredibly simple. But I nevertheless think that there should be an authoritative version in each vernacular, and the translations should be so prepared as to avoid technicalities and in a manner that would make the teaching of the *Gita* intelligible to the average man.

The suggestion is not intended in any way to supplement the original. For I reiterate my opinion that every Hindu boy and girl should know Sanskrit. But for a long time to come, there will be millions without any knowledge of Sanskrit. It would be suicidal to keep them deprived of the teachings of the *Bhagavad Gita* because they do not know Sanskrit.

Religious versus Fundamental Virtues

To me religion means Truth and *ahimsa* or rather Truth alone, because Truth includes *ahimsa, ahimsa* being the necessary and indispensable means for its discovery. Therefore, anything that promotes the practice of these virtues is a means for imparting religious education and the best way to do this, in my opinion, is for the teachers rigorously to practise these virtues in their own person. Their very association with the boys, whether on the playground or in the classroom, will then give the pupils a fine training in these fundamental virtues.

So much for instruction in the universal essentials of religion. A curriculum of religious instruction should include a study of the tenets of faiths other than one's own. For this purpose the students should be trained to cultivate the habit of understanding and appreciating the doctrines of various great religions of the world in a spirit of reverence and broad-minded tolerance. This if properly done would help to give them a spiritual assurance and a better appreciation of their own religion. There is one rule, however, which should always be kept in mind while studying all great religions and that is that one should study them only through the writings of known votaries of the respective religions.

For instance, if one wants to study the *Bhagavata* one should do so not through a translation of it made by a hostile critic but one prepared by a lover of the *Bhagavata.* Similarly to study the Bible one should study it through the commentaries of devoted Christians. This study of other religions besides one's own will give one a grasp of the rock-bottom unity of all religions and afford a glimpse also of that universal and absolute Truth which lies beyond the 'dust of creeds and faiths'. Let no one even for a moment entertain, the fear that a reverent study of other religions is likely to weaken or shake one's faith in one's own. The Hindu system of philosophy regards all religions as containing the elements of truth in them and enjoins an attitude of respect and reverence towards them all. This of course presupposes regard for one's own religion. Study and appreciation of other religions need not cause a weakening of that regard; it should mean extension of that regard to other religions.

In this respect religion stands on the same footing as culture. Just as preservation of one's own culture does not mean contempt for that of others, but requires assimilation of the best that there may be in all other cultures, even so should be the case with religion. Our present fears and apprehensions are a result of the poisonous atmosphere that has been generated in the country, the atmosphere of mutual hatred, ill-will and distrust. We are constantly labouring under a nightmare of fear lest some one should stealthily undermine our faith or the faith of those who are dear and near to us. But this unnatural state will cease when we have learnt to cultivate respect and tolerance towards other religions and their votaries.

Religious Instruction Framework

Teachers who teach under a common administrative system have no right to impart religious instruction according to their own viewpoint. As in the case of other subjects, religious instruction too must be given in accordance with the scheme provided by the administrative authorities. Every teacher will have his own method of teaching within that framework; however, such instruction may be imparted only in accordance with the ideals that have been laid down by the authorities with regard to religion. It is true that instruction in other subjects can be imparted by one who has read certain books on these subjects. That is not the case of religious instruction. It is never given through books.

The method of imparting this instruction is quite different from that followed in the case of other subjects. Whereas the latter is communicated through the intellect, the former can proceed from one's heart alone. Hence so long as the teacher is not steeped in religion, he should not impart religious instruction. Although in this manner the means of imparting religious instruction are different, nevertheless it is necessary to have a certain amount of understanding about the way in which it is to be done.

In other words, one cannot impart education which would encourage violence where non-violence has been accepted as the supreme dharma. Or, instruction antagonistic to other religions cannot be imparted where the ideal of love, tolerance and compassion towards all religions has been accepted as the ideal. In short, there can be no place for a state of anarchy with regard to religious instruction where its necessity has already been accepted.

SATSANG

It is true that we lack religious education in the country. Religious instruction can only be imparted through the practice of religion, not by exhibiting mere learning.

That's why someone has said: What is there that *Satsang*1 cannot do for a man? Who does not know the emphasis Tulsidas laid on the importance of *satsang* ? This does not mean that there is no need to read and understand religious books. But the need for books, etc., arises only after a man has had *satsang* and has purified himself to a certain extent.

If one starts studying religious books before this stage then instead of bringing peace this study could hinder the growth. This means that an intelligent man should put his religion into practice straightaway instead of worrying himself with all manner of questions. Then according to the maxim "as with the individual so with the world", one is bound to influence the other. If each one of us was to take care of one's self, nobody would need to worry about the others.

Ethical Teaching in Schools

Should religious instruction form part of the school curriculum as approved by the State? Do you favour separate schools for children belonging to different denominations for facility of religious instruction? Or should religious instruction be left in the hands of private bodies? If so, do you think it is right for the State to subsidize such bodies?

I do not believe in State religion even though the whole community has one religion. The State interference would probably always be unwelcome. Religion is purely a personal matter. There are in reality as many religions as minds. Each mind has a different conception of God from that of the other.

I am also opposed to State aid, partly or wholly, to religious bodies. For I know that an institution or group which does not manage to finance its own religious teaching, is a stranger to true religion. This does not mean that the State schools would not give ethical teaching. The fundamental ethics are common to all religions.

Ethics and Religion

Regarding religious education Dr. Zakir Husain thought that facilities should be provided for and time apportioned for religious education in our schools so as to enable those, who understood religion, to come and teach. More than that the Government should not undertake, if it wanted to avoid the appearance of undue interference.

Gandhiji said in reply, "You should talk it over with Maulana Saheb. I do not agree that the Government should provide religious education. If there are some people who want to give religious education of the wrong type, you cannot prevent it. If you try to do so, the result can only be bad. Those who want to give religious education may do so on their own, so long as it is not subversive of law and order or morals. The Governments can only teach ethics based on the main principles common to all religions and agreed to by all parties. In fact ours is a secular State."

Fundamental Ethics

Religious instruction in the sense of denominational religion has been deliberately omitted. Unless there is a State religion it is very difficult, if not impossible, to provide religious instruction as it would mean providing for every denomination. Such instruction is best given at home. The State should allow enough time for every child to receive such instruction at home or otherwise. It is also conceivable that the State should provide facilities for private tuition by those denominations which may wish to instruct their children at school provided that such instruction is paid for by such denominations.

As to the necessity of teaching equal regard for all religions, I personally hold strong views. Till we reach that happy state, I see no prospect of real unity among all the different communities. I regard it as fatal to the growth of a friendly spirit among the children belonging to the different faiths if they are taught either that their religion is superior to every other or that it is the only true religion. If that exclusive spirit is to pervade the nation, the necessary corollary would be that there should be separate schools for every denomination with freedom to each to decry every other, or that the mention of religion must be entirely prohibited.

The result of such a policy is too dreadful to contemplate. Fundamental principles of ethics are common to all religions. These should certainly be taught to the children and that should be regarded as adequate religious instruction so far as the schools under the Wardha scheme are concerned.

TRUE PRAYER

As feed food is necessary for the body, prayer is necessary for the soul. A man may be able to do without food for a number of days,—as Mac Swiney did for over 70 days—but believing in God, man cannot, should not, live a moment without prayer. You will say that we see lots of people living without prayer. I dare say they do, but it is the existence of the brute which, for man, is worse than death. I have not the shadow of a doubt that the strife and quarrels with which our atmosphere is so full today are due to the absence of the spirit of true prayer. You will demur to the statement, I know, and contend that millions of Hindus, Mussalmans and Christians do offer their prayers. It is because I had thought you would raise this objection that I sued the words 'true prayers'. The fact is we have been offering our prayers with the lips but hardly ever with our hearts, and it is to escape, if possible, the hypocrisy of the lip-prayer, that we in the Ashram repeat every evening the last verses of the second chapter of the Bhagavad Gita. The condition of the 'Equable in Spirit' that is described in those verses, if we contemplate them daily, is bound slowly to turn our hearts towards God. If you students would base your education on the true foundation f a pure character and pure heart there is nothing so helpful as to offer your prayers every day truly and religiously.

Prayer Meetings

Here is a letter written by a student to the Principal of a national institution asking to be excused from attending its prayer meetings:

I beg to state that I have no belief in prayer, as I do not believe in anything known as God to whom I should pray. I never feel any necessity of supposing a god for myself. What do I lose if do not care for Him and calmly and sincerely work my own schemes?

So far as congregational prayer is concerned, it is of no use. Can such a huge mass of men enter into any mental concentration upon a thing, however trifling it may be? Are the little and ignorant children expected to fix their fickle attention on the subtlest ideas of our great scriptures, God and soul and equality of all men and many other high-sounding phrases? This great performance is required to be done at a particular time at the command of a particular man. Can love for the so-called Lord take its root in the hearts of boys by any such mechanical function? Nothing can be more repugnant to reason than to expect the same behaviour from men of every temperament. Therefore, prayer should not be a compulsion. Let those pray who have a taste for it and those avoid who dislike it. Anything done without conviction is an immoral and degrading action.

Let us first examine the worth of the last idea. Is it an immoral and degrading act to submit to discipline before one beings to have conviction about its necessity? Is it immoral and degrading to study subjects according to the school syllabus if one has no conviction about its utility? May a boy be excused from studying his vernacular if he has persuaded himself that it is useless? Is it not truer to say that a school boy has no conviction about the things he has to learn or the discipline he has to go through? His choice is exhausted if he had it, when he elected to belong to an institution. His joining one means that he will willingly submit to its rules and regulations. It is open to him to leave it, but he may not choose what or how he will learn.

It is for teachers to make attractive and intelligible what to the pupils may at first appear repulsive or uninteresting.

It is easy enough to say, 'I do not believe in God.' For God permits all things to be said of Him with impunity. He looks at our acts. And any breach of His law carried with it, not its vindictive, but its purifying, compelling, punishment. God's existence cannot be, does cannot be, does not need to be, proved. God is. If He is not felt, so much the worse for us. The absence of feeling is a disease which we shall some day throw off nolens volens.

But a boy may not argue. He must, out of a sense of discipline, attend prayer meetings if the institution to which he belongs requires such attendance. He may respectfully put his doubts before his teachers. He need not believe what does not appeal to him. But if he has respect for his teachers, he will do without believing what he is asked to do, not out of fear, not out of churlishness, but with the knowledge that it is right for him so to do and with the hope that what is dark to him today will some day be made clear to him.

Prayer is not an asking. It is a longing of the soul. It is a daily admission of one's weakness. The tallest among us has a perpetual reminder of his nothingness before death, disease, old age, accidents, etc. We are living in the midst of death. What is the value of "working for our own schemes" when they might be reduced to naught in the twinkling of an eye, or when we may be equally swiftly and unawares be taken away from them? But we may feel strong as a rock, if we could truthfully say: "We work for God and his schemes." Then all is as clear as day-light. Then nothing perishes. All perishing is then only what seems. Death and destruction have then, but only then, no reality about them. For death or destruction is then but a change. An artist destroys his picture for creating a better one. A watchmaker throws away a bad spring to put in a new and useful one.

A congregational prayer is a mighty thing. What we do not often do alone, we do together. Boys do not need conviction. If they merely attend in obedience to the call to prayer without inward resistance, they feel the exaltation. But many do not. They are even mischievous. All the same the unconscious effect cannot be resisted. Are there not boys who at the commencement of their career were scoffers but who subsequently became mighty believers in the efficacy of congregational prayer? It is a common experience for men who have no robust faith to seek the comfort for congregational prayer. All who flock to churches, temples, or mosques are not scoffers or humbugs. They are honest men and women. For them congregational prayer is like a daily bath, a necessity, of their existence. These places of worship are not a mere idle superstition to be swept away at the first opportunity. They have survived all attacks up to now and are likely to persist to the end of time.

ESSENCE OF PRAYER

I am glad that you all want me to speak to you on the meaning of and the necessity for prayer. I believe that prayer is the very soul and essence of religion, and therefore prayer must be the very core of the life of man, for no man can live without religion. There are some who in the egotism of their reason declare that they have nothing to do with religion. But it is like a man saying that he breathes but that he has no nose. Whether by reason, or by instinct, or by superstition, man acknowledges some sort of relationship with the divine. The rankest agnostic or atheist does acknowledge the need of a moral principle, and associates something good with its observance and something bad with its non-observance. Bradlaugh, whose atheism is well known, always insisted on proclaiming his innermost conviction. He had to suffer a lot for thus speaking the truth, but he delighted in it and said that truth is its own reward. Not that he was quite insensible to the joy resulting from the observance of truth. This joy however is not at all worldly, but springs out of communion with the divine. That is why I have said that even a man who disowns religion cannot and does not live without religion.

Now I come to the next thing, viz., that prayer is the very core of man's life, as it is the most vital part of religion. Prayer is either petitional or in its wider sense is inward communion. In either case the ultimate result is the same. Even when it is petitional, the petition should be for the cleansing and purification of the soul, for freeing it from the layers of ignorance and darkness that envelop it. He therefore who hungers for the awakening of the divine in him must fall back on prayer. But prayer is no mere exercise of words or of the ears, it is no mere repetition of empty formula. Any amount of repetition of Ramanama is futile if it fails to stir the soul. It is better in prayer to have a heart without word than words without a heart. It must be in clear response to the spirit which hungers for it. And even as a hungry man relishes a hearty meal, a hungry soul will relish a heartfelt prayer. And I am giving you a bit of my experience and that of my companions when I say that he who has experienced the magic of prayer may do without food for days together but not a single moment without prayer. For without prayer there is no inward peace.

If that is the case, someone will say, we should be offering our prayers every minute of our lives. There is no doubt about it, but we erring mortals, who find it diffficult to retire within ourselves for inward communion even for a single moment will find it impossible to remain perpetually in communion with the divine. We therefore fix some hours when we make a serious effort to throw off the attachments of the world for a while, we make a serious endeavour to remain, so to say, out of the flesh. You have heard Surdas's hymn. It is the passionate cry of a soul hungry for union with the divine. According to our standards he was a saint, but according to his own he was a proclaimed sinner. Spiritually he was miles ahead of us, but he felt the separation from the divine so keenly that he has uttered that anguished cry in loathing and despair.

I have talked of the necessity for prayer, and therethrough I have dealt with the essence of prayer. We are born to serve our fellowmen, and we cannot properly do so unless we are wide awake.

There is an eternal struggle raging in man's breast between the powers of darkness and of light, and he who has not the sheet-anchor of prayer to rely upon will be a victim to the powers of darkness. The man of prayer will be at peace with himself and with the whole world, the man who goes about the affairs of the world without a prayerful heart will be miserable and will make the world also miserable. Apart therefore from its bearing on man's condition after death, prayer has incalculable value for man in this world of the living. Prayer is the only means of bringing about orderliness and peace and repose in our daily acts. We inmates of the Ashram who came here in search of truth and for insistence on truth professed to believe in the efficacy of prayer, but had never up to now made it a matter of vital concern. We did not bestow on it the care that we did on other matters. I awoke from my slumbers one day and realized that I had been woefully negligent of my duty in the matter. I have therefore suggested measures of stern discipline and far from being any the worse, I hope we are the better for it. For it is so obvious. Take care of the vital thing and other things will take care of themselves. Rectify one angle of a square, and then other angles will be automatically right.

Begin therefore your day with prayer, and make it so soulful that it may remain with you until the evening. Close the day with prayer so that you may have a peaceful night free from dreams and nightmares. Do not worry about the form of prayer. Let it be any form, it should be such as can put us into communion with the divine. Only, whatever be the form, let not the spirit wander while the words of prayer run on out of your mouth.

If what I have said has gone home to you, you will not be at peace until you have compelled your hostel superintendents to interest themselves in your prayer and to make it obligatory. Restraint self-imposed is no compulsion. A man, who chooses the path of freedom from restraint, i.e, of self-indulgence, will be a bondslave of passions, whilst the man who binds himself to rules and restraints releases himself. All things in the universe, including the sun and the moon and the stars, obey certain laws. Without the restraining influence of these laws the world would not go on for a single moment.

You, whose mission in life is service of your fellowmen, will go to pieces if you do not impose on yourselves some sort of discipline, and prayer is a necessary spiritual discipline. It is discipline and restraint that separates us from the brute. If we will be men walking with our heads erect and not walking on all fours, let us understand and put ourselves under voluntary discipline and restraint.

Sound Mind in a Sound Body

Exercise is just as essential to mankind as are air, water and food, though it is true that man cannot get on for a long time without air, water and food as he can without exercise. It is a fact of common experience, however, that one cannot enjoy really good health without exercise. We have to interpret exercise in the same way that we did "food". Exercise does not necessarily mean *moidanda*1 football, cricket or going out for a walk. Exercise means physical and mental activity. Just as food is necessary for the mind as much as for bones and flesh, so also is exercise necessary both for body and mind. If the body has no exercise, it is sickly and, if the mind has none, it is dull. Stupidity should also be regarded only as a kind of illness. It betrays sheer ignorance to describe as healthy a wrestler who, though adept at wrestling, is mentally a boor. There is a saying in English that he alone is healthy who has a sound mind in a sound body.

What is this exercise? Nature has so arranged things for us that we can be continuously taking exercise in one way or another. If we but think calmly enough, we shall see that a majority of people in the world live on agriculture. All members in a farmer's family have some form of exercise. It is only if they work eight, ten or even more hours every day in the fields or elsewhere that they can get their daily bread. They need no separate exercise for the mind. A farmer cannot work without applying his mind. He must be able to test the nature of his soil, must watch changes of weather, must know how to manipulate his plough skilfully and be generally familiar with the movements of the stars, the sun and the moon. However clever a city-dweller may be, every time he goes to a farmer's house, he feels altogether out of his element. The farmer can say how seed should be sown; he is familiar with all the by-ways in the vicinity and knows all the men in the neighbourhood. By looking at the stars he can judge the direction even at night. He can make certain deductions from the voice and speed of birds; for instance, when certain birds cluster or sing together, he sees in it a sign of the approach of the monsoon or some other similar phenomenon. Thus, the farmer knows enough of astronomy, geography and geology to serve his needs. He has to feed his children and has, therefore, some idea of the duties of man, and, residing as he does in the vast open spaces of this earth, he naturally becomes aware of the greatness of God. Physically, it goes without saying, he is always sturdy. He is his own physician, when ill. Thus, we can see, he does have an educated mind.

But all men are not going to be farmers. Moreover, these chapters are not being written for the benefit of farmers. The question is, what should those who have gone into business or some similar profession do in this regard? The farmer's life has been described at some length in order that we may find a rational answer to this problem, that we who are not farmers can arrange our way of life somewhat on the pattern of his and that we may realize that, in so far as our manner of living differs from the farmer's, we would enjoy poorer health. We can conclude from a farmer's way of living that a man should do physical work for eight hours a day and that of a kind that would stimulate our mental powers in the very process of doing it. Now, merchants and others certainly obtain mental exercise in the course of their work, but this is one-sided. A businessman does not know astronomy or geography or history, as the farmer does. He may be able to judge about movements of prices and may be proficient in the art of salesmanship, but this is not enough to exercise fully his mental faculties. In this type of work, the body does perform some movements now and then, but they are too slight to be of any account.

In the West, they have invented games like cricket for such people. Another way is to observe some days in the year as holidays, when more games are played, and to do some light reading by way of mental exercise. This is one method which we may consider. To be sure, spending time in sports does give some exercise to the body, but exercise of this kind does nothing to improve the mind. We can see the truth of this from numerous instances. What proportion of men of high intellectual calibre shall we find among those who regularly play cricket or from among the large number who play football? In India, what do we observe as regards the mental development of the princes who give their time to sports? Again, how many of those with well-developed intellectual powers are sportsmen? Experience shows that highly intellectual men are seldom sportsmen as well. The British nowadays are very much given to sports. Their own poet, Kipling has described these sportsmen as enemies of the mind, and adds that they will also prove themselves enemies to their country. In India, our intellectuals seem to have found a different way. They provide exercise for their minds but relatively very little or none for their bodies. These people are lost to us. Their bodies are enfeebled by excessive intellectual work. They are continually pursued by some ailment or other and just when they have gained enough experience to be of real use to the country, they pass away. From this we may conclude that neither exercising the brain alone nor the body alone is enough and also that exercise which serves no useful purpose, namely, that derived from sports, has little meaning. Real exercise is that which trains, continuously, both mind and body alike. He alone who takes such exercise can preserve good health. The farmer is the only such person.

Then, what are those to do who are not farmers? The exercise obtained from sports such as cricket leaves much to be desired. We must, therefore, think of a form of exercise something like what the farmer gets. Businessmen and others similarly placed can make a garden round their house and regularly spend two to four hours a day digging there. Hawkers get exercise from their own work itself. If we are living in a rented room, we should not raise any difficulty about working in another's land, for that would indicate a small mind. We would derive nothing but benefit from working on land, whosoever's it might be. The appearance of our house would be improved and we would have the satisfaction of having looked after another's land. It is necessary to say a few words for those who cannot find an opportunity to work on land or who do not favour such work in any circumstances. Apart from working on land, the best form of exercise is walking. It has been truly described as the king of physical exercises. Our *fakirs* and *sadhus* are very healthy. One reason for this is that they do not use horses, carriages or other vehicles. Their journeys are always performed on foot. There has been a famous American writer named Thoreau who has written a highly thought-provoking book on the subject of walking. According to him, the writings of one who refuses to leave his house on the excuse of lack of time and who undertakes no physical activity, are bound to be anaemic like himself. Speaking of his own experience, he says that when he wrote his best books he was doing his longest walking. He thought nothing of walking four or five hours at a stretch. Just as we cannot work when we are hungry, so it should be with exercise. We do not know how to measure mental work, therefore, we are not able to realize that mental work done unaccompanied by physical exercise will inevitably be dull and ineffectual. Walking results in rapid circulation of blood in all the parts of the body, promotes movements in every organ and strengthens it. One should remember that the arms move during walking. We obtain fresh air by going for a walk and behold the beauties of Nature. One should not take walks always in the same place or in narrow lanes but go out into fields and groves. We will then be able to appreciate in some measure the beauty of Nature. A walk of a mile or two can scarcely be called walking. A walk, to be worth the name, should cover ten or twelve miles. Those who cannot do this regularly can take long walks on Sundays. A certain patient, who used to suffer from indigestion, went one day to an experienced *vaidya*1 for some pills. The *vaidya* advised him to take short but regular walks. The patient protested that he was too weak. The *vaidya* realized that he was, in fact, a timid man. He thereupon took the patient with him in his carriage. On the way he purposely dropped his whip. The patient, out of politeness, had to get out to pick it up. The *vaidya* immediately drove off. The poor patient had to follow, panting hard for breath. The *vaidya* having made sure that the former had covered a fairly long distance, turned the carriage back, picked him up and told him that, since walking was the only medicine for him, he—the *vaidya*—had forced him to walk even at the risk of appearing cruel. By this time, however, the patient was ravenously hungry and had forgotten all about the whip episode. He thanked the doctor, went home and ate his fill. Those who are not in the habit of walking and suffer from indigestion and its accompanying ills should try the experiment.

11

Gandhian Values in Education

Mahatma Gandhi — the greatest of our leaders. He lit the imagination of the entire nation. There is a basic lesson of Indian History. Our people have always taken their moral standards from their rulers; the people have risen to great heights when they have basked in the glow of noble kings or leaders. The present generation is waiting for a leader who will make it relearn the moral values, and who will inculcate in the people, as Gandhi did, a sense of the responsibilities which fall on every citizen of a free society.

The waste of human ability energy and money on armament will continue unabated, and diversion of world resources to development will remain a pipe dream, so long as man does not learn the great lesson which Gandhi preached so convincingly in our own times-viz. non-violence is the law of our species. The diversion of world resources to development stands no practical chance of being heeded unless and until the balance of terror is replaced by the balance of terror is replaced, by the balance of reason.

Although it is true that India has been an integrated nation since olden times; it is also true that on the present context Gandhian values have special significance for national integration. Today communal amity has become essential for national integration and hence Gandhi gave it the highest priority. By communal unity Gandhiji did not mean merely paying lip service to 'bhaibhai-ism'. He meant it to be an unbreakable heart unity'.

In the religious context Gandhi emphasized that communal unity has to be based on equal respect for all religions. Everyone, Gandhi said, must have the same regard for other faiths as he had for his own. Such respect would not only remove religious rifts but lead to a realization of the fact that religion was a stabilizing force, not a disturbing element. Gandhi's basic axiom was that religion since the scriptures of all religions point only in one direction of goodwill, openness and understanding between men and men and between community and community.

Gandhiji regarded education as the light of life and the very source from which was created an awareness of oneness. Gandhi believed that the universality of religion can best be realized through the universalisation of education, and that such universalisation was the spring board for national integration. Harmony is not brought about about overnight. Gandhi advocated the process of patience, persuasion and perseverance for attainment of peace and love for harmony and was firmly convinced of the worth of gentleness as panacea for all evils.

Communal harmony had the pride of place in Gandhi's constructive programme. He taught us the dignity of labour as a levelling social factor that contributed to a national outlook in keeping with the vision of new India. he always believed that a nation built on the foundation of non-violence would be able to withstand attacks on its-integrity from within and without. Gandhi pleaded for the humanization of knowledge for immunization against the ideas of distrust among the communities of the nations and the nationalities of the world. He wanted to take the country from areas of hostility into areas of harmony of faiths through tolerance, so that we could work towards understanding each other. His mass contact programme was specifically aimed at generating a climate of confidence and competition and eliminating misgiving and misconceptions, conflicts and confrontation.

Gandhi also held that bridging the gulf between the well off and the rest was as essential for national integration as inter-religious record. HE said that we must work for economic equality and social justice, which would remove the ills caused by distress and bitterness. He said that we must work for economic equality and social justice, which would remove the ills caused by distress and bitterness. He stressed that the foundation of equality, the core of harmony will have to be laid here now and built up brick by brick through ethical and economic satisfaction of the masses.

Gandhian Relevance

It is 54 years since Gandhi was assassinated and there are all kinds of discussion in India and abroad on what Gandhi left for humanity and whether many of his teachings would survive the test of time. What even the passionate critic of Gandhi cannot miss is the string of activities along Gandhian lines one can see in almost all countries of the World now. If not in very significant measure there are very few countries in the world where something or the other in the name of Gandhi is not being organised.

In short there is a global non-violent awakening after Gandhi. What is the relevance of Gandhi in this all-pervading materialistic, agnostic and consumerist culture? It is precisely these three tendencies Gandhi fought all his life.

There is no denying the fact that Gandhi was deep rooted in his cultural and religious traditions. The phenomenal success Gandhi registered in far away South Africa fighting for human rights and civil liberties and later the adoption of the Gandhian techniques by Nelson Mandela and the subsequent revelations made by the former South African president De Klerk that he was greatly influenced by Gandhi's principles.

The year 1994 bore witness to the efficacy strategies and philosophy as could be seen from the manner in which the fight Gandhi began 100 years ago in South Africa i.e. in 1903 bearing fruits when the blacks and the whites in South Africa were able to work out a satisfactory solution to a peaceful transfer of power which resulted in the holding of elections and Dr. nelson Mandela taking over the reins of power.

In the American continent Martin Luther King's heroic fight for civil liberties on the Gandhian lines and his own admission that it was from Gandhi that he learnt his operational tactics also is not an isolated instance of the relevance of the Gandhian tactics. martin Luther King (Jr.) said, "If humanity is to progress, Gandhi is inescapable. He lived, thought and acted, inspired by the version of a humanity evolving towards a world of peace and harmony. WE may ignore him at our own risk."

Gandhi's contribution to the political awakening and freedom movement in different parts of the world and adoption of non-violence strategies which help both the opposing groups respect each other's sentiments and accommodating the news of others as much in common with UNESCO's decision to propagate the message of tolerance for humanity survival. Asia and African Continent particularly has seen peaceful transition power of power and social change, thanks to Gandhi's initiatives and teachings.

The name of Mahatma Gandhi transcends the bounds of race, religion and nation- states, and has emerged as the prophetic voice of the 21st century. he is remembered for his passionate adherence to the practice of non-violence and his supreme humanism. After the great Buddha and Jesus he once again demonstrated that non-violence could also be an effective instruments of social change.

Gandhi successfully demonstrated to a world, weary with wars and continuing destruction that adherence to Truth and Non-violence is not meant for individual behaviour alone but can be applied in global affairs too.

We can sum it all up by saying that it was Gandhi who, through his dedication, lifted the country from the British policy of 'divide and rule' and let the Indian masses form rivalries to reconciliation and from hostility to harmony. And in this the Mahatma was ably supported by his great disciples- Pandit Jawaharlal Nehru, Vallabhai Patel, Lal Bahadur Shastri, Maulana Abdul Kalam Azad and many others.

GANDHIJI—FATHER OF THE NATION

The period from 1920 to 1947 had been described as the Gandhian Era in Indian Politics. During the period, Gandhi spoke the final word on behalf of the Indian National Congress in negotiating with the British Government for constitutional reforms, and for chalking out a programme for the national movement.

Mahatma Gandhi led the national freedom struggle against the British rule. The most unique thing about this struggle was that it was completely non-violent.

Mohan Das Karamchand Gandhi was born on 2nd October, 1869 at Porbander in Gujarat. After finishing his early education in India, he sailed to England in 1891 and qualified as Barrister. In 1894, Gandhi went to South Africa in connection with a law suit.

The political career of Gandhi started in South Africa where he launched a Civil Disobedience Movement against the maltreatment meted out to Asian settlers. In 1916, he returned to India and took up the leadership of National Freedom Struggle.

After the death of freedom fighter and congress leader Bal Gangadhar Tilak on August, 1920, Gandhi became virtually the sole navigator of the ship of the congress. Gandhi had whole heartedly supported the British during the 1st World War (1914-1919). The end of war, however, did not bring the promised freedom for India. So Gandhiji launched many movements to force the British to concede India its Independence. The well known being: Non Co-operation Movement (1920), Civil Disobedience Movement (1930) and Quit India Movement (1942).

The British passed the Rowlett Act in 1919 to deal with the revolutionaries. Gandhi made the Rowlett Act an issue and appealed to the people to observe peaceful demonstration on April 6, 1919. Gandhi's call for peaceful demonstration met with tremendous response. It led to mass demonstrations in Punjab and Delhi. The Jallianwala Massacre (1919) was a sequel of this agitation.

The Indian people were shocked by the way the British conducted themselves. Gandhi them launched a non-co operation in 1920 against the British rule. On 12th March 1930, Gandhi started his Civil Disobedience with his famous 'Dandi March' to break the salt laws. Many leaders and persons courted arrest. Then followed the Gandhi-Irwin Pact for the participation of the congress in the Second Round Table Conference in 1931. On March 1942, Sir Stafford Cripps came to India with his proposals which were rejected by all political parties. The failure of the Cripps Mission led to unprecedented disturbances. Disillusioned and disappointed, the congress passed at Bombay the Quit India Resolution (August 8, 1942). The

British were asked to leave India forthwith. The moving spirit behind the resolution was Gandhiji. The Quit India Movement was the greatest challenge to the British empire.

Gandhi was a great leader, a saint and a great social reformer. He was pious, truthful and religious. He believed in simple living and high thinking. Every body who came in contact with him were so deeply influenced by his personality. He was a Champion of democracy and was deadly opposed to dictatorial rule.

Gandhi showed India and the World the path of truth and non-violence. He believed that it was truth alone that prevailed in the end. Gandhi believed that real India lived in more than five lakh villages uplift. According to him India's real emancipation depended on Swadeshi i.e. boycott of foreign goods, use of khadi encouragement to village and cottage industries.

Gandhi began to work day and night for the freedom of his country. He and his brave followers went to jail again and again, and suffered terrible hardships. Thousands of them were starved, beaten, ill treated and killed, but they remained true to their master. At last his noble efforts bore fruit and on August 15,1947, India became free and independent.

Gandhi defeated the mighty British empire not with swords or guns , but by means of strange and utterly new weapons of truth and Ahimsa. He worked all through his life for Hindu- Muslim Unity and the abolition of untouchability. Gandhi worked hard for the upliftment of the Harijans, the name given by him to the untouchables. Gandhi declared untouchability a sin against God and Man.

Gandhi wrote his famous autobiography under the title 'My Experiments with Truth'. Gandhi always stood for communal harmony, but he himself was shot dead by a religious fanatic Nathuram Godse on 30th January, 1948. The whole World mourned his death.

Some one had quipped: "If they had not thrown Gandhi out of the train in South Africa, the English would not have too much trouble from him." Gandhi, the young Attorney, vowed to oppose such unfair treatment-through non-co operation and other non-violent means.

Gandhi's ultimate search was for righteous conduct. The means are more important than the end, he maintained; with the right means, desired ends will follow. In time, he was proven right- almost always. His struggles and actions were but external manifestations of his struggle to evolve his own value system. Mahatma Gandhi better known as the father of Nation because it was he who got freedom for us. He was the maker of Modern India.

Gandhian Religion

Ahimsa, peace and non-aggression are the hallmarks of Gandhian Doctrine. Many years have gone by but *the luster of the Gandhian Religion* remains undimmed. Invading forces have descended on India but Gandhi's ideals have remained indestructible.

The Gandhian religion is not merely for Hindus, not merely for India, but for the whole world. The Gandhian philosophy is not only essential for the rebirth of the Indian nation but also for the re-education of the human race.

It is becoming clear that at this supremely dangerous moment in human history, the only hope for mankind is Mahatma Gandhi's principle of non-violence. The Gandhian doctrine, the ultimate realization must involve tolerance and understanding, peace and goodwill, and recognition of the immense variety of paths by which the soul can fulfill its ultimate destiny.

The Gandhian religion, which is primarily concerned with spiritual development, is of special significance in our age, which is marked by the obsolescence of the materialistic civilization. In fact, Gandhi laid the foundation of mathematical and scientific knowledge. They measured both time and space. Let us look at some of basic conclusions reached by ancient insights, which have become the fundamentals of the modern Gandhian Philosophy. Gandhiji perceived the principle more clearly and understood its implications even more deeply.

The virtues of self-discipline, self restraint and self-development which are the main-stay of Indian Dharma and Gandhi culture, are as fully relevant today as they were many years ago. Therefore we must go all out to preserve the Gandhian religion., In fact, Gandhi was a great soul who preached the essential unity of all religions and the basic unity of all humanity.

In recent times unity ahs been sought to be undermined by forces, internal as well as external out to destabilize us. So it is now time for India to show the world that we are one as a society, are too secure in our spiritual strength and national heritage to be so easily uprooted. This is a gigantic task but we have not shirked it.

In India we are a highly religious society, wholly secular in character. Gandhi was deeply religious person but he was clear in mind that the state should be secular-He stood for the maximum possible distance between religious concerns of individuals and the state's obligations towards its citizens. Gandhi also clearly stated that secularism did not mean opposition to religion. He also said that the state had to honour all religions equally without attaching itself to a particular faith.

Strange as it may seem, there is a religious essence at the core of secularism and even the modern secular West has recognized it. In Europe it ahs permeated all spheres of life, and even the French speak of there being something eternal about religion as the basis of life. It has been universally accepted that secularism is not a denial of religion. On the contrary it means tolerance and respect for all religions- what one can call- the hospitality of faiths.

Gandhi's religious quest for truth had no geographical limits. His political activities were but an avocation to his religious mission. The centre- most point of Gandhi's religious philosophy is the inviolable sacredness of life and the consequent sinfulness of bloodshed. "Since we have no power to create, we have no power to destroy", was his belief.

Gandhi taught us, learning in the quest for national integration- is the crying need of the hour. Thus both as an ideology and as a policy, Gandhian religion acquired worldwide acceptance. Along with Mahatma Gandhi, other Indian leaders also contributed to strengthening of the secular spirit of India.

The three basic factors militating against translation of the ideal of human unity into action are religion, nationalistic politics and economic ideologies. Religions are different roads converging to the same destination. Mahatma Gandhi said, " The need of the moment of not one religion, but mutual respect and tolerance of different religions. We want to reach not the dead level but unity in diversity. The soul of all religions is one, but it is encased in a multitude of forms. The latter will persist to the end of time".

People representing a variety of cultures, languages, and creeds have to be woven into one nation, one people, free of communal or religious divides, free of conflict, devoted to the building up of a climate of confidence and co-operation. This is indeed a big task and we need all the patience and perseverance if we have to accomplish it. We have been able to absorb the shocks of history because of our deeply ingrained spiritual qualities, and we must have faith that the same spiritual will help us overcome the current crises.

We are in a much better situation than, say, Britain with its Ireland and Scotland problem, Canada with its Quebec problem, Spain with its Basque problem as well as several Countries in Africa and West Asia where the old creed of fundamentalism. now coupled with the new creed of ethnicity is challenging the concept of nationalism.

Can we face the challenge of Gandhi's ideals and ideas? They have not yet been fully utilized. The revolutionary Gandhi, who was far ahead of his times, has not been fully understood by the younger generation. Gandhi's thoughts need to be disseminated amongst our youth. It is the ideas, which have a stupendous role in taking the human society forward; towards the desired goal.

Bibliography

Bhikhu Parekh, *Gandhi*, Oxford University Press, 1997.

Catherine Clement, *Gandhi: Father of a Nation*, London: Thames & Hudson, 1996.

Dhananjay Keer, *Mahatma Gandhi: Political Saint and Unarmed Prophet*, Bombay, 1973.

Fischer, Louis, *The Life of Mahatma Gandhi*, New York: Harper & Brothers, 1950.

Gandhi, Mohandas Karamchand, *Gandhi's Autobiography: The Story of My Experiments with Truth*, Washington, D.C.: Public Affairs Press, 1954.

_____________, *Satyagraha in South Africa*, Ahmedabad, India: Navajivan Publishing House, 1950.

_____________, *The Essential Gandhi*, An Anthology edited by Louis Fischer. New York: Random House, 1962.

_____________, *The Wit and Wisdom of Gandhi*, Edited with an Introduction by Homer A. Jack. Boston: The Beacon Press, 1951.

Geoffrey Ashe, *Gandhi*, New York, 1969.

George Woodcock, *Mohandas Gandhi, for the Modern Masters series*, New York: Viking Press, 1971.

Judith Brown, *Gandhi: Prisoner of Hope*, Yale, 1990,

King, Martin Luther, J.R., *Stride Toward Freedom: The Montgomery Story*, New York: Harper & Brothers, 1958.

Krishna Kripalani, *Gandhi: A Life*, 1968.

Louis Fischer, *The Life of Mahatma Gandhi*, New York, 1950.

Mosley, Leonard, *The Last Days of the British Raj*, New York: Harcourt, Brace & World, 1961.

Nanda, B. R., *Mahatma Gandhi: A Biography*, 1st ed., 1958; expanded edition, New Delhi: Oxford UP, 1981.

Nehru, Jawaharlal, *Mahatma Gandhi*, Calcutta, India: Signet Press, 1949.

Prabhu, Ramachandra Krishna, *This was Bapu: 150 Anecdotes Relating to Mahatma Gandhi*, Ahmedabad, India: Navajivan Publishing House, 1954.

Raghavan Iyer, *The Moral and Political Writings of Mahatma Gandhi*, New York and Delhi: Oxford UP, 1989.

Robert Payne, *The Life and Death of Mahatma Gandhi*, Dutton, 1969.

Sheean, Vincent, *Mahatma Gandhi, A Great Life in Brief*, New York: Alfred A. Knopf, 1955.

Tendulkar D. G., *Mahatma: Life of Mohandas Karamchand Gandhi*, New Delhi, 1951.

Index

Acharya Kripalani 98
Agricultural indebtedness 105
Ancillary processes 177
Ashram endeavour 74

Brahmacharya 77, 195, 197
Bureaucratic authorities 6

Champaran Satyagraha 54
Child education 188
Civil Disobedience Movement 286
College education 205
Colonization 2
Communal amity 281
Communal harmony 282

Dandi Salt March 2

Educational institutions 76
Elementary education 13, 14
Environmental degradation, 51
Epistemology 4
Ethical principles 80
Financial self-sufficiency 5

Gramseva-Dikshitas 102
Gross misapprehension 191

Human ability energy 281
Human habitation 191

Indian Christians 61
Indian Dharma 289
Indian National Congress 1
Industrialization 9
Infant education 171
Intellectual development 114, 116
Intellectually-stagnated discourse 53
International commerce 76
Inter-provincial communication 88

Jawaharlal Nehru 12
John Ruskin 5
Journal Yasnaya polyana 6

Liberal curriculum 14
Life-breath of millions 104
Literary education 76
Literary training 64
Lloyd George 88

Maganlal Gandhi 71
Mahabharata 196
Mahavidyalaya 93
Materialistic civilization 289
Mohandas Karamchand Gandhi 1
Montessori Education 178
Mulk Raj Anand 16
Muslim children Arabic. 75

Nathuram Godse 288
National education 202
National Higher Education 90

National Planning Committee
(NPC) 12
National service 82
National University 204
National Vidyapiths 101
New Gujarati Pathashala 183
Non Co-operation Movement 286
Nursery Education 179

Oral teaching 180

Phoenix Ashram 71
Physical education 80
Pranayam 200
Primary Education 179
Primary education 89

Quit India Movement 287

Rabindra Nath Tagore 170
Radicalism 52
Ramayana 196

Salt Satyagraha 100
Satyagraha Ashram 73
Scientific education 178
Secular education 61
Secular programme 11
Self-supporting education 109
Self-supporting universitites 208
Snatakas 195
Socialism 104
State-supported arrangements 14
Suicidal cleavage 205

Tolstoy Farm 62
Transformation 52
True National Education 84

United Nations General Assembly
1

Vedas 191
Vidyapith 99, 200
Vinitas 195
Vocational training 205

Western civilization 2